CITIZENSHIP

CITIZENSHIP

edited by
Geoff Andrews

LAWRENCE & WISHART
LONDON

Lawrence & Wishart Limited
144a Old South Lambeth Road
London SW8 1XX

First published 1991

© Lawrence & Wishart, 1991

Each essay © the author, 1991

Photoset in North Wales by
Derek Doyle & Associates, Mold, Clwyd
Printed and bound in Great Britain by
Mackays of Chatham, Kent

Contents

PART III – NEW EUROPEANS

PART IV – CITIZENSHIP AND NON-CITIZENS

PART V – BEYOND CHARTER 88

CONTENTS

Preface

The debate about citizenship has continued to gain momentum during the editing of this book, with developments in Eastern Europe and demands for constitutional reform at home, in particular ensuring that citizenship remains a live issue and a concept which needs substantial reassessment.

The idea for this collection came from two *Marxism Today* events with which I was involved: 'Redefining Citizenship' which took place in Oxford in May 1989 and the 'New Times' weekend, where citizenship was one of the featured themes, held in London in October 1989. I would like to thank all those involved in the organisation of these events. I am grateful to Anthony Barnett, Jon Bloomfield, David Held, Martin Jacques and David Selbourne for helpful suggestions and comments; to Iva for translating the Civic Forum poster; to Matt Seaton at Lawrence & Wishart for his advice, support and friendship. I have also learned a great deal from conversations with Caroline Ellis about citizenship over the last eighteen months and I owe a debt to her enthusiasm.

Some of these essays have appeared in earlier versions: David Held's piece is adapted from 'Citizens and Citizenship' which appeared in *New Times* (edited by Stuart Hall and Martin Jacques, Lawrence & Wishart 1989); Michael Ignatieff's 'Citizenship and Moral Narcissism' is adapted from an essay published in *Political Quarterly* (vol 60 no1), which also appeared in *New Statesman & Society* (3 February 1989); Geoff Mulgan's 'Citizens and Responsibilities' is reprinted from *Marxism Today* (September 1990); Fred Steward's essay is substantially revised from the original which appeared in *New Times*; Jon Bloomfield's essay is reprinted from the original which was published in *Marxism Today* (January 1990); Simon Watney's essay is adapted from the original which appeared in *Identity: Community, Culture, Difference* (edited by Jonathan Rutherford, Lawrence & Wishart 1990); John Osmond's articles first appeared in *Planet*; Bhikhu Parekh's essay

9

CITIZENSHIP

is adapted from an article first published in *Britain: A Plural Society* (Commission For Racial Equality 1990); my own 'Universal Principles' first appeared in *Marxism Today* (August 1990); Paul Hirst's 'Labour and the Constitutional Crisis' is adapted from a paper given at a Charter 88 Seminar.

Geoff Andrews
September 1990

Introduction

It is some coincidence that exactly two hundred years after its modern origins, citizenship should return in situations equally dramatic and revolutionary. As with the revolution of 1789, in the revolutions of 1989 *ancien régimes* were toppled by a spontaneous movement of popular sovereignty – 'people power'. In the mainly non-violent emancipation from subjecthood (in this case, state socialism), ideas of universal rights, freedom of expression and political liberty, formed the basis of a popular will. After 1989, few will question the significance of the term 'civil society'.

Like 1789, the rebirth of citizenship will alter the international political landscape. However, the new citizenship arguments will take place in the context of the decline, rather than the foundation, of nation states. Citizenship in its new expressions will not be founded exclusively on the basis of 'national sovereignty', but will depend upon new international obligations.

The revolutions in Eastern Europe have been accompanied by a more sedate discussion of the rights, duties and status of citizenship in places where it has been assumed to have existed for centuries. The debate in Britain, the starting point for this collection of essays, has gained momentum over the last couple of years, with the rights and responsibilities of the individual, constitutional reform, European integration and the future of the planet forcing citizenship to be reconsidered. All the main political parties (not to mention intellectuals and pundits) have sought to lay claim to the language of citizenship in one way or another.

This book has two related objectives. The first is to identify the points of departure for the different claims on citizenship. This requires us to 'historicise' the idea of citizenship. What has propelled citizenship at this moment to a prime position in so many otherwise divergent political agendas? What is the substance of the new politics of citizenship? Where does subjecthood end and citizenship begin?

In Britain citizenship has emerged as an ideological escape-route for both the right and the left. On the right, the language of citizenship – and specifically Douglas Hurd's notion of 'active citizenship' – has been a further indication of the end of Thatcherite hegemony as it attempts to shed its uncaring, self-interested image. Thatcherism has sought, belatedly, to recover a tradition of communitarianism in Conservative ideology, dating back to an earlier Victorian period in which the virtues of self-help were combined with a moral obligation to help worthy causes.

For the left, citizenship has been the focus for a new concern with rights. Individual freedom has assumed a much more prominent place in socialist thinking in an attempt to depart from both the experiences of 'real socialism' and the paternalist state bureaucracy of Labourism. It is liberty rather than equality that socialists now turn to with enthusiasm, with personal freedom given a greater prominence in most left agendas, including Labour's own 'Looking to the Future', than the redistribution of wealth.

The left's attempt to project itself as the representative of liberty is one element of a wider concern with the status of the individual within civil society. Against the background of the erosion of civil liberties and the abuses of executive power in the Thatcher era, together with the unfair electoral system and a long list of civil injustices by the state, a more fundamental attempt has been made to consider the constitutional basis upon which our democratic and political settlement has been founded. This has been the project of Charter 88, launched from the *New Statesman* three hundred years after the last constitutional settlement, the so-called Glorious Revolution.

Charter 88's arguments for constitutional reform are beginning to have a profound effect on political debate. In particular, Labour – which the Charter has targeted as the most realistic vehicle for constitutional change – has moved significantly on most of the Charter's demands.[1] It is shifting ground virtually every day on the question of electoral reform: the Party constituencies and regions are putting increasing pressure on the leadership for a fairer system of voting. While Labour stops short of arguing for a written constitution, it has been sufficiently moved to recommend a Charter of Rights, which it argues (together with other critics of Charter 88), would not be subject like a Bill of Rights to the interpretations of a reactionary judiciary, but could be revised on the authority of an elected second chamber. At the time of writing, the debate over legal reform is the most contentious between Labour and the Charter, with the former appearing to accept the need to incorporate the European Convention on Human Rights into British law.

Charter 88's proposals would entail a transformation of the British constitutional system which has also proved to be a major issue on which the left seeks common ground with the centre, and in particular the liberal tradition, on what has previously been unfamiliar territory. Citizenship appears – in the dimensions of constitutional reform – as a historic compromise between socialists and liberals. This raises wider questions and the second purpose of the book, which is to locate the new politics of citizenship within the context and prospects of the left.

The left's endorsement of citizenship has not been unanimous nor is it without problems. Despite its progressive origins citizenship, for the left in Britain until recently, has carried a reactionary meaning. It was identified with control of immigration and the succession of Nationality Acts that placed conditions on aspiring (usually non-white) citizens. This is the citizenship idea of the Tebbit cricket test, in which citizenship is offered on assimilationist grounds, that people have the right to residence if they conform to cultural preconditions. 'Citizenship' in this context is the ideological yardstick for measuring the entitlement of 'worthy' applicants to residence. Such preconditions imply exclusion and intolerance.

Suspicion that the right's more recent ideological manoeuvres have produced another exclusive idea of citizenship is emphasised in Ruth Lister's recent book.[2] In this case, the citizens are 'successful, self-reliant, enterprising, consuming and property-owning', the subjects are those in poverty whose means prevent them from belonging to the enterprise culture (the symbol of full citizenship). Lister's argument is that, despite the rhetoric of community, the 'active citizens' are those able to stand alone, independent before the market, their freedom guaranteed by economic rather than social rights, from the 'dependency culture' – the welfare state – the right's symbol of subjecthood.

Another left suspicion of the term 'citizenship' derives from the nature of its universal identity. It has often been argued that a concept which has historically been underwritten by a patriarchal, eurocentric and heterosexual consensus, did not admit those whose 'private' identities were different. Cultural and gender difference challenges the historical idea of the citizen. However, there are indications that citizenship can remain an emancipatory ideal without entering a new theoretical jungle. New arguments are being produced which are redefining the rights, responsibilities and status of citizens, in the light of difference.

Citizenship therefore offers the left the possibility of ideological renewal: it could even become the much mooted 'Big Idea', which has been missing from left politics generally and above all from Kinnock's tough pragmatism. The potential of a new politics of citizenship which reasserts the language of community and the extension of democracy, and which offers the prospect of a more vibrant civil society with more public trust in elected representatives and greater freedom of expression, would certainly confront the despoliation of a decade of Thatcherism. But it will not be easy for the left. Socialist ideology finds itself ill-prepared for many of the citizenship values. Individual freedom has been absent from 'real socialism', and has not until recently figured highly in the British left's priorities. It is over 40 years since the left in Britain enjoyed a moral authority where ideas of 'fairness' and 'a sense of community' formed the basis of social cohesion, and then only in the aftermath of war. T.H. Marshall's dream that the postwar 'citizenship' welfare settlement, would be a 'new common experience' rather than merely a 'cash benefit' was not realised.[3]

Citizenship cannot become another episode in a 'rethinking socialism' saga – the latest flavour of the month in which socialists at last come clean about what we have always believed in. Rather citizenship should provide a focus for a wider engagement between socialists and liberals. An assessment of the relationship between the collective and the individual, liberty and equality and (critically) the community and the environment is now beginning to emerge. This book is intended as a contribution to that debate.

Notes

[1] The Charter's four political priorities, as stated in its *Summary of Prospects and Plans for the Nineties*, are: the incorporation of the European Convention on Human Rights into British law; to persuade the Labour Party to support electoral reform; to help secure the establishment of a Scottish Assembly; and to help achieve a Freedom of Information Act.

[2] Ruth Lister, *The Exclusive Society: Citizenship and the Poor*, Child Poverty Action Group, London 1990.

[3] T.H. Marshall, *Citizenship and Social Class*, Cambridge University Press, Cambridge 1950, p58.

Part I – The Rediscovery of Citizenship

Goering reached for his revolver when he heard the word 'culture'. Now it is tempting to do the same when people talk about 'citizenship': the great, but wholly indistinct, thing that parties and voters agree we should have more of … but is there anything concrete hidden in the clouds of rhetoric, or has the idea of citizenship reached a stage of vacuity?

Professor Alan Ryan, *The Times*, 12 September 1990

Between State and Civil Society: Citizenship

David Held

For more than two decades, citizenship could scarcely have been described as a central issue on the political agenda.[1] In fact, the concept seemed rather out-of-date. To the extent that it carried a deep political charge at all it was in relation to questions of immigration and emigration. Something, however, has recently changed.

A number of different factors seem to have propelled the return of citizenship to the top of the political agenda. Some derive from the experience of Thatcherism itself: the dismantling of the welfare state; the growing centralisation of power; the erosion of local democracy. Some factors have a wider, more 'global' context: the growth of regional autonomism and nationalism in Scotland and elsewhere; the prospects for greater European integration; the growing pace of international interconnections or globalisation.

These changes have been accompanied by shifts in attitude towards the idea of citizenship on both right and left of the political spectrum. It used to be fashionable in some sections of the left to dismiss the question of 'rights' as, largely, a bourgeois fraud. But the experiences of Thatcherism in the West and of neo-Stalinism in the East have gradually shifted the left's thinking on this question. The shift on the right is more uncertain. Thatcherism's drive towards unrestricted private accumulation, its attack on public expenditure and its critique of the 'dependency culture' made it the natural enemy of citizenship in its modern, welfare-state form. Yet anxiety within some sections of Tory opinion about the *anomie* of 'enterprise culture' has fostered the promotion of the 'active citizen'. Given the current tussle over its meaning, it may be worth establishing some of the fundamentals of citizenship.

From the ancient world to the present day, all forms of citizenship have had certain common attributes. Citizenship has meant a reciprocity of rights against, and duties towards, the community. Citizenship has entailed membership, membership of the community in which one lives one's life. And membership has invariably involved degrees of participation in the community. The question of who should participate and at what level is a question as old as the ancient world itself. There is much significant history in the attempt to restrict the extension of citizen rights to certain groups: among others, owners of property, white men, educated men, men, those with particular skills and occupations, adults. There is also a telling story in the various debates about what is to count as citizenship, and in particular what is to count as participation in the community.

If citizenship entails membership in the community and membership implies forms of social participation, then citizenship is above all about the involvement of people in the community in which they live; and people have been barred from citizenship on grounds of class, gender, race and age among many other factors. Accordingly, the debate about citizenship requires us to think about the very nature of the conditions of membership and political participations.

To put the point another way, if citizenship involves the struggle for membership and participation in the community, then its analysis involves examining the way in which different groups, classes and movements have struggled to gain degrees of autonomy and control over their lives in the face of various forms of stratification, hierarchy and political oppression. A concern with citizenship in its fullest sense is coterminous with a concern for issues posed by, for instance, trade unions, feminism, the black movements, ecology and those who have advocated the rights of vulnerable minorities like children. Different social movements have, then, raised different questions about the nature and dimensions of citizenship.

A reflection on the nature of citizenship rights helps to define the issues a little more sharply. Citizenship rights are *entitlements*. Such entitlements are public and social (hence Mrs Thatcher's antipathy towards them). They are 'of right' and can only be abrogated by the state under clearly delimited circumstances (for example, in the case of imprisonment). However, though citizenship is a social status, it is defined – its benefits are defined – in terms of individuals. Individual citizens enjoy entitlements on the basis of a fundamental equality of condition, which is their membership of the community. Citizenship, therefore, combines in rather unusual ways the *public* and *social* with the *individual* aspects of political life.

Citizenship rights establish a legitimate sphere for *all* individuals to pursue their actions and activities without risk of arbitrary or unjust political interference. Early attempts to achieve citizenship involved a struggle for the autonomy or independence of individuals from the place in which they were born and from prescribed occupations. Later struggles have involved such things as individual entitlement to freedom of speech, expression, belief, information, as well as the freedom of association on which trade-union rights depend, and freedom for women in relation to marriage and property.

The left critique of this position – essentially the liberal conception of citizenship – is by now quite familiar, and carries considerable weight. It centres on the emphasis, in the language of rights, on *individual* entitlement, but contains several strands: first, the degree to which individuals are 'free' and the nature of that 'freedom' is open to question in capitalist democracies; second, everything depends on how freedom is defined, for the freedoms which interest the liberal right refer primarily to a very narrow arena of action in the marketplace; third, citizenship rights, particularly in Britain, are largely defined negatively, so that, for instance, there are no laws preventing us entering the Ritz or buying property in Docklands or applying for most jobs. Whether in fact we have the means or the capacity, let alone a positive entitlement, to do or achieve any of these things is quite a different matter.

This relates to the tension, often noted, between 'formal' and 'substantive' rights. The citizen may formally enjoy 'equality before the law' but, important though this unquestionably is, does he or she *also* have the capacities (the material and cultural resources) to choose between different courses of action in practice? Do existing relations between men and women, between employers and employees, between the different social classes, or between blacks, whites and other ethnic groups, allow citizenship to become a reality in practice? This question lies at the centre of the 'politics of citizenship' today. Any current assessment of citizenship must be made on the basis of liberties and rights which are tangible, capable of being enjoyed, in both the *state* and *civil society*. If it is not given concrete and practical content, liberty as an abstract principle can scarcely be said to have any very profound consequences for everyday life.

So there is a great deal of substance to the left's critique of the liberal conception of citizenship. On the other hand, this critique may have led the left too often to dismiss the significance of rights altogether. We must certainly test every 'formal' right we are supposed to enjoy against its substance in practice. But this does not mean that the formal definition of rights (for example, in a constitution or bill of rights) is unimportant, or a matter of 'mere form', as is often claimed.

What this line of reasoning suggests is that the 'politics of citizenship' must come to terms with, and attempt to strike a new balance between, the individual and the social dimensions of citizenship rights. These two aspects are interdependent and inseparable; neither on its own will suffice.

Despite some justifiable scepticism about citizenship rights, the left's engagement, in my view, has traditionally been muddled and confused. For instance, the orthodox left has generally regarded the state as the only force of sufficiently compelling weight to bring to bear against the power of property and capital. As a consequence, in the left's lexicon of citizenship, the state is not inimical but essential to the very idea of citizenship.

This view is partly right: it is difficult to see how a proper conception of citizenship could be established with full social and public status, or how the means to ensure its effectiveness could be secured, without the intervention of the state. On the other hand, citizenship also entails the protection of the citizen *against* the arbitrary exercise of state power. The weaknesses and limitations of a purely 'statist' conception of citizenship have become much more obvious in the light of recent history, both in the West (with the decline of the social-democratic vision of reform) and in the East (via the crisis of Communism). There is, then, a tension in the left's position on citizenship since it both depends upon, and can be threatened by, the state.

One strategy of the left has been to try to resolve or by-pass this difficult issue by dissolving the whole question into that of democracy itself. The development and extension of public democracy, it is thought, will resolve all these knotty problems. This, in turn, has led to the left's advocacy of collective decision-making as a resolution to all the problems of citizenship. The 'democratic' solution is in many ways attractive, but it presents certain real difficulties. It is vulnerable to the charge of having failed to address the highly complex relations in modern societies between individual liberty, distributional questions of social justice and democratic processes. And it poses the extremely awkward issue of whether there are to be any specifiable limits to democracy (such as, for instance, whether minorities should be protected from 'assimilation' or enforced conformity).

The challenge, then, is to think through the meaning of citizenship without falling prey to some serious objections arising from oversimplified and lazy conceptions of the 'state' or 'democracy', which themselves contain problems. One point which has already emerged can be stated clearly. There is a need to formulate and give institutional expression to, the demands of citizenship and democracy as closely-related issues; *but it is important to keep these questions distinct*. Democracy can only really exist on the basis of 'free and equal citizens', but citizenship requires some specification, and some institutional and political protection, separate from and beyond the simple extension of democracy. In short, in the relationship between citizenship and democracy a new balance is entailed, a new settlement between liberty and equality.

Evidently the parameters of such a 'new settlement' need further definition. It appears that a plausible resolution of some of the dilemmas of contemporary politics can only be provided if enhanced political participation is embedded in a legal and constitutional framework that protects and nurtures individuals, and other social categories, as 'free and equal citizens'. This requires us to recognise the importance of a number of fundamental tenets, often dismissed because of their association with liberalism: for example, the centrality, in principle, of an 'impersonal' structure of public power; the need for a constitution to help guarantee and protect rights; a diversity of power centres; mechanisms to promote open debate between alternative political platforms; an institutional framework of enforceable and challengeable rights.

For the left in particular, the implications of these points are, I believe, profound. For a socialist democracy to flourish today it has to be reconceived as a *double-sided* phenomenon: concerned, on the one hand, with the reform of state power and, on the other hand, with the restructuring of civil society.[2] This involves recognising the indispensability of a process of 'double democratisation' which means, in practice, the interdependent transformation of both state and civil society. Such a process must reject the assumption that the state could ever replace civil society or vice versa. It must defend thereby, on the one hand, the liberal principle that the separation of the state and civil society must be a permanent feature of any democratic political order and, on the other hand, the Marxist notion that this order must be one in which the power to make decisions is no longer subject to private appropriation. The aim would be progressively to equalise the power and, thereby, the capacity of men and women to act in the key realms of political and social life – in other words, to acquire full citizenship. To put the point another way, a socialist democracy would only be fully worth its name if citizens had the actual power to be active as citizens, to enjoy a bundle of rights which allowed them to command democratic participation and to treat it as an entitlement. Such a bundle of rights should be seen as identical with, and integral to, the very notion of democratic rule itself. It is a way of specifying certain socio-economic conditions for the possibility of effective democratic participation. One final question remains unanswered: to what political entity does the democratic citizen belong? Everywhere the sovereignty of the nation state itself – the entity to which the language of citizenship refers, and within which the claims of citizenship, community and participation are made – is being eroded and challenged. Externally, the processes of economic, political, military and ecological interrelation are beginning to undermine the status of nation state as a sacred and self-sufficient entity. The rise of regional and local 'nationalisms' are beginning to wear away at it internally. The historical moment seems to have passed for trying to define citizens' claims and entitlements in

24

terms of membership of a *national* community. Equally, ecological disaster – whether in terms of pollution, damage to the ozone layer or the 'greenhouse effect' – does not acknowledge national boundaries and frontiers. The threat of ecological disaster creates the conditions for giving priority to the claims of humanity and *its* needs, the language of the citizens of 'Planet Earth', rather than the language of the nation-state democracies.

These are real and complex problems besetting any attempt to develop a modern conception of citizenship, and they cannot and will not be easily resolved. On the other hand, they may represent difficulties, but they do not constitute reasons for giving up the idea of citizenship.[3] In the meantime, there is *no* world political community to which we can formally 'belong', and the nature and quality of *our* particular 'membership' of *our* specific political community remains a pressing issue: unless we resolve it for ourselves, it will be resolved for us.

Notes

[1] This paper was delivered at the 'New Times' conference organised by *Marxism Today*, 27-29 October, 1989. It draws on a number of sources, where different elements of the argument are elaborated: 'Citizens and Citizenship' (with Stuart Hall) in *New Times: The Changing Face of Politics in the 1990s*, edited by Stuart Hall and Martin Jacques, Lawrence and Wishart, London 1989, pp173-188; my 'Citizenship and Autonomy', in *Political Theory and the Modern State*, Polity Press, Cambridge 1989, pp189-213; and my *Models of Democracy*, Polity Press, Cambridge 1986, chapters 8-9.
[2] See my *Models of Democracy*, *op.cit.*, and John Keane, *Democracy and Civil Society*, Verso, London 1988.
[3] For a fuller treatment of these issues see my 'Democracy, the National State and the Global System', in *Political Theory Today*, Polity Press, Cambridge, forthcoming.

Citizenship and Moral Narcissism

Michael Ignatieff

A new figure of speech – the 'active citizen' – is popping up in the political vocabulary of the Conservative Party. In speeches by the Prime Minister and the Home Secretary, the active citizen is frequently evoked: the good-hearted, property-owning patriot, who serves as an unpaid JP if asked, does jury service, gives a day a week to meals on wheels, checks that the old-age pensioner next door is tucked in on cold days, and so on. The accent is on good neighbourliness, public spiritedness and, above all, on property. For it is property that makes the active citizen active. Without property, a citizen cannot be independent; without the income of property, an individual will not have the leisure necessary to be a good citizen. Without property, the citizen is passive, a ward of the state, a dependent on the benefit cheque, the social services and the council housing department.

The active citizen is an idea deployed defensively: to lumber Labour as the party of state tutelage and to rebut the persistent and damaging charge that Conservatism is the party of greed and selfishness. The active citizen is also an image meant to take the party on the offensive, to give Conservatism an ideological hold on just about everyone's wishful best image of themselves: as the good neighbour, the concerned and active member of the community.

The rhetoric of the active citizen is modern Conservatism's latest attempt to create a genuine and believable language of community. What is interesting is that it cannot make itself believable: each hymn to the active citizen is shadowed by unstated but menacing disapproval of the passive citizen. Each evocation of the heart-warming traditions of

English voluntarism ends up as yet another party-political attack on the dead hand of Labourist statism.

Try as it might, Conservatism cannot make it to the unifying higher ground. Its language of citizenship, intended to unite, only serves to divide. The reasons for this are complicated. In the first place, society is too riven by the radically unequal consequences of the Thatcherite boom to be sewn back together with patches of rhetorical flannel. More importantly, Conservatism is itself riven between the vestigial communitarianism of its ageing grandees and the radical individualism of its present leader. If the Conservative image of citizenship is ambiguous, it is because Mrs Thatcher came to power in 1979, not to reform the civic contract between state and citizens, but to rip it up and begin again.

The political counter-revolution that brought Margaret Thatcher to power can be understood as an attack on the citizenship of equal entitlement in postwar liberal democratic society. Citizenship has its active modes (running for political office, voting, political organising) and its passive modes (entitlements to rights and welfare). The ideal of citizenship current in postwar Britain gave special emphasis to the passive mode: equal entitlement to family allowance, free health care, the dole and the old age pension. This citizenship of shared entitlement came to be understood in the Conservative thought of the late 1970s as a coercive bargain between strangers which abridged the liberties of both rich and poor while infantilising the poor.

In the irreparable ruination of the socialist tradition which did so much, alongside liberalism, to put the postwar civic contract into place, it is tempting to return to the classical discourse on citizenship – to seek to reconstruct the intellectual case for a vision of society as a political community to set against the market individualism of conservatives.

Since the Greeks, philosophers languishing under venal or despotic forms of human rule have been inspired by an ideal of a public realm in which the individual debates and deliberates on the public good, transcends the limits of private interest and becomes what Aristotle said a man truly was – a political animal. The republican myth of citizenship which traverses Western history from Cicero and the Roman republics through the early Italian city states of the thirteenth century, Calvin's Geneva and the English Commonwealth became, with the emergence of market society in the eighteenth century, the major vernacular for the criticism of the selfishness and lack of public spiritedness in modern market man. In Rousseau's *Discourse on the Origin of Inequality* (1755), for example, the myth of citizenship – like the myth of the primitive savage – inspired a threnody on the corruption of political virtue by market greed.

It was Marx who forged the intellectual junction point between a Rousseauian doctrine of citizenship which had declined into moral jeremiad and an emergent socialist critique of capitalist modernity. In the early 1840s, Marx subjected the myth of citizenship to devastating scrutiny. Modern man, he concluded, was riven by the conflict between his identities as *bourgeois* and as *citoyen*: the former expressed his real interests; the latter fabricated a merely legal equality. In the market he lived as an unequal competitor, in the *polis* he was only nominally a rights-bearing equal. The doctrine of communism, hammered out then, can be seen as an attempt to envisage a form of political society in which the contradiction between *bourgeois* and *citoyen* would be reconciled. Socialist production would create the conditions of affluence and leisure which would allow communist men and women to realise the Aristotelian ideal and overcome the split between private interests and public good. Marxism, in this interpretation, was an attempt to render the ideal of citizenship applicable in modern economic conditions. It failed because the command economy is incompatible with either democracy or efficiency and because its politics never entrenched and protected private rights.

Yet if communism failed to find a way to enact the ideal of citizenship in modern conditions, Marx's indictment of bourgeois citizenship was surely correct. The social history of citizenship in late nineteenth-century and early twentieth-century Europe can be understood schematically as an attempt to reduce the contradiction Marx had discerned between real inequality in the market and the formal equality promised by the civic contract of modern democracies ruled by universal suffrage. This struggle was led from below by working-class and feminist organisations, assisted from above by middle-class liberals or socialists repelled by the contradiction between the formal and the real. It was in struggling against this contradiction that an essentially individualistic market society created the modern interventionist state.

The history of the welfare state in the twentieth century can be understood as a struggle to transform the liberty conferred by formal legal rights into the freedom guaranteed by shared social entitlement. Given the tendency of markets to generate inequality, the state was called upon, by its own citizens, to redress the balance with entitlements designed to keep the contradiction between real inequality and formal equality from becoming intolerable. From this history of struggle was created the modern social-democratic polity: formally neutral on what constitutes the good life, yet committed to providing the collective necessities for the free pursuit of that good life, however individuals conceive of it.

The Conservative counter-revolution has rewritten the history of citizenship in order to drive home a very different message. Largely under the influence of Hayek and Popper, post-war European conservatism viewed the history of collectivism as a conspiracy against liberty. The citizenship of entitlement throttled both the market and the liberty it was intended to enhance. This style of argument about the welfare state set up an enduring antithesis in Conservative thought between the market (realm of liberty, initiative, responsibility, efficiency) and the citizenship of entitlement (realm of regimentation, collectivism and bureaucratic despotism).

Instead of confronting Conservative mythology head-on, many British liberals, social democrats and former socialists have taken refuge in a lament for the vanished civilities of postwar British citizenship and in pious homilies against market values. Lament for the lost values of civic spirit may be nothing more than harmless sentimentality but becomes pernicious when it casts a fog of illusion over the real failures and limitations of the postwar experiment in citizenship. When, moreover, the rhetoric of citizenship is used, not to understand market society but simply to express moral distaste for the vulgarity of market values, it becomes a form of moral narcissism – that, is a rhetoric of complacency whose result is to reassure those who cannot bear the moral complexity of a market society that they are sensitive and superior beings.

What the losing sides in politics do not need is complacent conviction of the superiority of their values. They need to think hard about why they lost, about why the treasured words and fastidious distaste they keep expressing have led them into a theoretical and practical *cul de sac*.

Evoking the idea that we should be citizens, and not just predators, in the Thatcherite rat-race may warm the heart but it casts a veil over inconvenient questions. Specifically, under what economic regime is citizenship, either active or passive, actually possible? Since at least Rousseau's time, the political theory of citizenship has confronted the reality of the market economy and it has never fully met the challenge of reconciling an egalitarian community of citizens with a free market. Rousseau believed that market processes would subvert the equality and selflessness required for virtuous civic deliberation, and he could see only one way in which actually existing civic republics, at sea in the market economy, could survive: by creating a fortress economy, immured from the tides of international competition without and inequality and selfishness within. This sort of answer – eerily echoed across the centuries by the import-control socialism of the late 1970s – escapes the reality of the market economy with a leap into political science fiction.

Yet such leaps cannot conjure the difficulty away. Rousseau was right: market economies do generate substantial inequalities; indeed they require them and reward them. But a political community of citizens requires a rough equality of rights and at least a rough equality of starting conditions. Any invocation of citizenship as an ideal that is not just heart-warming words has to make its peace with the indubitable efficiency of markets and then to define and implement its redistributive goals in such a way that they do not crush the liberty that equality of opportunity exists to enhance.

The second difficulty, which has dogged the language of citizenship throughout its history, concerns what is a political question and what is not. What questions should be left to the determination of the market or to private reason and what should be collectively decided?

In general terms, the strength of the market case is that given the infinitely contestable nature of the argument about collective distribution of national income, it is both more efficient and more democratic to leave this argument to be worked out in each home, by each private individual determining how much income to devote to current consumption, and how much to education, saving for retirement and so on. Political allocation of these choices, free-market ideologists maintain, is to infringe the rights of those individuals who want to spend either more or less than the democratically agreed mean. A defence of citizenship must, therefore, be able to show that for a majority of citizens, collective choices produce results superior to those reached by private allocation of income.

The third difficulty, connected to the second, concerns representation. We are a long way from Athens: democracy is dead in the modern world. Since it is dead, we must delegate, and as soon as we delegate, either to a bureaucrat or a politician, the question of whether they represent their interests or our own arises. All systems of representation present a problem of accountability and this problem has dogged social-democratic politics in the postwar world.

It is no accident that the citizenship ideal of postwar liberals and social democrats stressed the passive quality of entitlement at the expense of the active equality of participation. The entitled were never empowered because empowerment would have infringed the prerogatives of the managers of the welfare state. Housing estates were run 'in the name' of the citizens by council housing departments who had no desire to surrender any of their delegated powers. Tower blocks were run up 'in the name of' working communities whose wishes, had they ever been consulted, would have been for the repair and refurbishment of their existing low-rise housing.

Postwar social democrats talked in terms of the enabling and facilitating state and never faced the empirical evidence that the interests of the state – its officials and politics – were sometimes in opposition to those of ordinary citizens. The language of the state as servant of its citizens encouraged public sector unions to equate their interests in the collective bargaining process with the interests of the citizens their members were said to serve. The rhetorical shell-game in which trade-union power spoke the language of public service might have been avoided had there been a more robust awareness, in postwar social-democratic language of citizenship, of the need for countervailing power, checks and balances, safeguards of the rights of citizens against their representatives.

Postwar social-democratic thinking about citizenship never pursued its rhetoric about accountability to the point of devising sanctions ordinary citizens could use to punish incompetence or unresponsiveness in the state bureaucracies. Ordinary citizens believe, rightly or wrongly, that no one in the public service is ever punished for a mistake. Again the plausibility of market solutions is that – under competitive conditions at least – the consumer enjoys the sanction of going elsewhere.

These failures of social democracy need to be reiterated because so many people on the losing side of politics persist in believing the heart of the Conservative case is an appeal to greed alone. *Enrichissez-vous* is certainly a more appealing gambit than 'Who is my brother's keeper?' Yet the core of the electoral case made for the free market by the British Conservatives in 1979 was not just that it would enrich the British people, but that it would also enfranchise and empower them. Creating a market in council house properties freed the better-off tenants from the dead hand of the council housing department; denationalisation and share-sales offered workers a 'piece of the action' in their own companies.

In place of the fictive identification of workers with their enterprise offered by public ownership, Conservative legislation delivered what many workers believe to be a real identification with the prospects of the company. Any counter-attack which attempts to counterpose the noble principles of citizenship to the venality of private greed will fail because it misunderstands the fundamental appeal of these measures: they appear not merely to enrich, but also to empower. Criticism of them works only if they can be shown to do neither.

If the core of the anti-Thatcherism case is that a politics of selfishness poisons the well-springs of altruism and lays waste the welfare institutions that reproduce solidarity, then the counter-attack will have first to confront the ambiguous impact of the postwar welfare state on social solidarity. For the impacts are markedly paradoxical. When, for example, social workers take over the caring functions formerly discharged by family members, there is both a gain and a loss: dependent individuals may be better cared for in institutional or public settings, and family members, particularly women, will be freed to enter the labour market or otherwise use their time as they wish. But it is occasionally the case that a sense of family obligation suffers, and community ties among strangers may be weakened when everyone comes to believe that 'it's the council's job'.

The welfare state did encourage the emergence of new styles of moral self-exculpation, not only among welfare dependants but among the tax-paying public. 'It's the council's job' became everyone's first line of defence when confronted with vandalism, the neglect of civic property, or more seriously, abuse of children or abandonment of the aged. In public housing especially, the maxim 'everybody's property is nobody's property' helps to explain the all too frequent downward spiral of neglect.

If the idea of citizenship is in trouble these days, it is because practical experience did not always validate the postwar civic ideal that public goods would extend civic solidarity. In some cases – the health services – it did. The National Health Service still enjoys popular support despite its increasing inefficiency and squalor because it incarnates the primal equality on which political citizenship is based, equality of the body in the face of illness and death. But in other areas, like public housing and education, the delivery of the services themselves was often either so mediocre or so undemocratic, that individuals were only behaving rationally when they opted out whenever their income allowed them to.

Further, when Labour proved unable to manage the corporatist bargain between labour, capital and the state, and the economy began to stagnate, the resultant decline in the quality of public goods simply hastened the exit of the vocal and the highly paid. For these groups, the citizenship of the 1970s seemed to be a poor bargain indeed: higher and higher levels of taxation for declining levels of public service.

Faced with the crisis of confidence in public goods, opponents of Mrs Thatcher have unfailingly succumbed to the moral temptation of defining themselves as the altruists, the ones who care, against the supposedly selfish hedonism of the Conservatives. But to describe the welfare state in the language of caring is to misdescribe it, and to deceive. The civic pact of the welfare state was not between 'haves' and 'have nots', between care-givers and care-receivers. The break with Poor Law principles was explicit and deliberate. The basis of a citizenship of entitlements was the insurance principle and universality of benefit: everyone contributed and everyone benefited. The effects may have been regressive – the middle class did disproportionately well out of the welfare state – but this was the inevitable result of the Beveridgian intention to ground social solidarity on equality of

33

entitlement, rather than on the rich helping/caring for the poor.

To continue to describe the welfare state as a 'caring institution', and to pose as the political party that 'cares', is to think of entitlements as if they were a matter of moral generosity, when in fact, they are a matter of right. Moreover, anyone who has endured social security waiting rooms will be surprised to hear that their particular combination of squalor and officiousness is an instance of 'caring'. Only someone who has not actually been on the receiving end of the welfare state would dare call it an instance of civil altruism at work.

The language of citizenship is not properly about compassion at all, since compassion is a private virtue which cannot be legislated or enforced. The practice of citizenship is about ensuring for everyone the entitlements necessary to the exercise of their liberty. As a political question, welfare is about rights, not caring, and the history of citizenship has been the struggle to make freedom real, not to tie us all in the leading strings of therapeutic good intentions.

I do not want to live in the 'caring society' beloved of Labour and SDP party political broadcasts, because it evokes for me the image of a nanny state in which the care we get depends on what the 'caring professions' think it fit for us to receive. I would prefer to live in a society which struggles to be just, respects and enhances people's rights and entitlements. The pell-mell retreat from the language of justice to the language of caring is perhaps the most worrying sign of the decadence of the language of citizenship among all parties to the left of Mrs Thatcher.

Were liberals, social democrats and socialists to work themselves free of the seductive pleasures of moral superiority and false nostalgia they might be able to devleop a robust alternative vision to market Conservatism. As long as it is believed that such an alternative depends on mobilising those well-springs of civil altruism, and that such well-springs are being steadily poisoned by Thatcherian greed, there can be little grounds for hope at all. But the history of citizenship sketched at the outset would show that the twentieth-century citizenship of entitlement was not built on altruism so much as emerging awareness of the indissoluble interdependence of the private and public.

Put another way, the history of citizenship of entitlement is a history of freedom, not primarily a history of compassion. People have struggled to extend and defend public transport, health care, unemployment insurance and pensions because these provide the starting conditions that make individual freedom possible. That awareness of the structural dependence of private freedom on public provision is as strong now after a decade of Mrs Thatcher as it ever was. Poll data consistently indicate support for high levels of public expenditure in the fields of health, education, and social welfare.

It is notorious that neither in Margaret Thatcher's Britain nor in Ronald Reagan's America has public expenditure diminished as a percentage of GNP. In Britain the privatisation of public assets has not brought down the levels of state expenditure in the economy. The income windfalls from privatisation have been used to maintain expenditure on welfare, manpower training, unemployment benefit and health services, while lowering levels of taxation for the better-off. Rolling back the frontiers of the state has been a matter of playing at the margins.

It is here that modern Conservatism reveals its incoherence: in the increasing gap between its anti-statist rhetoric and its public expenditure performance, and in its larger failure to appreciate the extent to which private satisfactions depend, in the modern world, on share entitlements. The pathologies of modern living – pollution, overcrowding, despoliation of the common heritage of nature, exhaustion of natural resources – repeatedly bring home to any citizen the extent to which the satisfactions of private consumptions are vitiated when the environmental regulation that only the state can enforce is absent.

Private affluence is a humble but important human good, but it becomes a hollow when 'enjoyed' amid public squalor. Understanding this does not require altruism, compassion or even very much civic pride. It requires nothing more than a pair of eyes to see.

There is, it turns out, a deep incoherence in Conservative attitudes towards their central value – freedom. Conservatives believe the polity exists to maximise private freedom but do not believe the polity should provide the means to enable all citizens to be free. It is this incoherence that an alternative politics has to exploit. There is nothing wrong with Mrs Thatcher's values: putting freedom first is what liberal society has always stood for. There is nothing wrong with enterprise, initiative, personal responsibility or even the lawful pursuit of private profit. What is incoherent is believing these goals can be achieved without a citizenship of entitlement, without the shared foundation that alone makes freedom possible.

Citizens and Responsibilities

Geoff Mulgan

Some like to read the history of the last 200 years as a faltering but unmistakable accretion of freedoms and rights. The idea of citizenship is one way of giving form to this progress. An alternative view sees the last 200 years as an increasingly frenzied abuse of the powers of industrial society, as the use of new freedoms was not tempered by any sense of limit. Both views have a solid base at the start of the 1990s, ensuring that their reconciliation will be one of the decade's most difficult challenges.

In this essay I want to argue that a third theme, as persuasive if less clearly defined than the other two, offers a way of bringing these two conflicting outlooks into line. It can be summed up in one word: responsibility.

Having become a dull and dusty word, perhaps a bit too pious for the late twentieth century, responsibility is again being invoked by people as diverse as Vaclav Havel, Prince Charles and Jesse Jackson. Strong commitments to an ethos of responsibility can be found in the feminists' comparison of the male lust for power without responsibility and the caring spirit of reproduction and nurture, and in the green slogan about thinking global and acting local. In rhetoric of corporate responsibility it is being used, sometimes cynically, by businesses eager to show their commitment to community. In Douglas Hurd's 'active citizenship' and Chris Patten's failed attempt to introduce green taxes there is evidence of the right's unease with the irresponsibility of 1980s Thatcherism.

These arguments about responsibility resist easy appropriation. They are neither obviously right-wing nor left-wing. They challenge both the unfairness and amorality of the market and the diffusion of responsibility brought about by large-scale industrial socialism. They suggest that the world's deficits of responsibility can be solved only by linking a strong individual ethic with a new affirmation of what it means to live as part of a community. There is a special reason why these arguments are pressing for the British left. Although it has begun to convince people that it can offer material well-being, a more balanced and whole prosperity, and although it has come to feel more in season than the right, the left has found it hard to occupy the moral high ground. It still lacks a moral centre and still remains vulnerable to the charge that it is short on principle and substance.

Across the world three historic crises have forced these issues on to the political agenda. The first has been the collapse of communism. A large part of its failure was practical, an inability to make things work. But equally important was its failure to be responsible, either in the sense of being accountable to those on the receiving end of decisions or in the sense of having an ethos of responsible behaviour. Instead, power corrupted and absolute power corrupted absolutely. Marxism-Leninism offered no guidance as to how individuals should use power, or about their standards of truth and propriety. As a result many of the most magnetic ideas in the East today come from those who assert the obligation of the individual and community to truth and responsibility. Havel, Sakharov and Fang Lizhi have all invoked high standards of personal behaviour as a starting point for any credible politics. All have denounced the way a totalitarian, corrupted and amoral society corrodes any sense of individual responsibility.

The second crisis has been that of the environment. The green movement calls to account the responsibility not only of politicians and industrialists but also of the human species. Humans are held to bear responsibilities to other species and to life itself. A retreat from industrial civilisation is justified on the grounds that only then can human power be brought into line with humans' capacity to use it responsibly. Meanwhile, in its more immediately political forms, the green movement has successfully called for regulations and taxes to make the polluter pay, for a more responsible ethos of consumption and for the state to impose responsibility on to those who cause damage. The political and the personal are seen to be intimately linked, and one of the great appeals of green ideas is their claim that the individual can act in practical, everyday ways, rather than waiting for states to find collective solutions.

The third crisis arises from the legacy of Reaganism and Thatcherism. Responsibility was always an important element in neo-conservative rhetoric. It underpinned the claimed moral superiority of the right. The left could be characterised as spending without earning, as creating dependency and sapping the self-responsibility of people and communities. It could be shown as engaged in a perpetual search for alibis, blaming every ill on society or others. Under socialism the buck would never stop. The right promised that it would reverse the irresponsibility of socialism by reducing people's dependence on the state. Margaret Thatcher's proud boast of her first administration was that it had achieved a shift away from a state which was 'totally dominant in people's lives and penetrated almost every aspect of life to a life where the state did do certain things, but without displacing personal responsibility …'.

Ironically it is now the arriviste right that seems the very acme of irresponsibility. Far from raising standards of behaviour, Thatcherism and Reaganism brought a serious decline. An expansion of individual freedom for some was not balanced by a sufficiently strong sense of social duty. Far from ushering in a more responsible society, the right created the conditions for greed, indifference and carelessness to flourish. The result has been both a political and a moral crisis for the right. It has failed to square its libertarianism and its conservatism. It has failed to convince that its policies for increasing responsibility are more than a weak apology for cuts in public services. And it has failed to forge a true 'moral majority' behind its programme.

These three crises, of communism, of the environment and of the right, present both opportunities and dangers for the left. The opportunities arise because a sense of mutual obligation is central to why most people think of themselves as socialists. It is the moral core of socialism as personal credo, as opposed to the socialism of scientific analysis and world-conquering movements. It is what carries the left to the moral high ground. The dangers come from the fact that the left still shies away from the implications of a strong ethos of individual responsibility. It still feels more comfortable concentrating responsibility in the hands of the state and of remote collective institutions. It is still ill at ease with the suggestion that socialised forms can dissipate responsibility as much as the market. It is still ambivalent about arguments that emphasise ethos and morality over structure and interest, universal values over political economy.

These problems have not been solved by the left's recent shift away from an inflexible statism towards a more libertarian and permissive stance. If anything they have been exacerbated. By concentrating too narrowly on the need to devolve power and on the virtues of freedom, issues of responsibility have been pushed to the margins. This is all too apparent in today's fashionable code-words. The words 'enabling', 'empowerment', 'citizenship' and 'consumerism' promise a dispersal of power away from an oppressive and monolithic state. State power is to be broken down and distributed fairly. Citizens are to be given clearly-defined rights.

As a result of this new rhetoric of enabling, right and left now speak remarkably similar languages. Where the new right suggests granting people entitlement in the market, the left proposes to give them powers through local democratic institutions or constitutionally guaranteed rights. Where the right offers tax cuts, subsidised council-house sales and utility shares, the left offers regional assemblies and citizens' rights, training credits and denominational schools. The exchange has gone in both directions. But while the right has learned the power of libertarian radical-democratic and populist arguments, the left the organisational virtues of markets, both have lost something. Both have become embarrassed by moral arguments. Both have come to see power as a commodity that can be distributed and parcelled up, the state as a body that can choose to give this or that section of the population units of empowerment. Once received, power is simply there to be used. A Santa Claus state dishes out powers without making demands on those receiving them. Left and right compete as to the attractiveness of what is to be distributed.

For parties to be engaged in a competition to wither away the state is certainly novel historically and not without its attractions. But amid the celebration, difficult questions are coming to the surface. There is widespread unease about the implications of a more fragmented, heterogeneous world. A broken-up state in a broken-up society seems to imply an inevitable loss of universal solidarities and mutual responsibilities. There is unease that the left's ideas about citizenship should end up as nothing more than a package of rights without obligations, a programme for a loose society in which relationships are contingent and undemanding. This despite the fact that many are asking whether, to paraphrase John Kennedy, the question is not what the community can do for you but what you can do for it.

I shall come back to these questions later. At this stage it is enough to reflect that each step towards dismantling the state is deeply ambivalent. The right often seems to want to devolve responsibilities without distributing the power (and the money) to bear them. The left often seems to want to devolve power while silently assuming that the state still bears the final responsibility for outcomes. Both, meanwhile, are sometimes less than honest about the fact that each step towards decentralisation helps to solve the state's legitimation crisis precisely because it allows government to absolve itself of responsibility. Whitehall walks away, and politicians find a perfect alibi. Having privatised and devolved, they can simply shrug their shoulders and say, 'None of my business', when something goes wrong.

This is also true of reforms to the machinery of government. The new right used to argue that the classic impulse of politicians and bureaucrats is to build empires. Yet throughout the 1980s, states of all political stripes have happily divested themselves of functions. Recent studies offer an explanation. Like the modern corporation, the most rational and perceptive modern bureaucracy aims to maximise its power and minimise is responsibilities. To do this it slims itself down to a strategic core and hives off all operational functions. While maintaining strategic control and all the perks of power, it too can shrug its shoulders when anything goes wrong.

The dangers of an imbalance between power and responsibility also apply to the individual, and to the question of freedom. The last year has seen an orgy of praise for freedom. Left, right and centre justify their actions as expanding the realm of freedom. It is the one unquestioned ideal, with almost no visible enemies outside Beijing, Baghdad and a few other forsaken places. This is in almost every way a good thing. To anyone living under alien tyranny there is nothing more important than freedom. It is a pressing, almost palpable need. It is the necessary condition for life itself. But come the revolution it turns out that while freedom may have been a necessary condition it is sufficient for nothing. It doesn't give any clues as to how to behave to others; how to share; how to think; or how to feel. It tells us nothing about judgment, about right or wrong. It simply defers from the social to the individual all the big problems. At its worst the rhetoric of freedom represents the conquest of meaning by vacuity.

Few today use that clear distinction between freedom and licence, between freedom, and freedom to do the right thing, that dates back to St Augustine and beyond, and that makes a link between politics and personal morality. We now assume that the only worthwhile freedom is the freedom to do wrong, freedom without restraint. This may be the curse of an era that still lives in the shadow of utopian ideologies. Utopias maximise freedom. They never maximise responsibilities, though it is arguable that the bearing of responsibility is as much an end of human potential as the exercise of freedom. In this sense utopias are childlike. Like the worst demagogues, they promise without demanding.

Marxism shares all these weaknesses. It has been notoriously silent on the problems of power and freedom. While much of its intellectual labour went into detailing the manifold forms of power, economic, ideological and cultural, it was easy to succumb to the utopian belief that in the future power could be eliminated and replaced by freedom without compromise. If the end is a society without power, states and mediating representatives, then there are no problems of responsibility.

The one realm where the left has consistently spoken a language of responsibility is around accountability. This idea has a long history. The democratic and later the socialist revolution promised to bring power into line with responsibility and accountability. Instead of the caprice of kings and the indifference of bankers, public actions would be open to scrutiny and judgment. Anyone exercising power would have to stand or fall by their record. Government would become accountable and transparent, responsive and responsible. Those on the receiving end of power would have a chance to know what was done in their name.

There are still strong echoes in today's left. Freedom of information acts, co-determination in companies, democratic accountability in local affairs, in education and public services, can all be counterposed to the accretion of invisible and (literally) irresponsible power by national government, transnational companies and organisations. This is all to the good, especially in an opaque society like Britain. It remains true that there are far too few lines of accountability, whether within firms, between service providers and users, or between planners and planned. It remains true that the continued modernisation of socialist ideas depends on finding appropriate forms of accountability in work, welfare and government.

The problems arise when answerability works in more than one direction. We might all agree that the powerful should be answerable to the powerless. But should those without power be answerable to each other, perhaps when they pollute, when they take each other's jobs, or when they choose a distinct lifestyle? And should the individual be accountable to the community or the state, the employee to the employer, the young to the old? Here a libertarianism that leaves the individual with no obligations looks like a cul-de-sac. It leaves community as contingent, social responsibility as nothing more than an effect of free-floating conscience.

Much of the policy debate of recent years has been shaped by the fact that the new right thought it had an answer to precisely these problems. Their answer, which is still influential on political discourse throughout the world, can be summed up in two words: private property. According to the theory, property rights provide the best means for creating a responsible society. This applies as much to the home-owner as to the small business. The democratic component of popular capitalism is that owners are accountable to themselves, not others. If there are enough owners then society becomes more democratic, but without the built-in irresponsibilities and upward bidding of electoral democracy.

Meanwhile, the same market which empowers also restrains and disciplines. To extend its virtues, the public sector is sold in parcels, public goods turned into private ones. Cento Veljanovski's book on privatisation reflects the theory in its title, *Selling The State*. The rationale is that the property owner takes the long view, conserving and husbanding resources. By contrast the individual who shares a tiny part of a collectively-owned good has little immediate incentive to value it.

43

According to the theory, property inculcates care, collectivism carelessness.

These ideas are attractively simple. But their very simplicity makes them unbalanced. For while it is true that while anyone living by the laws of the market has to spend only what they earn (within admittedly broad limits), to plan and to care for their assets, it is equally evident that all markets bring strong incentives to evade responsibilities: to pass costs of health, training and environment out on to the community, and to devalue the future that is left to later generations. Property rights seem to foster care within narrow limits only at the price of carelessness in relation to the rest of society.

These are not the only reasons why a property-based market is an inadequate foundation for a responsible society. Today's markets are not like the face-to-face ones of the past. Their complex global interconnections make it hard to see the links between decisions and outcomes. Producers and users, owners and employees, investors and managers, are distant from each other, and the rhetoric of popular capitalism hides a reality in which ownership is extraordinarily diffuse. The opacity of modern capitalism undermines its claim to responsibility. It is easy to evade responsibilities. It is easy to justify a decision by reference to abstract market forces. And in one of the worst symptoms of an irresponsible system, it is easy for the provider of an amoral product, whether a dishonest newspaper or an addictive drug, simply to blame the public which demands it.

These contradictions between ideal and real markets do much to undermine the right's case. But from a philosophical point of view there is a much more basic reason why market-based theories of private property fail to offer a convincing vision of a more responsible society. Responsibility is both etymologically and philosophically a social concept. It means, literally, 'answerability'. It is an idea born of the assumption that people live in communities and that they answer to each other. It fits much better in a worldview that recognises that collectivities have identities, aspirations and memories, a worldview that accepts that there is such a thing as society, than it does in a philosophy founded on the separate and selfish individual.

The remainder of this essay draws on these roots to suggest how the left might begin to construct its view of a more responsible, and self-responsible, society. These are sketchy notes rather than a complete or wholly coherent vision. But they do at least suggest a path we might choose to follow. We could start with four basic principles. The first is that responsibility can be good for you. People are social as well as individual creatures. They often find themselves through groups and collective identities and through the obligations these entail. What marks out the socialist tradition is the belief that responsibility to others brings out the best in human nature. The political problem is to tap people's desire to be responsible in the same way that the economic system taps their more selfish desires for material well-being.

The second principle is that the buck has to stop somewhere. The challenges and dangers of responsibility are inseparable from its benefits. Unless we ask individuals and institutions to carry the can for their own actions we will soon slip into a world of alibis and evasions. If responsibility is diffused we can assume that irresponsible action will follow.

The third principle is that we should favour individual responsibility where possible, but collective responsibility where necessary. Without a strong sense of mutual obligation, without a sense that the community can help people to take responsibility for their own lives, society runs the risk of sliding into mutual indifference. Without collective provision, principles of individual responsibility can simply translate into policies that pile responsibilities onto the weak.

The fourth is that, wherever possible, the political system should seek to establish a congruence between power and responsibility. It is hardly progressive to distribute responsibilities to the powerless. And it is not sustainable to distribute power unless those exercising it are responsible for how it is used. These principles represent a possible starting point, not a destination. They suggest the questions to be asked of policies and programmes, rather than the shape these would take. Nevertheless, it is possible to suggest where they might lead.

At a personal level, they might imply criminals being required to compensate victims; individual granting training and education credits, and greater control over planning work, education and retirement. They might imply a greater devolution of control over services, as in the Danish model where parents are entitled to a fixed sum for organising their children's schooling. The City's monopoly over pension funds might be breached by giving individuals the right to use some of their accumulated pension assets to invest in friends and relatives.

At the level of the neighbourhood, these principles might imply collective responsibility for cleaning, childcare or lighting, and direct contractual relationships with service providers. They also suggest strict environmental auditing and payments by firms which produce excess waste and pollution; clearly-defined obligations for firms to stakeholders other than shareholders; and, as is already the case, laws making unions liable for the effects of disputes. Going further, one could imagine companies having clear contractual obligations to their workforces as a whole, covering such things as employment security, training and health. In the public sector, utilities or council departments could be made directly liable for their failure to deliver a service, with management salary levels directly tied to performance. Investors could be required to share some responsibility for the actions of those they finance. Tax laws could discourage capital from skipping from industry to industry, always seeking the effortless exit.

In welfare we could ask of any reform whether it really does create the conditions for people to escape dependency. If it is simply a guise for cutting funds like many 'workfare' schemes, and like the restructured social fund, if the independence it offers is not practical and useable, then it should be opposed. If on the other hand it enhances people's human capital, and their access to the means for an independent life; if it gives both responsibility and the power to use it, then it should surely be supported.

There are also implications for government itself. One is that there is a need for restraints on governments' power to create money, to spend in the short term and to respond too readily to the upward bidding of democratic politics. If government acts irresponsibly, whether in monetary policy or in the conduct of its ministers, then it is hard to expect the rest of society to adhere to high standards. Self-restraint is essential if the left is successfully to answer those on the right who would turn the state, in David Stockman's vivid words, into nothing more than a 'spare and stingy creature'.

The list could go on. There are questions about how empowerment can be made meaningful for women who bear the greatest burden of domestic responsibility; about the full range of environmental responsibilities, from waste reduction through to the obligations of drug companies; about moving towards a system of payment according to responsibility. None of these issues is simple or one-dimensional. Any programme for fostering a more responsible society immediately runs into tensions, not least the age-old tension between freedom and equality. Granting neighbourhoods the responsibility for managing their own litter collection, or granting regions autonomy over economic decision-making could rapidly lead to heightened inequalities. A stronger collective sense of mutual responsibility may ease these tensions, resolving them, as it were, on a higher plane. But they do not disappear. Each step towards greater diffusions of power and responsibility brings risk and danger. Each step makes freedom into a weight as well as a release.

The ideal of a more responsible society lends no easy answers. It doesn't offer a simple map to the moral high ground, not least because there are now many moral high grounds, and because any ethos of responsibility appropriate to a plural society must respect the distinct responsibilities of the doctor, the teacher, the journalist, the police officer and the parent. But such an ideal does at least point in the right direction. It does at least pass moral responsibility away from the great institutions and back to a more human scale.

To the sceptical socialist I would offer three very different reasons why, difficult as they are, these questions cannot be fudged. The first is that it is precisely the most powerful institutions which are most immune to responsibility. No convincing radical programme can leave them untouched. Most governments have guaranteed themselves an extraordinary panoply of immunities and barriers against redress. Limited companies have done the same. Since the invention of limited liability in the mid-nineteenth century, the licensed irresponsibility of the capitalist enterprise has been beyond question and there is only one real relationship which involves responsibility, the relationship of directors and shareholders. All others, whether workers, consumers, or those polluted or inconvenienced, are simply bystanders.

There was a time when the labour movement took the view that if you couldn't beat them it would be better to join them. At the beginning of this century the trade unions won many legal immunities.

Most of these have been taken away during the 1980s while those of the firm and those of the professions, which regulate themselves precisely to limit the danger of them being held responsible by the outside world, remain largely intact. The labour movement could seek to go back to the days of state-sanctioned privilege. But it would surely be more astute, and more in tune with the times, to argue instead for a removal of all unjustifiable immunities.

The second reason for not shying away from the difficult problems of responsibility follows from the first. The same impulse to protect privilege with immunities also lies behind the phenomenal spread of insurance: the idea that mistakes and misfortunes can be planned against and paid for in advance. In the free market it is now possible to be insured against anything from damages claims to libel. In the USA it is possible to sue a host for allowing you to get too drunk to drive safely, and to sue a doctor or lawyer for outcomes that in another society might be ascribed to bad luck. Under the sway of the actuarial table responsibility is replaced with probability. Uncertainty is replaced by calculable risk. Insurance is not in itself a bad thing. It was one of the building blocks of the welfare state. It is one of the signs of a civilised society that people can defend themselves against adversities. Allowed to run rampant, however, insurance always tends to favour the strong over the weak, the rich over the poor. Allowed to run rampant, it undermines the very idea that people are responsible for their actions.

The third reason for taking these questions seriously is that it is hard to imagine any viable future for socialist ideas unless they can be answered. If socialism isn't rooted in some notion of what makes people tick and of what makes communities work together, then it is hard to see how it can remain distinct from any other political tradition. If it is just a more generous shopping list of citizenship rights, then it is hard to see why people should believe in it, rather than just voting for it. It may be politically rewarding simply to promise a progressive extension of freedom. But it is not legitimate to claim that such a position is socialist, or that it tells us how shared values can be upheld and how we can avoid the contingency of a society in which, to use Albert Hirschman's distinction, exit always takes the place of voice.

The right has flunked its historic opportunity to win this argument. It has turned out to be a prisoner of its own history, of the interests that sustain it and of the unbalanced enterprise culture of the 1980s that smirked at the idea of civic obligation. The challenge for the left in the 1990s is whether it can assert a convincing vision of a more responsible society, or whether it too is a prisoner of its own vested interests and of its own past.

Social Rights and the Reconstruction of Welfare

Raymond Plant

The idea of citizenship has played a major role in mainstream political debate in the past couple of years. The Conservatives have made the idea of the 'active citizen' a central part of their attempt to blunt the effect of the economic individualism which they espouse elsewhere. For the Liberal Democrats, Paddy Ashdown has argued in his book *Citizen's Britain* for a view of citizenship which links it to the idea of entitlement. It has loomed large in the 'New Times' debate initiated by *Marxism Today*. In particular, Charter 88 has argued that we need to develop a culture of citizenship in Britain as a basis for a new constitutional settlement which will underpin the workings of a bill of rights and a written constitution.

Although it has adopted a purely reactive role so far, it is very important that the Labour Party is not intellectually isolated on this important political issue. Unless it develops its own views on citizenship, it may well find that an idea which fits naturally into its own framework of values and political vocabulary has been hijacked by other parties in much the same way as 'freedom' was by the new right in the late 1970s and since. The idea of citizenship is certainly not alien to the traditions of the Labour party, and indeed formed part of the labour movement's original intellectual basis (particularly that part of it which was influenced by the growth of new or social liberalism in the 1880s). Political philosophers of that period, such as T.H. Green, D.G. Ritchie (an early Fabian), and R.B. Haldane (Labour's first Lord

Chancellor), made citizenship central to their political creed. As a result, they influenced labour intellectuals such as R.H. Tawney, Mansbridge and politicians such as Ramsay MacDonald.

Many of the ideas in Labour's Policy Review and in its 'Aims and Values' document cry out for a theme such as democratic citizenship which would link together what are, individually, highly attractive ideas into some kind of synthesis. In addition, given its significance in Labour's intellectual origins, a rediscovery of citizenship would put current 'revisionist' policies into some perspective and help to defuse the criticism that they are rootless and opportunistic.

However, making the idea of democratic citzenship central to the ideological modernisation of the Labour Party does mean that two entrenched attitudes which are at best indifferent, and at worst hostile, to citizenship, have to be faced. The first is the class-based approach to politics central to Marxism: this sees the ideal of democratic citizenship as fatally flawed because it assumes some shared set of common values, some conception of a common good in which the *rights* and *duties* of citizenship can be articulated. In the view of many Marxists, these common values of citizenship embody a very high degree of ideological distortion. For Marxists, there cannot ultimately be shared political and social values in a society divided on class lines which follow, in the final analysis, the contours of private ownership. There is a basic clash of interests between those who do and those who do not have property rights in the means of production and those who own capital and those who do not. Ultimately these class differences yield different social and political interests. Those who look to the ideal of democratic citizenship gloss over these fundamental cleavages of class and class interest, and the pursuit of the ideal is essentially an ideological obfuscation. This Marxist argument originates in Marx's own essay *On The Jewish Question* in which he argues that the current inequalities in the ownership of the means of production, and the different economic, social and political interests to which this necessarily leads, cannot be overcome by a purely formal overlay of the supposed common values of citizenship.

The issues involved here are immense in their complexity and in their theoretical elaboration, but they have never been satisfactorily resolved within the Labour Party because it has been the heir to both the Marxist and the liberal approach to citizenship. For much of its history, the Labour Party has not had to solve this ideological dilemma since it was assumed that the social rights of citizenship could be extended without too much trouble in a growing economy and that Conservatives would seek to accommodate such rights with their own ideology. For much of the postwar period, this is what happened. However, since the defeat of the Heath government and the growth of a more militant and confident right in the Conservative Party, this has no longer been the case. Far from the Conservatives accommodating themselves to the constant extension of a set of social and economic rights of citizenship, they have sought to cut back such rights in the interests of individual, consumer choice. Instead of accepting citizenship as a political and social status, modern Conservatives have sought to reassert the role of the market and have rejected the idea that citizenship confers a status independent of economic standing.

In its response, the Labour Party has no option but to clarify its ideological position on these issues. The Marxist will argue that the counter-attack of the radical right is to be expected because the extension of the social and economic rights of citizenship had gone so far in the postwar world to threaten the entrenched privileges of capital. In retrenching such rights, the Conservatives are making the world safe for capital accumulation. In the Marxist view, the Labour Party should also defend class interests which cannot be done by appealing to the common values of citizenship, because there are no real common interests on which such values could be based. Either the Labour Party has to go down this road, or it has to reassert its belief in citizenship in all its aspects: political, civic, economic and social. It is difficult to see how the ideological issue can be fudged any longer.

This is not the place for a full-scale analysis of the strengths and weaknesses of the Marxist view. However, two points are worth making. The first is that many Marxists in Britain are moving towards the citizenship approach in response to the changing circumstances outlined above. The second point which probably underlies the first is that in Britain today a narrowly class-based approach to politics is a recipe for purist impotence and glorious isolation on the left. The working-class base is diminishing all the time: as the phenomenon of working-class conservatism shows, the working class does not share one common class interest. The electoral arithmetic seems to imply that unless the Labour Party can reach out beyond its traditional class base to other groups in society, it will not gain power. Such an extension of appeal has to be based upon the idea of citizenship which cuts across class and makes some appeal to precisely those common values which Marxists are keen to deny by their emphasis on conflict.

The idea of citizenship, particularly when it is understood in terms of individual rights, also runs up against another entrenched attitude on the left, namely the importance of the idea of solidarity. The labour movement has, it is argued, made most of its gains through the solidarity of workers, particularly in unions, and that this kind of collective action and solidarity is to be preferred to individualised ideas about rights. But the unions themselves are changing their attitudes here, largely under the influence of the European Social Charter. Some unions seem prepared to trade in the solidarity of the closed shop, for the protection of the individual rights of workers which they see embodied in the Social Charter. There are also difficulties with a simplistic idea of solidarity in the modern world: it clearly persists in unions which represent workers in firms where there is a common work culture, in which people live in the same areas, go to the same clubs and so on – the best example being the NUM's relation to mining communities. However, such working conditions are becoming the exception rather than the rule. Now that, in T.S. Eliot's phrase, we 'live dispersed on ribbon roads' it is not clear that there will be the depth of solidarity, forged by a common life, for unions to draw upon. The acids of individualism have eaten away at these old forms of solidarity and unions now seem prepared to replace an appeal to collective solidarity and discipline, most clearly exemplified in the closed shop, for a more individualised set of rights at work.

Citizenship also contrasts with the other view of the future of socialism in Britain, namely that it should be seen in terms of interest groups – that the Labour Party should become a coalition of interest groups, particularly those representing minorities, following the model perhaps of Jesse Jackson's 'rainbow alliance'. However, there are well-known and deep-seated difficulties associated with interest group politics of this sort for a party which has national aspirations. There are two sorts of difficulties here. The first is that policy-making is likely to turn into securing a bargain between the major interest groups represented in the party and this is likely to express the lowest common denominator of agreement, rather than some form of policy worked out to meet needs which are identified independently of these interest group pressures within the policy-making process. Secondly, to see a party as essentially a coalition of interest groups is to put the political cart before the horse. Unless a party has a set of core aims and values against which it can test and evaluate interest group aims, then it will fall prey to the most powerful interest groups within the coalition and the political principles of the party such as social justice will just become a 'fig leaf' disguising this domination of the most powerful groups.

There must be some institutional filter for interest group claims at the policy-making level and the most obvious candidate here is a set of integrated values and principles around the idea of citizenship. None of this is to deny the importance of interest groups in a modern democratic society – on the contrary, but their claims do have to be tested against and matched with core political values. Indeed, their claims might well be enhanced by being put into a framework which would seek to determine from a socialist perspective what the rights and obligations of citizens should be in a more democratic and more egalitarian society.

The common basis of citizenship is to be found in an account of basic rights and obligations, beginning with civil and political liberties: the freedom to speak and publish, freedom of association, freedom of movement, due process of law, freedom from illegitimate coercion, freedom from physical assault, torture and so on. The protection of these sorts of rights requires legislation which proscribes various interferences in the life of one citizen by another or by a group of citizens. However, in the case of many of these rights, the most serious encroachments are made by governments themselves. There are two ways forward here. The first is to say that elected representatives in parliament have to be trusted to make sure that the government stays its hand when proposing actions which impinge on civil liberties and to ensure that unwritten constitutional conventions in this field are maintained and continued. However, the history of the past eleven years seems to show that there is no reason to think that MPs will be willing or indeed capable of restraining a government when it is set upon such a course. The alternative is to go for a bill of rights.

However, there are several reasons why the left has been suspicious of such legislation. The first is the idea of the mandate. The claim here is that political parties are given a mandate by the electorate and, armed with this democratic legitimacy, government should not be constrained by a bill of rights. In other words, a bill of rights is regarded as expressing one set of political preferences. Why should these be entrenched and constrain the political preferences of future generations? However, this argument is currently enfeebled by the fact that it is wholly unlikely that any government in the foreseeable future will be elected by a majority of the votes cast in a general election. While a government may enjoy a majority in the House of Commons, in all probability it will have been elected on less than a majority of the popular vote. Even if it had there are still serious questions about the doctrine of the mandate. The idea of the mandate appeals to a notion of democratic legitimacy, but there is more than one interpretation of what this might mean and certainly a majoritarian conception of democratic legitimacy is not the only one. It certainly is possible for majorities to take the most oppressive measures against minority groups and many would be worried by the claim that the idea of the democratic mandate legitimised this.

The other major objection to the bill of rights on the left is that we cannot trust the judges who would have to interpret the rights defined in such a bill. This is an important issue but, on the other hand, it is fundamental to politics in a large-scale society that someone has to be trusted to defend rights and over the last few years Parliament has not shown itself very strong in this area. A bill of rights should also be set in the context of a more general reform of the legal system and of legal education to try to break down some of the antediluvian practices of the legal profession which act as a break on a wider recruitment of barristers from whom judges are normally selected.

Many on the left, particularly supporters of Charter 88, have recently argued for the incorporation of the European Convention on Human rights into British law. Critics have claimed that this would entrench a right to personal property and act as a brake on redistributive taxation which a Labour government might want to introduce. But this would be a matter of interpretation. The Convention only entrenches a general right to personal property: it does not in any sense define what the limits or boundaries are to this and it certainly does not necessarily mean an unlimited right to the ownership of income – otherwise taxation of any sort would be a violation of property rights.

In any case, the idea of citizenship is not just concerned with civil and political rights, vitally important though these are. The left also has to articulate and defend a concept of social citizenship, and this has two broad aspects. The first is that citizenship as a status confers some rights to resources such as income, health care, social security and education. The second aspect is that citizens should be empowered more as consumers whether in the market or in the public sector. It also implies that as we have equal civil and political rights as citizens – that is, equality before the law – the distribution of the *social means* of citizenship should be as fair and as equal as can be attained without infringing the other rights of citizenship.

The first of these issues, namely that of citizenship conferring rights to resources, has been thought to raise intractable problems in terms of guaranteeing resources as rights. It is argued that rights are absolute and carry along with them some notion of enforceability, whereas resources are scarce and finite and cannot be subject to enforceable claims.

Despite claims to the contrary, this is equally a problem with rights in the civil and political sphere. These rights also carry with them resource implications. Obviously if we were a community of saints and people did not coerce, interfere with, or assault one another, then these rights could be respected in a wholly costless way. But in the real world a right to physical security involves expenditure of police services, on courts, prisons, probation services and street lighting. These are all key ways of protecting civil and political rights and they all involve costs. If we believe that we have a right to the protection of civil and political rights, then we cannot draw a distinction between civil and political rights on the one hand, and social and welfare rights on the other, because the latter involve resource constraints in the way that the former do not. We run up against resource constraints in each area of rights and these problems have to be solved by political negotiation and decision. What we spend on public provision to meet needs, whether these are civil and political needs or social and economic ones, is therefore a matter for full democratic debate.

This observation begs a major question: if all rights run up against resource constraints, in what sense are individual rights enforceable? For example, in the Baby Barber case two years ago, a young child was initially denied a heart operation in a Birmingham hospital because at that time the Health Authority did not have the resources to undertake it. The parents appealed to the courts, which refused to intervene. One thing that this case demonstrated was that there was *no* individually enforceable right to health care, precisely because of resource constraints. Similarly, as recent history has shown, there is no right under the education acts to the services of a teacher if there is a shortage of teachers. The same is equally true in the area of civil and political rights. If my house is burgled, I do not have an individually enforceable right to the services of a policeman. The Chief Constable has the duty to deploy his forces in what he regards as operationally the most effective way, and as an individual I do not have a right to enforce a visit by a policeman to my property. I have such a right only if the Chief Constable is failing, as a matter of policy, to enforce a particular set of laws.

Since the time of Marshall's great essay on *Citizenship and Social Class*, we have become accustomed to talk about 'social rights'. But what Marshall meant by social rights was not that these would be individually enforceable but that the state had a *general* duty to provide *collective* services in the fields of health, education and welfare: he did not envisage that these would yield individual entitlements, as is clearly illustrated in the examples above. As the Labour Party Policy Review says 'rights without the means of enforcement are a shame'. So do we have to say that because all rights come up against the limits of scarcity, they are not genuine at all? – a question which would apply equally well to the protection of civil and political rights as to securing social and economic rights.

If we see this as a general problem about rights which do involve resources, then there are several courses of action open. The first is that in certain areas of social rights, particularly in the social security field, it *is* possible to define rights to specific resources in a strictly enforceable way. If a claimant falls into a particular category governed by a rule which confers a right upon people in that category, then that particular individual has an enforceable right to that resource. There is no particular difficulty in this case and setting out benefits in terms of rights and strict entitlements would at one and the same time empower the claimant more and reduce the discretionary (potentially discriminatory) power of the social security officer. Another area in which conferring enforceable rights is not particularly problematic is in procedural rights in the public sector. In health this could include a right to medical records, a right to change a GP, a right to an appointment at a specific time and so forth. In education the national curriculum could be seen as conferring enforceable rights on parents for the provision in schools in terms of subject coverage and teaching methods relating to methods of assessment and the right to a periodic report on the child's progress.

In personal social services, the idea of a contract between the social worker and the client has become established: the client is given a right through the contract to negotiate the scope, nature and objective of the relationship between the client and worker. However, all of these cases represent *procedural* rights, often in the form of access to information of various sorts. Important though this is in creating greater equality of power between the professional provider of the service and the recipient, they are nevertheless circumscribed, because they confer little in terms of rights to resources or services. Such procedural rights are of limited value for education in a place like Hackney, for example, where children are turned away from school because there are not the resources to teach them; or in health care, where the procedural rights only operate once one is within the system, whereas the most basic right is access to the system itself. So can there be a right to health care or education in the *substantive* sense of a right to the services of a teacher or a doctor, or does the fact of scarcity mean that these will always be aspirations rather than rights?

There are two ways forward here which have to be considered if social rights are ever to be enforceable. The first is through the idea of performance indicators and the need to link entitlements to such indicators. The second is through conferring the entitlement less in terms of the provision of the service and more in terms of cash or a cash surrogate such as a voucher. In the case of performance indicators, it should be possible in each area of the public sector to work towards specific standards for service delivery which would then yield rights or entitlements in the expectation that these indicators would be met. If they are not, there would be scope either for compensation or alternative provision to the particular local delivery of the service. In some areas of the public sector some progress has been made: one much quoted example is the cleansing department in Islington in which the public have come to see themselves as having a right to a particular type of service (for example, bins emptied within a specified period and a right to two dustbins). There is no reason why the same process could not be pursued in other areas of the public sector. The Prison Officers Association is pressing for the introduction of basic rights for prisoners which would establish at least a minimal standard of accommodation, training and exercise for all prisoners. Of course, such entitlements have to be developed by negotiation against a background of scarce resources. But while they are not absolute rights to a particular type of treatment, they do define a set of bench marks or minimum standards. This type of development could be applied over time to other public services, in education and health particularly.

Free-market conservatives believe that this efficiency and degree of responsiveness to consumer demand can only be produced by competition and 'market discipline'. The social rights approach, however, disputes this and takes the view that there are ways of empowering people through entitlements linked to performance indicators. These sorts of solution are particularly relevant in the fields of education and health where there is no possibility of moving over to a free-market position, not least because of popular sentiment. The proposal also links together two key themes of the left: democracy and rights. In the earlier distinction between positive and negative rights, I said that – even in the case of civil and political rights – the resources to protect those rights are in fact negotiated through political processes, and that there is in no sense an *absolute* right to an absolute degree of protection. If this process of negotiation were to be democratised to a fair degree through the participation of Police Authorities, Community Health Councils and other bodies, helping to work towards performance indicators and methods of enforceability in the public sector, then this could in fact strengthen both rights and democracy at the same time. It would also lessen the power of producer interest groups and professional authorities to decide what is good for the rest of us and delivering services on their terms rather than ours.

A more radical approach to the question of entitlement is through vouchers in which the entitlement is defined in cash terms. This idea is not generally popular on the left because it is associated with the radical free-market right. It clearly has major limitations, particularly in the health sector where medical needs can not be clearly measured as a voucher would be and where the onset of the need is unpredictable. But if we are to take the issue of the enforceability of rights seriously then we cannot just rule out vouchers on *a priori* grounds, particularly in those cases where the needs are limited and predictable. Two examples spring to mind which have been discussed by policy analysts on the left. The first is in child care which has been proposed (in a *New Socialist* article) by Patricia Hewitt, formerly Kinnock's press secretary. The second in education by Julian Le Grand in his essay 'Markets, Equality and Welfare'.[1] There is no space here to discuss their proposals in detail, but one of the merits of a voucher system is that they could have a redistributive effect if the voucher was worth more to those people living in areas of high deprivation as indicated by the 'Z' score system of the Department of the Environment. Again, if social rights are to be plausible and not just rhetorical, we have to look at a range of ways in which they could become enforceable: in some restricted areas vouchers could be an effective way to achieve this aim.

The final point about rights which I want to discuss in this essay is the link between rights and duties. It might be argued that defining citizenship in terms of rights is far too limited and has to be linked to the *obligations* that citizens might be thought to have. There is nothing intrinsically anti-socialist about this, since some of the major contributors to the British socialist tradition, particularly R.H. Tawney, wrote a good deal about the issue of obligation. If we believe that citizens do have a range of rights, do we also believe that they have obligations? This view has become popular on the right, largely as the result of the work of the American social policy theorist Lawrence Mead. Mead argues that social and economic rights to collective resources should not exist outside an obligation to society as a whole and, in particular, an obligation to work. So the right to social security for the able-bodied should not be unconditional; it should depend on willingness to and availability for work.

There are some major difficulties with this view which are worth exploring briefly. First of all the argument assumes that the possession of ordinary civil and political rights is dependent on having a particular moral character or on being particularly virtuous. The criterion of eligibility for the right is simply citizenship and not virtue. But in the context of social and economic rights, the claim now is that these rights *should* depend on discharging some moral obligations such as labour.

If, as I have suggested, there is no substantial difference between the two sorts of rights, then it is not clear why one sort should be unconditional and the other conditional on the discharge of obligations. It might of course be argued in defence of the obligation view that social rights as rights to resources imply that able-bodied people should contribute to the production of those resources which they want to claim as rights through labour or training. Yet we do not make civil and political rights conditional on contributing to the production of the resources necessary to secure such rights.

Defenders of the obligation view of citizenship dispute the point that it is really at the heart of my defence of social and economic rights, namely that rights are empowering, that enforceable social and economic rights in the welfare services and public sector empower those who hold them. The new right critics of welfare rights reject this view and argue that such rights create not power but 'dependency'. The reason for this is that social or welfare rights create, in effect, an economic and social status of citizenship *outside the market* where, to some degree, a person's entitlement is determined by non-market criteria. In the view of the new right this creates quite the wrong incentives for the worst-off groups in society who are encouraged to believe that others owe them a living and a status not earned by their own efforts. Far from creating a sturdy sense of independence, welfare rights in fact create a sense of dependency upon the welfare system and the bureaucracies which operate it. This argument was quite effectively summarised twenty years ago by Professor Pinker:

The idea of ... holding authentic claims by virtue of citizenship remains largely an intellectual conceit of the social scientist and the socialist. For the majority the idea of participant citizenship in distributive processes outside

61

the market place has very little meaning. Consequently most applicants for social services remain paupers at heart.[2]

This idea cannot be fundamentally altered in a capitalist society in which the idea of individual worth is settled more by the market place than it is by the idea of citizenship. Conferring social rights outside economic performance is not compatible with either the prevailing ideology or, more importantly, the self-understanding of those who are most likely to claim the rights. They are unlikely to see themselves as independent citizens claiming what is theirs by right, rather than essentially recipients of charity, whatever the rhetoric deployed to disguise this. This is why – according to the radical right – the receipt of state benefits for the able-bodied should be made dependent on work, because only then is there the appropriate reciprocity between rights and duties. The entitlements of citizenship have to be earned; it is not a status which confers rights to resources by itself.

No doubt there is something in this argument in its critique of the humiliating and debilitating effect of welfare clientism, but it does not necessarily imply the conclusion about 'workfare'. It neglects the project of trying to make the rights of citizenship more effective by making them more enforceable. There is, however, another aspect of the obligation argument which deserves some sceptical attention.

It is assumed for the reasons given by Pinker that entitlements have to be earned before they are regarded as real and therefore that work alone confers dignity, independence and self-respect which the passive recipient of rights cannot earn. But in the context of workfare, this argument needs to be treated with some caution. If benefits have to be linked to work, then the state must be the employer in the last resort. If benefits are linked to work, then work has to be somehow guaranteed on an individual basis. Another way of putting it is that if benefits are linked to work, then there must be an enforceable right to work and the only institution which can guarantee such a right is in fact the state. However, it is not clear that work guaranteed by the state will necessarily develop that sense of independence which workfare theorists are looking for. It may be the case that getting a job as the result of one's own efforts creates a sense of self-esteem, but it is not clear that this would apply if the state guaranteed work at all. It may well, in Britain, mean transferring dependency (and public expenditure) from the Department of Social Security to the Department of Employment.

Clearly the state would have to be the employer of last resort in any workfare system linked to the idea of citizenship, given Britain's current level of unemployment. This necessity conflicts sharply with the views of the new right on the labour market regulation and public expenditure. If unemployment benefit, to take just one example, were to be made conditional on work, then this would dramatically increase public expenditure in this field since such work would have to be found and manufactured by the state in those areas where the market cannot provide such jobs. This would be much more expensive than merely paying out benefit on an availability for work test. New right thinkers such as Lord Joseph continually complained in the 1970s about the way in which the nationalised industries were vastly 'overmanned' during that period. However, if the state was to link benefits to work, this kind of make-work would have to be increased dramatically.

Therefore the implications of a workfare, obligations approach to citizenship, poses problems for the new right on their own terms. This is not to say that the issue does not pose problems which the left has to face, since as I have already said, there is a tradition within British socialism which does link socialism with accepting obligations to the community. Perhaps the strongest argument for an obligations approach on the left is that the aims of a socialist society with regard to a fairer distribution of resources have to depend on those resources being produced (in order that these resources secure an adequate defence of civil and political as well as social rights). Those who are able-bodied and claim rights must be prepared to contribute to the production of these social resources. This is done by the majority through taxation, but for some it might be done through accepting an obligation to (socially useful) work.

The left cannot just remain content with reiterating the Marshall arguments about the social rights of citizenship. These rights have to be redefined in today's more individualistic and consumer-oriented context; and the issues of enforceability of rights and the reciprocity of rights and obligations will have to be developed in practice.

Notes

[1] Julian Le Grand and Saul Estrin (eds), *Market Socialism*, Clarendon, Oxford 1989.
[2] Robert Pinker, *Social Theory and Social Policy*, Heinemann, London 1971.

Citizens of Planet Earth

Fred Steward

The rise of green politics has a complex relationship with the new politics of citizenship. Green politics expresses aspirations of citizenship through its globalisation of the sense of community, combined with a new emphasis on individual responsibility. It also challenges the discourse of social citizenship by attributing enhanced status to an agency external to human society – the biosphere of Planet Earth.

Citizenship concepts concerning the rights and obligations of the individual in society, and the relationship between civil society and the state are highly pertinent to the analysis of political space created by the environmental movement. On the other hand, the centrality of nature and of internationalism to green concerns represents a different and problematic dimension to the focus of citizenship politics on society and the nation state.

At the same time, green politics has set the relationship of the individual and society in a dramatic new light. The green outlook is marked by a striking renewal of collectivism, universalism and social purpose: the individual is seen in the context of a global identity, the human species; the ecology of the planet is given a primary status which informs all policy issues; interdependence and sustainability set the terms for individual and social choice; and finally, the future of the planet is a fate shared by all and is therefore the overriding focus for common purpose and action. The rise of green politics represents a pattern of change in which collective identity and universal values assume a new status and significance.

However, the growth of the green movement is also associated with a new emphasis on individuality, diversity and choice. Personal responsibility for the consequences of one's actions has become a prominent theme on matters ranging from recycling newspapers to the purchase of fur coats. Decentralisation of economic power is expressed in relation to self-sufficiency and emphasis on small-scale local enterprise. Choice of new patterns of work and consumption for individual satisfaction and self-realisation are central to the green outlook. These aspects appear to reflect those broader economic and cultural shifts which in general have been appropriated by the political right.

These two contrasting dimensions, broadly of collectivism and individualism, are both of fundamental importance to an understanding of current processes of change and an assessment of new political potentialities. Our analysis must embrace the dynamic of their interrelationship rather than privilege one over the other: individuality and choice cannot be dismissed as peripheral to a new social purpose, while universal moral aspirations cannot be shunned as a slide toward bureaucratic control. The reality is that both of these elements have a valid place in the new context, and the left has been outflanked by the competing political currents engaging with both. The right has captured the terrain of individual space and consumer choice. The greens now hold the high ground of grand moral vision and all-embracing social responsibility, and are fast making inroads into the terrain of consumer choice.

The political options for the left include neither a 'realism' based on accommodation with a selfish individualism nor a new 'fundamentalism' justifying technocratic centralism. Instead we need to combine the collective and the individual, common purpose and personal choice in a new way. The greens offer some valuable insights into the possibilities. Both their agenda and their style are vital pointers to important new features of the social landscape, the context of any political action.

The power of green politics is precisely that it has responded to these changed circumstances and articulated a political philosophy and practice in a novel and imaginative way. We have witnessed the emergence of a new political culture which embraces a notion of individual responsibility along with one of collective strategy. The new green organisations of the 1970s such as Friends of the Earth, Greenpeace and the Green parties embody this culture and have shown a unique capacity to bridge the gulf between transformative politics and the reality of existing political institutions. At the individual level, people have shown an unprecedented willingness to change their habits and make new choices about personal consumption: the green consumer is no longer viewed as an eccentric, but instead as a growing and sought after market segment.

Regulatory agencies have been stimulated into action through effective use of established channels of expert evidence and media briefings. The culture is both eclectic and integrative, individualist and collective. Demands are made equally on personal lifestyle, government action and industrial management. Criticism of the inadequacy of bureaucratic rationality are accompanied by skilful use of expertise and reason in the presentation of arguments which affirm explicit environment-friendly values.

The openness and effectiveness of this political style is clearly underpinned by a clarity of common purpose. The timeliness of its practice is matched by a resonance for its philosophy. What is it that fosters a receptiveness to a new universal 'world-view' at the same time as reinforcing a commitment to choice and diversity? What ideas and values lie at its root?

Green thinking draws on a clear moral stance which is both a radical challenge to the existing order yet in tune with the times. There are two central values to the green outlook and these inform a range of green social and economic policies as well as specifically environmental issues. One of the core values is an emphasis on the importance of qualitative, as opposed to quantitative, objectives as a measure of social progress. The quality of life expressed through health and environment takes precedence over the quantity of material wealth. The wholesomeness of air, food and water are more central than the size of the pay packet. The beauty of the environment overrides the growth in GNP. Job satisfaction and the fulfilment of mixing work and leisure to personal taste are considered more important than restoration of conventional full employment. The other core value concerns the primacy of nature over society: human goals of all kinds are seen as dependent on the integrity and diversity of the biosphere. As a result, a politics concerned solely with the position of different social groups or the relationship between human beings, however radical, is seen as implicitly subordinating nature, the source of life, to a secondary position.

These core values pose an awkward challenge to the political discourse of both right and left. Neither the pursuit of individual sovereignty in the market place, nor the materialistic empowerment of the individual through a redistributive welfare state address this challenge. The essence of green politics requires a new space and paradigm within politics for its expression: for example, the new scope for choice between technological options must be adopted not simply as a better route to the fulfilment of diverse consumer needs but as an environmentally viable path to be followed. The green agenda demands both a reassessment of the fundamental objectives of a democratic economy and the adoption of broad strategic goals embodying the principles of quality of life and primacy of nature.

The exercise of choice within such a strategic framework is to be governed not by centralised institutions, however enlightened, but through a *decentralised* economic and political system relying on active individual consent by citizens. Such an approach has often appeared individualistic and utopian, sometimes criticised for neglecting the realities of power and the need for firm central direction. Yet, as the costs of ignoring such a strategy are becoming clearer, green solutions strike a more serious popular note than before: a decade ago suggestions that wind, waves and sun were serious options for energy policy were ridiculed; now they receive public money and scientific attention. Concern over food processing and additives was seen for many years as the preserve of the crank; now consumer pressure has put the quality of food at the centre of political attention.

The new conception of individual rights and social responsibility expressed by green politics is accompanied by the enhancement of civil society in relation to the state. This represents an important change both in the nature of environmental problems themselves and in the political process appropriate to their resolutions.

The original rise of industrial society carried with it a range of substantial and negative environmental effects. Air pollution from smoke, river pollution from toxic effluent, exhaustion of mineral and energy resources, despoliation of landscape through over-exploitation all took their toll. Such destructive consequences were gross and manifest yet in general were limited geographically and over time. Effects were usually confined within national boundaries and were evident within a short space of time, so that causality was direct and immediate.

The modern epoch has been marked by two striking developments concerning geography and time. The globalisation of industry and technology has dramatically increased our capacity for affecting the planetary biosphere. This is a consequence both of the scale of production and consumption and the speed of diffusion of technology into the world market. Product innovations ranging from motor cars to aerosol cans have global repercussions. In addition, new technologies like nuclear power embody features which transcend national boundaries in the event of catastrophe. In short, human capacity to affect the planetary environment appears to have reached a new order of magnitude.

Accompanying this development, there has often been an increased difficulty in ascertaining the relationship between cause and effect. Consequences are expressed much wider than both the workers in the industry and the direct consumers of its products. A local event like a nuclear plant melt-down has an impact across the world through the radiation released. Individual consumption decisions on the use of aerosols containing CFCs can affect planet-wide systems such as the ozone layer. Environmental impacts become increasingly cumulative and indirect. They are expressed over new and unpredictable time spans. Actions which in the past appeared sustainable, such as using the oceans as a source of food or a destiny for wastes, may rapidly precipitate critical thresholds for the survival of species like seals and whales. Events in the present such as burning fossil fuels and deforestation could have dramatic consequences for future generations through the greenhouse effect. On all of these issues the precise interpretation of the evidence is contested, yet the potential threat is one of unprecedented enormity.

To compound the daunting challenge of averting global environmental disaster, the new epoch carries with it new problems of handling

69

uncertainty and exercising political power. These have engendered a crisis in the structures of regulation and representation characteristic of the earlier order. The rise of mass production was accompanied by social pressure in response to environmental impacts which led to reasonably effective regulation. This occurred through the political and legal channels of the nation state: the Clean Air Acts got rid of the London smogs; planning legislation controlled the balance between town and country. Such national legislation was accompanied by the growth of administrative structures in which rationality and expertise were deemed the province of the professional, and social interests were confined to indirect representation. It was the era of the standing expert committee in which consensus was based on 'value-free' notions of detachment and reason. Partisanship and explicit values were regarded as introducing emotion and irrationality into a political process that would best succeed without them. Regulation was essentially a form of negative control over immediate and overt risks.

The growth of uncertainty and conflict between experts as to the severity of environmental risk has led to a recognition of the limits of rationality alone and an enhanced status for explicit values. There is widespread dissatisfaction with existing structures premised on professional exclusiveness and expert consensus. Instead there is pressure for an acknowledgement of uncertainty, for explicit representation of diversity in the regulatory process and for a positive commitment to pre-empting indirect and subtle threats. All of these shifts in attitude are expressed in proposals to facilitate direct expression of public interest groups and encourage a more open contestation of the 'specialist' knowledge and values underlying environmental decisions.

These changes signify the need for much more serious attention to the public availability of information and the nature of interest group representation within the political process. Freedom of information legislation is important to enhance the capacity of groups within civil society to analyse problems and articulate alternatives. Rights of consultation for such groups, and increased status as representatives within a pluralistic political process also need to be strengthened through appropriate legal and financial measures.

Two important factors that have contributed to this enriched role in civil society have been technology and knowledge. The new information technology makes it possible to combine decentralised activities within a wider, even global, strategy to a degree hitherto inconceivable. The capacity to handle complex information with great speed enables an interactive flow between centre and locality, producer and consumer, institution and individual. The intelligent application of technology makes the combination of central purpose with individual choice more feasible. At the same time, there is a spread of education and access to knowledge via the mass media and international communications technology. This has opened a global perspective to the individual which was simply inaccessible to previous generations. The consequences of technological change have therefore been double-edged: although human power to affect the planet has been unleashed on a frightening scale, the capacity for local control of technology and the economy has been enhanced. These two factors have combined to make the phrase 'think global, act local' actual rather than rhetorical. The local dimension of a politics that embraces both the global and the individual is expressed in a new emphasis on 'community', encompassing a desire for a smaller, more human scale of economic organisation and social activity.

Ecological objectives have to be pursued both through government regulation and consumer choice: there is neither a simple statist nor a pure market solution. The avoidance of new environmental risks will undoubtedly involve greater social regulation and control of business activities. The scale of these problems will require the use of the law to intervene in private business decisions to achieve a broader common purpose. At the same time, there needs to be a new ethic of personal responsibility. Consumer choice, expressed through the market, for environment-friendly products is a necessary complement to regulation. Such a social change of attitudes and objectives cannot simply be legislated for; it rests on a broader cultural and ethical shift in individual behaviour. However, it can certainly be assisted by encouragement through information and facilities addressed to the individual. At local level, this could involve local authorities providing the appropriate infrastructure. Decentralised decision-making requires shifts in perceptions of the individual's relationship to the environment. Only in this way can otherwise conflicting roles of tenants/residents, consumers and workers, be resolved.

CITIZENSHIP

The politics of citizenship is developing very much in tandem with the issues of individual/collective and civil society/state relations raised by the emergence of green politics. However, there are three areas of considerable importance to green politics which are more problematic in their implications for citizenship. These concern the relationships of modernism with tradition, nature with society, and international with national sovereignty.

The concept of citizenship is closely associated with the liberation of the individual from the constraints of tradition and community. Its expression was linked to the modernising forces of science and progress, from the age of Enlightenment onwards. Yet green thought also embodies a powerful sense of tradition and the maintenance of links with the past. The identification with cultural continuity has been prominent in the recent debates on the built environment, reflecting the urban dimension to green politics. Many environmentalists share a desire for a smaller scale to our immediate environment and for the preservation of tradition and identity through building to blend with the past. The motivation behind the emphasis on community and continuity need not be a conservative desire to narrow horizons or seek to remain static. Instead intimacy and heritage may be adopted as legitimate values within a dynamic global perspective.

'Nature' and 'tradition' are two values that are central to the green philosophy and represent an explicit challenge to the modernist virtues of 'technology' and 'change'. For some critics of green 'fundamentalism', such a challenge represents a return to the reactionary or romantic idealisation of a pre-modern era in which, in fact, the individual was subordinate to the claustrophobic power of subsistence and superstition.

There seems no *a priori* reason why 'nature' and 'tradition' should necessarily be linked to political conservatism. Choice over future paths of economic and technological change could give greater weight to nature and community without denying the value of human technical endeavour or succumbing to social stasis. The 'new times' are an opportunity for the elaboration and assertion of such values in the context of both material progress and social and personal liberation.

Behind this engagement with the reject values of modernism lies a need for a synthesis of a new type, which must not simply offer modifications confined within the narrow ideological framework of modernism. The categories of 'technology' and 'change' have indeed changed: 'technology' has correctly been shown to have shifted from process to product, standardisation to differentiation, production to consumption; 'change' has been transformed to accommodate social diversity rather than impose homogenity, strategy rather than planning, consumer choice rather than state ownership. But whatever the importance of these insights, they need to be accompanied by a re-evaluation of the fundamental objectives of political change prompted by the green 'project'.

The politics of citizenship runs into a second major problem in its encounter with environmentalism. The concept is formulated to deal with the relationship between the individual and the community within human society, but the fundamental issue addressed by green politics is the status of nature as separate and distinct from human society. Does nature have *rights* and if so, then how are they to be articulated and represented in a discourse of social citizenship? In more realistic terms, how are the 'rights of nature' to be protected against incursion and violation by human society?

At one level, the setting of firm criteria for environmental protection through state regulation can partly fulfil this latter objective, although the initial impulse and motivation to adopt such rules remains dependent on an explicit social recognition of nature's rights. At another level, the fundamental question of the rights of nature requires structural political reform to allow a more effective, if still indirect, representation of the planet's interests.

Such reform would depend on a new relationship of alliance between popular movements and professional experts in the assessment and control of environmental risks. The changing nature of environmental threats means that anticipation of uncertain risks becomes more important than action based on proof of past harm. This type of action will rely on an enhanced role for popular environmental interests to represent explicit ecological values in the political process. Decisions will give greater weight to caution in the face of uncertainty and will reflect a less cavalier attitude to development which might infringe the rights of future generations. This will involve a change in the dominance of the expert and the professional in this field of political decision-making and a broadening-out of the traditionally narrow rationality applied to environmental risks. At the same time, the complexity of global risks will offer new challenges for science and knowledge in the analysis of such issues and the uncovering of obscure and unexpected causes of environmental damage. The role of the professional will be enhanced, but as part of a more *broadly representative* political process. New types of political institution will be needed to combine these popular and professional forces.

Since nature cannot speak for itself until too late, its interests rely on human agencies acting as its advocate. At its greatest (but perhaps least realistic) extent such a role of advocacy would be as impersonal and as powerful as the state itself. Alternatively, a more pluralistic path would rely on the direct representation of movements and organisations articulating environmental concerns and a greater separation of powers between forces promoting human material goals and those expressing the protection of the planet. Generally, advocates of green politics regard authoritarianism as antithetical to their aims, and this latter path is both more likely and more acceptable.

The final problem posed by green politics to the normal discourse of citizenship is its emphasis on the international level of political decision. This inevitably implies a loss of sovereignty on the part of the nation state which has been the traditional locus of enforceable citizen rights and obligations.

The new features of environmental concern have challenged these established political forms. There are serious limits to the capacity of sovereign national government to deal with threats to the environment, and priority will increasingly go to new international and supranational forums for the resolution of such issues. Ecological interdependence at a global level has to inform the international political agenda.

Citizenship of planet earth, then, embodies a new sense of the universal political subject beyond the context of the traditional nation state, and a refreshed awareness of equality in terms of our shared dependence on nature. Global citizenship expresses the right to a common human inheritance regardless of nation – the rainforests and coral reefs, as well as the earth's planetary resources of atmosphere, ocean, genetics. The concept also embodies an economic right to choice in terms of material consumption and lifestyle which should not simply be either constrained by poverty or facilitated by wealth. The concomitant *obligations* of citizenship involved an acceptance of the growing need for international and global regulation of industry and the environment, which itself entails a necessary foregoing of some elements of local and national sovereignty. Individual citizens also owe a duty of care to the planet in terms of minimising resource consumption and pollution.

This represents an optimistic prospectus for a green global citizenship, and yet it offers a perspective of participatory democratic change which transcends the limited constitutionalism of the current debate on citizenship. The environmental crisis which we face is forcing the recognition at every level that political action and industrial regulation by individual nation states are not adequate to the challenge; supranational, even global co-operation is essential. At the same time, green politics has successfully fostered a culture of local, community activism and personal responsibility that is the envy of the advocates of orthodox social citizenship. The concept of the 'green citizen', then, commands a unique potential for progressive consensus: the future of the Earth and its citizens depends upon the realisation of that potential.

Citizenship and Feminist Theory

Anne Phillips

The current interest in citizenship brings together what had come to be regarded as separate concerns, for it restates the centrality of specifically political rights, yet does this in a language of activity and participation. One of the messages it sends out is that political rights and freedoms matter: that citizens need guarantees of their civil and political liberties; that governments should be elected and not arbitrarily imposed. None of this may need saying in 1990s Europe, except that it reverses the direction of so much previous socialist thought. For a variety of reasons (many of them good) socialists have been wary of attaching undue significance to the political realm, and have stressed the prior importance of economic and social relations. Political equality can accommodate itself all too easily to structural inequalities in the distribution of wealth and power, and yet these systematically undermine any formal equality in rights. The point has become blunted through so much repetition, though to my mind it still retains its edge. The problem is that socialists then became too dismissive of the 'merely' political, and sometimes blurred the distinctions between democracy and dictatorship until they virtually disappeared. The new emphasis on citizenship is a deliberate corrective to this tradition of socialist thought.

Citizenship does more, however, for it also expresses growing frustration with the fragmentation and passivities of contemporary life. In the contrast it implies between citizen and subject, it calls for more active participation, more substantial 'citizen' involvement and control. As is frequently noted, this is meant to span responsibilities as well as rights, and it inspires memories of Athenian citizens rotating among themselves the responsibilities for democratic rule, or Rousseau's virtuous men who never missed a general assembly. In the debased version favoured in official circles, the emphasis is almost exclusively on responsibilities, and refers to activities in the social rather than political realm. Despite the grandiose title, the 'active citizen' then becomes a bit of a busybody keeping the neighbours in line, or a self-appointed social worker who does the work for free (or rather, for the moral self-gratification). In contrast to this perspective, I consider citizenship most useful and meaningful when it is considered as a primarily *political* term. In particular, I want to look at some of the implications of recent feminist arguments, especially the growing literature that challenges apparently gender-free categories and subjects them to severe critique.[1] Starting with 'humanity', moving on to 'equality', 'rights', 'freedom', and 'democracy', feminists have queried most of the basic concepts of political thinking, arguing that theorists have always built on assumptions about women and men, though they have not always admitted (even to themselves) what these were. One of the most common tricks of this trade is to smuggle real live men into the seemingly abstract and innocent universals that nourish political thought.[2] The 'individual' or the 'citizen' are obvious candidates for this form of gendered substitution.

The old taunt that used to be thrown at those who talked in terms of citizens is that outside the sometimes life-or-death situation of those who migrate from one community to another, becoming a citizen may not make much difference to one's life. One disadvantaged group after another has fought lengthy battles to be included on the list of people entitled to citizenship, only to find that social justice and equality still eluded them. The traditional explanations for this have followed one of two routes. The first (which is heavily indebted to Karl Marx's arguments in *On The Jewish Question*) notes that citizenship is fundamentally a political category, and cannot therefore deal with substantial inequalities in the social and economic spheres. The polemical advocacy of citizenship is emphatic on this point: equal citizenship is extended to people *despite* all their differences of birth, education, occupation, gender or race. It is a slippery slope from saying that these differences should not count, towards saying that they don't even matter. Socialists were quick to spot the disturbing implications for class inequalities, while feminists have been equally speedy in noting the implications for gender. There is no procedure that has proved itself so well suited to disguising women's oppression as the division into public and private spheres; by directing our attention to specifically political or civil equalities, citizenship helps obscure what goes on in the home. As feminists often remarked in the early years of the women's liberation movement, the equal right to vote barely scratches the surface.

The second approach is perhaps more pertinent to what citizenship subsequently became. Against the background of postwar welfarism, T.H. Marshall reconceptualised citizenship as an evolving complex of civil, political and social rights, and thus gave more real substance to the term. In this later version, the term 'citizen' no longer signalled a readiness to accept the 'merely' political as sufficient. The problem now was that the concept of citizen could *incorporate* (a metaphor that is used with more than casual intent by contemporary feminist theorists) even more characteristics of the dominant groups. In her critique of the patriarchal welfare state, for example, Carole Pateman notes that Marshall wrote in a right to employment as part of his conception of citizenship rights, but did so just at the point when architects of the welfare state were constructing man as breadwinner-worker and woman as dependant-wife.[3] If employment is taken as the mark of citizenship and one of its inalienable rights, does this mean women are not yet full members, that their citizenship is still second-class? Similar arguments apply to the citizen responsibility for defending his (sic) country, for women are almost universally excluded from conscription, and even when they sign up voluntarily for the armed forces, they are not expected to join in combat roles. Does this indicate that their citizenship is partial, and help confirm them in a subordinate role?

Such questions give a new feminist twist to an older socialist suspicion, and suggest that the citizen is less universal in scope than 'he' likes to pretend. Socialists used to criticise the concept as an abstraction from the social realities of capitalist and worker, landlord and tenant, rich and poor; feminists now stress the way it abstracts from differences between women and men. This is not just a re-run of the same issue, for sexual difference raises particularly tangled questions about the relationship between the social and biological, and how much of what we call sexual difference is open to future change. Partly because of these issues, feminist theorists are divided over where to go next, and while some look to reformulations that will finally eliminate masculine bias, delivering us concepts that are genuinely gender-free, others reject any kind of grand abstraction, seeing this as an epistemological strategy which inevitably imposes one sex as a norm.

My main concern in this essay is an exploration of the kind of politics that citizenship implies. I have suggested that citizenship refers us back to the traditions of civic republicanism; if this is so, then it also refers us forward to a revitalised politics that will transcend the self-interest and parochialism of today. Discussion in Britain has perhaps been overly distracted by the non-political citizen espoused by conservative thinkers, but from Hannah Arendt onwards there has been a substantial (if largely American) literature that sees the citizen in explicitly political terms. Citizenship has been set up in direct contrast to the huckstering politics that deals only in individual and group interests; and this has generated an impressive critique of liberal democracy, pressure-group politics, and the capitulation to market interests.[4] These arguments stress the need to reclaim the specifically political arena, and they envisage a world in which people will be able to transcend their more private, localised interests and tackle what should be the community's common concerns.

The last surge of interest in a more active democracy took place in the 1960s and 1970s, when 'participatory democracies ... appeared everywhere like fragile bubbles'.[5] In these heady days – which witnessed the emergence of the women's liberation movement, but also a renewed impetus towards the democratisation of the workplace – the gulf between half-hearted and serious democrats was thought to overlap with the division between those who stressed the political and those who stressed the social or economic spheres. Democracy was felt to be impoverished and ineffective precisely because it had been restricted to the purely political realm: it dealt only in the elections of governments and not in the substance of popular control. If democracy were to mean more than the four- or five-yearly foray into the polling station, it had to be extended and applied elsewhere. Those who campaigned for a more active and participatory democracy thus redrew the boundaries of what counted as 'political', identifying the hierarchy and authoritarianism of the workplace and, in the case of the women's movement, the most intimate textures and relations of personal life.

Feminists have pointed to the division that then developed between those who thought primarily in terms of workplace democracy, and those who looked to the more sweeping 'democratisation of everyday life'. Carole Pateman, in particular, has stressed how very orthodox most proponents of participatory democracy remained in 'forgetting' the domestic realm.[6] But whether the emphasis was exclusively on the workplace, or more radically on a full spectrum of class and patriarchal power, both sides seemed to agree on one thing. The route to a more active and enabling democracy lay outside the conventionally political sphere.

Citizenship potentially reverses this trend, for it restates the 'political' and looks to this for our greater fulfilment. Participation 1970s-style dealt largely with what its critics called the micro-level: the housing estate, the local nursery, the community centre, the place of work. Radical politics centred more on movements than on political parties, and what defined these movements were often group identities of gender, race, sexuality or nationality. There was a growing commitment to a politics based on difference, a sense of the heterogeneity of contemporary societies, and a greater awareness that representation had to be balanced between groups. Examples of this include the increased importance of women's sections in the Labour Party, of women's caucuses in a number of trade unions, and of procedures for improving women's representation; a less conclusive example is provided by the debate about black sections inside the Labour Party. It would be easy to overstate this trend, but in the decline of a specifically class-based politics there has been more recognition of the claims of different social groups, and more self-organisation around their needs. The politics of the women's movement is only one manifestation of this.

Citizenship 1990s-style points in a new direction, and in their preliminary exploration of 'Citizens and Citizenship', Stuart Hall and David Held rightly note that difference is 'the joker in the citizenship pack'.[7] If 'citizen' implies a contrast with 'subject', it also implies a contrast with all the more differentiated descriptions of capitalist and worker, male and female, black and white, for it accentuates the rights and responsibilities we share. It is a concept that deliberately abstracts from those things that are particular and specific, and seems to lift us onto a higher terrain. Differences between one group and another then appear more negatively as problems, for the task is to ensure that no group is excluded by virtue of its peculiarities and position, and that equal citizenship is extended to all. More strongly even than this, citizenship often propels us towards an ideal of transcendence, a greater collectivity in which we get beyond our local identities and concerns. When we are called upon to act *as citizens*, we are by implication not acting simply as women or men, black or white, manual worker or professional, homeowner or council tenant, however powerful these affiliations are that bind us to a particular social definition or location.

How, if at all, does this relate to the earlier emphasis on different social groups? British socialists have been somewhat schizophrenic on this issue, and if discussions of citizenship help clarify the muddle, this will itself be a major advance. Consider the politics of the last fifteen years: much political rhetoric was expended in stigmatising those who are out only for themselves, and while conservatives usually exempted entrepreneurs and city folk, socialists made fewer exceptions. Both sides seemed to unite in condemning trade unionists for their narrowly selfish concerns. Those lucky enough to work in the private sector were attacked for pursuing their own wage claims regardless of either the requirements of the economy (this was the main conservative argument), or (from a more radical perspective) the interests of lower paid workers, women, the unemployed or retired. Those in public sector employment were frequently criticised for setting their own conditions as workers above the needs of the clients they should serve. In an age hardly characterised by altruism or generous deeds, 'sectional interest' nonetheless became a term of condemnation or contempt, meaning exclusive concentration on the narrow interests of your own little group.

At the same time, many socialists were celebrating a politics based on group identity, while feminists were arguing the importance of organising around one's own needs and concerns. Group identity seemed to be good, while group interest was bad – or did it depend on which kind of group? What exactly was the dividing line between pressing one's own selfish and sectional interest, and organising around your needs as a disadvantaged or oppressed group? Was it positive or negative to be partial? Should politics begin from where you are, or start with wider concerns?

Two contributions by US feminists help clarify the questions I want to raise. In a 1985 article on 'Citizenship with a Feminist Face', Mary Dietz developed a powerful critique of the new 'pro-family' feminism, as represented in the United States by Sara Ruddick and Jean Bethke Elshtain.[8] Both these writers had turned to women's experience as mothers as an antidote to a male metaphysics, and Elshtain in particular saw mothering as the basis for a new politics of compassion that would reconstruct the political sphere. Mothers do not put their own interests first, for they can never forget the vulnerability of the human child. Women can therefore bring to politics a kind of morality and civic virtue that will displace the (implicitly masculine) selfish materialism that so much dominates today.

While Dietz shares the ideal of citizenship as transcending localised claims, she has no time for the argument that this can be nurtured in the private, family realm. She sees the loving and protective relationship between mother and child as qualitatively different from the egalitarian relationship between citizens, and argues that it is only in moving beyond the intimacy of family relations that people learn what citizenship is about. 'Women who do not venture beyond the family or participate in practices beyond mothering cannot attain an adequate understanding of the way politics determines their lives'.[9] In other words, 'To be a good mother is not in itself to have the requisite capacity for citizenship. (Good) mothers may also be (good) citizens, but their being (good) mothers does not make them (good) citizens'.[10] Citizenship is an explicitly political activity, in which people who are equals address collective and general concerns.

Iris Young shares with Dietz her emphasis on the specifically political nature of citizenship, but not the notion that citizens pursue general concerns. In 'Polity and Group Difference: a Critique of the Ideal of Universal Citizenship', she argues that universal citizenship carries three distinct meanings, the least contentious of which is that citizenship should be extended to everyone regardless of who and what they are. 'Citizenship for everyone, and everyone the same *qua* citizen'.[11] This gets linked however to two further ideals: that citizenship is universal as opposed to particular, common as opposed to differentiated; and that citizenship means everyone being treated the same. In a society marred by group oppression and subordination, these latter meanings end up confirming the dominance of privileged groups.

> In a society where some groups are privileged while others are oppressed, insisting that as citizens persons should leave behind their particular affiliations and experiences to adopt a general point of view serves only to reinforce that privilege; for the perspectives and interests of the privileged will tend to dominate this unified public, marginalising or silencing those of other groups.[12]

It should not be a condition of citizenship that people have to 'forget' their own perspectives or grievances, and turn their minds to so-called wider concerns. On the contrary, she argues, a democracy should establish mechanisms through which oppressed groups are directly represented *as groups*. Here she suggests three possible elements: that public resources should be made available to support the self-organisation of such groups so that they can reflect on their experiences and interests; that these groups should then be enabled to make their contribution to social policy, and decision-makers obliged to consider their views in formulating policies that will affect their group; and that the groups should have a right of veto over specific policies that directly affect them. (Two examples she suggests of this last consultative mechanism are reproductive rights for women, and the use of reservation lands for Native Americans.) She goes on further to challenge the ideal of equal treatment, and argues for 'special' as well as universal rights. When society is socially differentiated, then citizenship must be equally so.

The two perspectives are not directly opposed: Mary Dietz is criticising maternal thinking as paradigm for citizenship, while Iris Young takes issue with American democrats who have seen citizenship as the antithesis to particular interests and as the realisation of a majoritarian common purpose. But between them they suggest some searching questions about the politics of citizenship: Iris Young refers explicitly to the American idea of a 'rainbow coalition' as part of the basis for her critique, and she draws on this as a potential model for the 'heterogeneous public' in which groups can work together but retain their identity, and not be swallowed up in a 'unified' approach. There is considerable overlap between this and the ideas that have surfaced in discussion of 'new social movements', and yet Young builds on the rainbow coalition to raise problems about what citizenship means.

The point on which Dietz and Young agree is that citizenship refers to common membership of a shared community, and in that sense at least, it calls on us to acknowledge others as being of equal account. Outside our activity as citizens, we can more legitimately ignore what other groups think. It would be absurd to expect workers to take the perspective of employers when they put forward their annual claim; or women to worry about hurting men's feelings when they organise a movement of their own. In our capacity as citizens, by contrast, we are necessarily reminded of other people's claims. The point Iris Young stresses is that this happens adequately enough through the very fact that we engage in politics, have therefore to discuss with others and reach a decision that seems fair and just. By virtue of this alone, we are obliged to acknowledge others as citizens and arrive at conclusions that they too can accept. We should not *also* be asked to take a 'general perspective', for this general perspective is an 'Establishment' myth.

Both writers then arrive at the absolute primacy of politics. For Mary Dietz, citizenship means leaving the 'private' world of family or neighbours or work, and becoming involved in more general concerns. For Iris Young, citizenship means organising politically around one's group identity, but then interacting with others in order to decide what policies should apply. They may differ over whether citizenship also involves a particular state of mind, but they see it as taking place in a public arena. Both are miles away from the kind of active citizen who picks up the litter but never gives a thought to the political issues of the day. And despite Iris Young's emphasis on group identity as being a necessary and legitimate part of citizenship, they are also a long way from those arguments that sought to dissolve distinctions between the public and private.

Stuart Hall and David Held argue that because the rights of citizens are often rights that people hold *against* the state – guarantees, that is, of certain freedoms and autonomy in social life – citizenship 'therefore combines, in rather unusual ways, the public and the social with the individual aspects of political life'.[13] This is true enough if we concentrate on rights, but from the perspective of democratic participation, citizenship returns us emphatically to the political sphere. It is not about 'democratising everyday life', nor about enhancing people's participation in their places of work or study.

The point I am stressing is that this marks a break with much of the radicalism of previous decades, which tended to side-step the political and concentrate on transforming and democratising the economic and social spheres. It certainly marks a break with much of what feminists have understood by 'the personal is political', for instead of reshaping politics to cover any arena in which there are relations of dominance and power, the discourse of rights and entitlements affirms a division between public and private spheres. Iris Young argues elsewhere that there should be certain aspects of our lives that we are entitled to treat as private, but no aspect that we are compelled to treat in this way.[14] For example, we should have the right to keep our sexual lives to ourselves and not be expected to answer public queries about what we do in bed. At the same time, however, we should also be entitled to demonstrate publicly on all sexual issues, and none should be excluded from public discussion as inappropriate or trivial or better suited to a private domain. This retains much of what feminists have meant in stressing the political nature of what used to be dismissed as personal or private concerns, but it does so in the context of a distinction between public and private space. The implication, to give another example, is that we would be acting as citizens if we publicly campaigned for men to take a full share in the household tasks; we would not, however, be acting as citizens when we sort out the division of labour inside our own home. In the older language of democratising everyday life, each of these was equally 'political'. In the new language of citizenship, only the one that takes place in a public arena can seriously contend for the name. Again, the point is not that we should stop arguing about who does the housework, just that citizenship acts on a different and more limited terrain.

There are those who will be unhappy with this conclusion, though I myself find it acceptable, so long as it is not used to disparage the more 'private' work of transforming personal relations. Being a good citizen is not the same as being a good mother; nor is it the same as being a good feminist; nor is it the same as being a good neighbour. There *is* a kind of jump from the way we relate to people in our more private, and even group relations, to what goes on in political interaction. The women's movement has rightly reduced this gap by arguing, for example, for greater consistency between the ideals people espouse in politics and the way they live out their daily lives. Even after this narrowing of the gap, however, something still remains: politics is a particular kind of activity, and not to be dissolved into everything else.

Though this signals a new direction, it is less at odds with recent developments in feminism than might be expected, since the importance of the specifically 'political' is in many ways being reclaimed. There is, for example, renewed interests in what can or cannot be done through the more orthodox channels of public policy and official legislation, and there has been a substantial shift from the anti-statism that characterised much of the earlier years of the women's liberation movement in Britain.[15] A different, but related, example is the emerging critique of 'identity politics', with arguments that stress the explicitly political alliances which can be forged through organising for common objectives, instead of the experience-led identities that arise from shared racial or sexual oppression.[16] With the growing emphasis on politics *per se*, there is more chance of bridging the gap between feminism and the language of citizens.

The preoccupations that underpin much of the current interest in citizenship are ones I fully share. We do need to reassert the importance of the specifically political, and we do need to campaign for more active involvement and control. It is still an open question, of course, as to whether these are best approached through the concepts of citizen and citizenship. In a period in which feminist theorists are exploring the problems in abstract universals, citizenship looks an unpromising avenue to pursue. Without careful attention to the issues raised by Iris Young, it threatens to foreclose the awakening recognition of group identity and difference. So while there may be no *necessary* incompatibility between feminism and the language of citizens, much hard work will have to go into ensuring that this is so.

A language that has been harnessed on the one side to the anti-politics of the active citizen, and on the other to the limited constitutionalism of Charter 88, does not look particularly encouraging. We will perhaps look back in another ten years' time to this flurry of activity to see it as a peculiar abberation, testifying more to the crisis in previous modes of analysis than any real insights such concepts allow. What nonetheless attracts me to these debates is the tradition of civic republicanism and the urgency of political action to which citizenship seems to refer. The new emphasis on our role and aspirations *as citizens* raises important questions about the limits to a 'democratisation of everyday life', and helps us to look again at the relationship between the political, economic and social spheres. Citizenship restates the importance of political activity, and if people can only retain enough critical awareness of the pitfalls, it might yet prove itself as a way of dealing with the politics of an extraordinary time.

Notes

[1] A leading figure in this line of critique is Carole Pateman. See her *The Sexual Contract*, 1988, and *The Disorder Of Women*, 1989 (both published by Polity Press, Cambridge). See also the essays in Carole Pateman and Elizabeth Gross (eds), *Feminist Challenges: Social and Political Theory*, Allen and Unwin, London 1986; and Carole Pateman and Mary Lyndon Shanley (eds), *Feminist Interpretations and Political Theory* (forthcoming, Polity Press); Anne Phillips, 'Universal Values and Sexual Difference: Feminist Political Theory', in Michèle Barrett and Anne Phillips (eds), *Feminist Theories Today*, and Anne Phillips, *Engendering Democracy* (both forthcoming, Polity Press). Specifically on citizenship, see also Ursula Vogel, 'Under Permanent Guardianship: Women's Condition Under Modern Civil Law', in K.B. Jones and A.G. Jonasdottir (eds), *The Political Interests of Gender*, Sage, London 1988.
[2] I owe this phrase to the article by Beverley Thiele, 'Vanishing Acts in Social and Political Thought: Tricks of the Trade', in Carole Pateman and Elizabeth Gross (eds), *Feminist Challenges*, op.cit.
[3] Carole Pateman, 'The Patriarchal Welfare State', in Carole Pateman, *The Disorder Of Women*, op.cit.
[4] See, for example, Hannah Arendt, *The Human Condition*, University of Chicago, Chicago Press 1988; Sheldon Wolin, *Politics and Vision*, Little, Brown and Co. Boston 1960; Benjamin Barber, *Strong Democracy: Participatory Politics for a New Age*, University of California Press, Berkeley 1986. For a fuller discussion of these and how they relate to feminist concerns, see Anne Phillips, *Engendering Democracy*, op.cit.
[5] Jane J. Mansbridge, *Beyond Adversary Democracy*, Basic Books, New York 1980, p22.
[6] Carole Pateman, 'Feminism and Democracy', reprinted in Pateman, *The Disorder of Women*, op.cit.
[7] Stuart Hall and David Held, 'Citizens and Citizenship', in Stuart Hall and Martin Jacques (eds), *New Times*, Lawrence & Wishart, London 1989, p177.

[8] Mary G. Dietz, 'Citizenship with a Feminist Face: The Problem with Maternal Thinking', *Political* Theory, no.13(1), 1985. The two works she discusses are Sara Ruddick, 'Maternal Thinking', *Feminist Studies*, no 6, 1980; and Jean Bethke Elshtain, *Public Man, Private Woman*, Princeton University Press, Princeton 1981.
[9] Dietz, *op.cit.*, p32.
[10] Ibid., p31.
[11] Iris Marion Young, 'Polity and Group Difference: A Critique of the Ideal of Universal Citizenship', in *Ethics*, no 99, 1989, p250.
[12] *Ibid.*, p257.
[13] Hall and Held, *op.cit.*, p177.
[14] Iris Marion Young, 'Impartiality and the Civic Public', in Seyla Benhabib and Drucilla Cornell (eds), *Feminism As Critique*, Polity Press, Cambridge 1987.
[15] A recent collection of essays on Australian feminism discusses tensions between 'grass-roots' and statist feminism: see Sophie Watson (ed.), *Playing the State: Australian Feminist Interventions*, Verso, London 1990.
[16] See, for example, Pratibha Parmar, 'Other Kinds of Dreams', in *Feminist Review*, no 31, 1989.

Part II – Citizenship and Socialist Decline

The only thing *for* which we can combine is the underlying ideal of socialism; justice and liberty. But it is hardly strong enough to call this ideal 'underlying'. It is almost completely forgotten. It has been buried beneath layer after layer of doctrinaire priggishness, party squabbles and half-baked 'progressivism' until it is like a diamond hidden under a mountain of dung.

George Orwell, *The Road to Wigan Pier*

Who Would be a Socialist Citizen?

David Selbourne

The journal *Socialist Citizen*, whose provenance is an Oxford college, offers itself to subscribers with a testimonial. The first and second sentences of this testimonial (by Anthony Barnett) declare that 'Britain is not a democracy. It is a parliamentary dictatorship which generates both anger and resignation'.

I have been staring at these falsehoods for some time, instead of setting out straight away on my main task, which was to discuss whether the concept of the 'socialist citizen' is a contradiction in terms. Several thoughts come to mind about the silly assertions before me. The first, a somewhat Socratic consideration, is that the question of citizenship, being in part a moral question, cannot be properly discussed by anyone – whether on the left or the right – without at least some attempt to be truthful.

The second is that at a time of left frailty, when its projects lie around its feet in political ruins, and its intellectual pretensions seem to those not on the left to be more suspect than ever, the burden of truth rests particularly heavily upon the left's shoulders as it tries – in any way it can – to resurrect its ideological fortunes.

The third consideration is gloomier. It suggests that the left, despite everything, continues to find it difficult to tell the truth *at all* on a large number of subjects. It is almost as if strenuous falsehood about the past, the present and the future – whether as the product of utopian illusion, wilful rigging of the record, or arrogant presumption – is a characteristic feature of socialist thought-processes. Here I have only the space to suggest that the metaphysical historical certainties and 'scientific laws' to which Marxism came to be reduced proved deeply corrupting to the spirits of empirical inquiry and open-minded speculation, including those who knew that Marx's Marxism was always more than this. As for Leninism, it merely justified the abuse of authority, intellectual authority included. (And even the meekest 'democratic socialist' is not immune to such corruptions.)

To return to the assertion that 'Britain is not a democracy'. I recall talking in February 1988 to the late Milan Simecka, the Czech author of *The Restoration of Order*, one of the finest of all books on socialist falsehood. The new generation of Czechs, he told me, was 'quite different' from the previous one. Young people were 'more dangerous to the system than we were'. In what way? I asked him. 'Because they are normal. We were deformed by our experiences. We were deformed by our education. We were deformed by our reading. We were deformed by what we believed. But for them Marxism is absolute nonsense.'

In other words, we – Marxists, ex-Marxists, Leninists, socialists, ex-socialists, 'left-wing progressives' – may all be liars, capable of seeing 'dictatorship' in the parliamentary system (and its defects) just as we once saw, or thought we saw, the 'dialectic' in the complexities of social change and evolution, or transcendental virtue in the proletariat. There is, in addition, something deeply reactionary – because Leninist – in the term 'parliamentary dictatorship' itself: it is a term of exploded political art not empirical judgment, the product of reflex not reflection.

Moreover, such reflexes are all the more striking at a time when even the most hard-bitten of ex-Communists and ex-socialist propagandists in Eastern Europe have been setting us examples of (belated) truth-telling. Efforts to recover the true records of their national pasts, after decades of Party-inspired falsehood, have everywhere accompanied the present upheavals; events, institutions and individuals are at last being called by their right names, the victims of past lies have been rehabilitated, and what everybody always knew has been, or is being, admitted.

Above all, the 'socialist democracies', 'workers' democracies', 'people's democracies' and the rest of it are now recognised to have been dictatorships of a party élite or a single, crazed individual, and former 'counter-revolutions' have been recategorised as 'popular uprisings'. What has been at issue in this process of re-naming has been respect for human reason, grounded in that knowledge which is based on actual experience. Affronts to countless minds have been, or are being, cancelled; there has been a huge rebellion against socialist lying. Yet we are still stuck *here* with left ideologues who, in the name of the truth, can declare that 'Britain is not a democracy'. Look hard at this proposition, and you look directly into the eye of left intellectual failure.

The sense of such falsehood, and of how significant it is, is with me a very deep one. A liberal-minded idealist in search of principles to live by, I found my way, with many others of my student generation, into the left world of the 1960s. But much more than that: I became a self-proclaimed Marxist, overawed (for good intellectual reasons) by Marx's powers as historian, as philosopher, as economist, as writer, as guru of an alternative world order. In his pages were certitude, force of mind, and a broad reach of knowledge. There was also a seductive intellectual schema to be explored, both jesuitical and talmudic, with as many rooms in its vast mansion as in Ceausescu's palace in Bucharest.

In my responses to all this there was a nonconformist scepticism too – as in most British Marxists who did not take leave of their senses – but I preferred, during most of the 1970s, the reassurance of belief in an overarching theory of history and a philosophy of knowledge. In my hands I had, or often thought I had, a cabbalistic key to the secrets of earth and heaven. In the late 1970s and into the 1980s, gradual apostasy led the way to intellectual freedom, with its uncertainties and confusions but also with its possibilities of creative renewal. The theory of Britain as 'not a democracy' recalls what I came at that time to fear and dislike most: the left half-truth, the mingling of objective fact with the ideologue's fancy, the hot air of faction, the intellectual rigmarole of left-wing role-playing.

I also gradually found – as in recuperation from a long illness – that it was only outside this asphyxiating hospital ward of left intellection that the complexity of things took on their true dimension. It was then that I discovered that life, as Alexander Herzen memorably put it, is more stubborn than theory; saw that the schemata of the left cannot encompass the embarrassing diversity of human experience; and came to know that such assertions as that 'Britain is not a democracy' are juvenile. The counter-proposition that Britain's is a flawed democracy whose flaws require to be amended, but a democracy – liberal, pluralist, parliamentary – for all that, is beyond the reach of the left demagogue. Its very lack of rhetoric disqualifies it. True it may be, but it is not a manly enough assertion for the barricade; it cannot make a slogan. Above all, it is not half so appealing (to what remains of the left) as a tough-sounding falsehood designed to raise flagging spirits.

There are false notes being struck, too, in the debate among socialists about 'citizenship'. But here, at least, there are arguably some excuses. For one thing it is unfamiliar ground to those who have spent their ideological lives on the old issues of class and state, exploitation and collective 'struggle'. The very language of citizenship is alien. More particularly, the question of individual citizen rights – to say nothing of individual duties, to which I will come later – is, in the Marxist canon, ineffably *bourgeois*. Indeed, for many on the left, the debate has more than a whiff of betrayal about it.

After all, 'true' democracy, especially to a Marxist, is not a thing of the here and now but of the classless and egalitarian future. Hence today's Britain cannot be a democracy, by definition. To insist that it *is* a democracy, a flawed but, mature and functioning, liberal democracy, still strikes left reactionaries as heretical. The further obvious suggestion that ours is precisely the kind of democracy to which the post-socialist world in Eastern Europe is aspiring remains, for most, absolutely beyond the pale of left acceptance. Yet the left, with few other ideological devices remaining open to it, is being driven towards the 'politics of citizenship': a politics (of liberal democracy) in which most of the left can scarcely believe, and for which little or nothing in its own intellectual past has prepared it.

As I understand it, the 'new' left case on citizenship runs as follows. Britain is 'not a democracy', but it could in the interim – before becoming what now remains unspoken – be democratised. That is, it should be made possible for 'everyone' to participate in the (regrettably capitalist) civic order without the obstruction of removeable economic, social, juridical, educational, sexual and racial disabilities. To help achieve this end, the citizenry must be 'empowered' (by various means) to assert its rights against that which renders its citizenship (for many) a dead letter, while our political and other institutions are made more open and accountable to a citizen body which is itself increasingly conscious of its rights, and increasingly able to defend and advance them. 'Tyranny' – even a Ceausescu-like tyranny, for some – threatens, or already exists, in the present dispensation. Remedy is urgent.

There are several levels to this argument, from which, it should be noted, the word 'socialism' is increasingly absent. The first and most visible is the shallow, opportunist level, in which the politics of 'democratisation' is most obviously a last throw of the socialist dice, *faut de mieux* or *in extremis*, and as such is not worth discussing. The second, equally shallow level, which I have already touched upon, consists of pure falsehood. The allegation that Britain is a 'dictatorship' is not true in any sense which has meaning. The third level, or substratum, contains (and compresses) two and a half thousand years of debate around the 'problematic' of democracy, its purposes and its limits, its rights and its duties, and the best design of the institutions who should express it. At the fourth level, there lies buried – or unarticulated in the left's current presentation of the citizenship issue – the premise, shared in their different ways by Aristotle and Marx, that men and women can find their true selves only in the *polis*, or community; that is, as members of the body politic.

Underneath this lurks the oldest political question of all, one which the left, after more than a century of immersion in varieties of socialist theory, is barely able to ask, let alone adequately answer: namely, what is the nature of this body politic to which the citizen (allegedly) wishes to gain greater access? The left's simple old answer – that the body politic in question is 'capitalist', *tout court* – has served it for a hundred years and more, can serve it no further, and it has found no other. No wonder that the no-longer-socialist left now finds itself in limbo; or that it sees in the cause of citizenship the hope of political salvation.

The 'Empowered Citizen' of the left's alternative Utopia is a strange being, unknown to political philosophy. According to the programme for empowerment, he or she can lay claim to rights of every description: political rights, economic rights, social rights, educational rights, cultural rights, sexual rights and so on. They include rights to the basic necessities of life and to fundamental political freedoms; ('socialist') rights of unfettered access to the state's welfare protections, but also ('non-socialist') rights to an autonomous or self-governing existence; rights, in the name of democracy, to individual or collective participation in the political process, but also rights to withhold support from, and even attack, that process on the grounds that it is 'not democratic'; rights to act as a citizen, but also rights to choose not to; above all, the right to be treated by the state as a citizen in whatever circumstance. Much of this is a contradictory nonsense, though to the left it by no means seems so.

In this (amoral) Utopia, the state has correlative obligations to meet its Empowered Citizens' large-scale demands and expectations: the duty to protect and provide, the duty to empower and enable, the duty to desist from interference with the exercise of the above-mentioned rights, and the duty to tolerate citizen objections, in whatever form expressed, to its actions. Citizen rights and state duties, in this utopian schema, are perfectly congruent, as they need to be. But of citizen duties and state rights there is rarely more than a token mention; more often, not a whisper.

Fatally for the left, the trouble with the word 'duty' is that it is seen to be a 'right-wing' word and a 'right-wing' virtue. It suggests the forelock and the flag, the parade-ground salute and the bent knee of the servant. But the left's concept of citizenship cannot acquire legitimacy or command assent in a liberal democratic culture – and even less in a 'parliamentary dictatorship' – when its content is frequently no more than the unilateral assertion of a set of rights against the state. In such a form (lacking all sense of commensurate obligation on the individual citizen's part) it is mere rhetoric. No civil society could rest upon it.

Moreover, it is an elementary proposition, which holds good for post-socialist left political theory as for any other, that without respect for the rights of other free and independent citizens, equally empowered in the new Utopia, the whole project must either collapse in disorder or be rescued by the very 'dictatorship' against which the doctrine of the Empowered Citizen is pitted in the first place. There is little or nothing about respect for the rights of *other* Empowered Citizens to be found in the texts of the new citizenship doctrine. Perhaps the very word 'respect' seems Tory.

And who, in what remains of left circles, would dare argue that if there is a *right* to participate, there is also a *duty* to participate in the civic order? Or, harder still, that a right to welfare protection carries with it certain duties, including duties to the self? (Self-management has many dimensions.) Such obvious arguments are now almost unheard of on the left, though they were commonplace enough in 1945, when the postwar welfare state was being established. But the principal reason for these silences – silences which are unique in the ancient history of debate on these questions – is not hard to find.

It is that the debate today is not what it seems: we are, in fact, faced not with a genuine and fully-engaged argument about citizenship, but with the search for an alternative means of attracting the uncommitted to the left enterprise, at a time of ideological debacle. And since the discussion on the left is for the most part a hollow one, albeit on subjects of importance for every libertarian, the difficult questions – such as those which concern citizen duty – can be given short shrift, or sidestepped entirely.

We must also ask who this 'citizen' is, standing so unexpectedly at the heart of the new left project. Is he, or she, not the 'individual' – with his or her 'individualism' – about whom left authoritarianism has always felt so uneasy, and for good reason? And who, or what, is the '*socialist* citizen', when we are, at these very moments, living through a revolution *against* socialism and *for* citizenship in Eastern Europe and the Soviet Union? Who would be a socialist citizen when the claims of 'collective man' and his Party are giving way, by free choice, to the 'dictatorship' of parliaments, the separation of powers, independent judiciaries and the anarchy of market freedoms? Who would be a socialist citizen when the very word 'comrade' – 'over there' where they have been right through this socialist business and out the other side – arouses only recoil and hatred?

The 'citizen' is an inhabitant of the city; in Roman times, or perhaps in all epochs save ours, an individual with determinate rights and known duties, protected by those rights but ready to be summoned to his duties. (The Latin root of the word for citizen, *civis*, is derived from the verb 'to summon', *cieo*.) The term also signifies membership of a community of inhabitants – inhabitants with common political rights and duties – but betokens nothing of a specific socio-economic order. As a word, 'citizen' (we can now see) is grander in scope than 'socialist'; indeed, 'socialist' has served only as a limiting, qualifying and disabling adjective when affixed to nouns like democracy, citizen or culture in the countries of Eastern Europe.

But these were 'not really socialist' countries, declares the left apologist, seeking to rescue something from the political wreckage (just as the 'not really democratic' argument is used *here* for a related, ulterior purpose). In what way were they 'not really socialist'? 'Not really socialist', goes the apologist's answer, because they were Party tyrannies, 'Stalinist', 'bureaucratically deformed', unaccountable to the people, and so forth. (In other words, they were – like the British parliamentary system – 'not democratic'.) Yet were they not also founded upon the moral claims of the collective, upon the superior legitimacy of public property and public interest over private property and private interest, and upon a preference for non-market allocations of rewards and resources, in accordance with classical socialist – and not merely communist – principles?

Of course they were. And, equally undeniably, states and economies founded upon these principles have failed in practice. Indeed the failure has been so great that communists the world over have been forced into silence, or (worse) driven to become 'democratic socialists', 'social democrats' and even free-market followers of Hayek. The variant British outcome, the politics of citizenship, is a particularly eclectic response to this crisis.

However eclectic, is it nevertheless ideologically coherent in its own terms? The answer must be no. Any effort to reconcile the claims of individuality with atavistic forms of socialist aspiration (however disguised and 'modernised') is equivalent to an attempt to square the political circle. Such an attempt is both implicit and explicit in much of the current debate on citizenship. Ideological failure, tragically, is therefore already inscribed upon it.

Let us go into this a little further, since it is the heart of the matter. What is it exactly about socialist – and now much post- and ex-socialist – aspiration that itself militates against the new commitment to the citizenship ideal? First, socialism is emancipatory in theory but *dirigiste* in practice, and as a doctrine, or cluster of doctrines, attracts too many instinctive authoritarians. (In my experience, the more 'fraternal' the more authoritarian.) In consequence and secondly, the beneficiary (or victim) of socialist organisation is generally the object of such organisation; the ideal citizen, and often the real citizen too, is a subject. Thirdly, socialism in practice (at its worst) has shown insufficient respect for the integrity, even the physical integrity, of the person; but the citizenship ideal seeks to protect it. Fourthly, socialism is a politics and economics of 'social justice', ostensibly designed to widen life-chances for the majority, but whose pursuit in practice compresses (for most) the range of personal choices; even the least socialist of social democrats is ill-at-ease with a politics rooted in individual preference. Yet citizens, in so far as they see themselves as independent contractors and stand upon the very rights which define their citizenship, will (unhappily) choose to act at least some of the time – and, more usually, most of the time – in ways which are not compatible with any plan for 'social justice'. Fifthly, every socialist (at least in theory) is above all an egalitarian, who aspires not only for equality of opportunity for all, but a rough equality of outcome; in this respect, once a socialist always a socialist. Citizens, however, aspire above all to be treated as individuals who are equal in the matter of their civic rights and duties to other individuals.

Sixthly, socialism in all its variants contains, and for some is defined by, a philosophy of the general good, in which the individual good is held – often without inquiry, and sometimes with great ruthlessness – to reside. But the ideal of the citizen, at least in theory, refuses to concede such authoritarian (or collectivist) priority to the civil society of which the individual citizen is a member. Instead, it strives (at its best) for a balance between the safeguarding of citizen rights against the prevailing system of power, and insistence upon the performance of citizen duties. Socialism, even in its enfeebled social-democratic form, has never conceived of its purposes in this fashion.

For socialism, finally, the community or collectivity is more than the sum of its individual parts. But the citizen *is* that individual part, and the idea of citizenship rests upon it. Ultimately, and despite Rousseau, these are not reconcilable philosophical positions. Neither socialist wishful thinking nor socialist special pleading will make them so: there is no squaring this circle.

Supposing that 'citizenship socialists' were openly to abandon their socialism entirely – as many have now done in private – would their difficulties be over? No, and not least because the ground on which they would be (and are already) trying to stand is ideological territory long occupied by others on the right and in the centre of the political spectrum.

Moreover, those brought up with a traditional left 'mind-set', whether Marxist or not, make it embarrassingly apparent that they are emotional and intellectual interlopers on the old terrain of liberal democracy. Indeed, it is a high price to pay for decades of ideological isolation and intellectual arrogance that the left – socialists and ex-socialists alike – make less convincing liberal democrats than do many rightists. Can an ex-Marxist, or indeed any kind of socialist, enter fully into the spirit of a debate on, say, the nature of the contract between state and citizen in a free society? The socialist, or ex-socialist, merely reveals how alien he is to the whole subject when he declares – as a macho reflex – that the free society in question is 'not democratic', while simultaneously making demands for rights within it. And to cap it all, such demands rest upon an arrogant left pretension – shameless at a time when 'socialist democracy' has been so discredited – that there is available to us, if only we set about it under left leadership, a 'deeper democracy' to which the left is privy, and to which it alone holds the key!

This 'deeper democracy' is the democracy to which the Empowered Citizen beckons us. So far as I can make out, it is a democracy which (as ever) promises us the benign state – presumably to be ruled by high-minded left intellectuals – 'real accountability', 'genuine' or 'grassroots' participatory democracy, community and workplace self-management, a heavenly social justice, paradisal relations between the sexes, and a quality of individual freedom of which liberal democrats and right-wing libertarians alike can know nothing. It is not much more than the old socialist Utopia in modern (that is, individualist) guise, and with old questions of property, class and Party discarded under the weight of ideological failure.

To switch from this fantasy world to the world in which we actually live – the liberal contractual society, founded on market and commodity relations – is to move well out of reach of the left ideologues, the new citizenship theorists included. A true contact between the left and the actuality we inhabit requires a still impossible acceptance as *legitimate* of the capitalist basis of the social order upon which the left makes its various demands; it requires a still impossible recognition that 'socialism' can achieve in practice only ameliorations of the social market economy, and that it has lost the moral right to aspire further; and finally it requires a still impossible acknowledgement that the political goods procured to the citizen through the agency of liberal-democratic institutions can be improved upon (in some respects) by left political action, but cannot be 'transcended' by any of the existing forms of the broader left project.

It is hard for a socialist, or even ex-socialist, to accept as true not only that the liberal capitalist state has legitimate rights over its citizens, but also that there is now a duty upon the left ungrudgingly to concede it. But in the absence of such acknowledgement, the left's debate about citizenship is a debate conducted *in vacuo* – rightly perceived by those not on the left to be largely rhetorical. It is only when the liberal-democratic (and anti-socialist) consensus comes to be openly embraced by the left, and the left ceases to be socialist, that a left politics of the rights and duties of the citizen might acquire a true legitimacy and a real content.

Can this still be correctly termed a *left* politics? Yes, in the sense that, today, to be 'on the left' should mean, above all, vigilance in the defence of the liberal-democratic capitalist order, with its precariously balanced citizen rights and unrespected citizen duties. Defence against whom? Against its right-wing and authoritarian enemies, socialist reactionaries included. In any case, no real choice now exists in the matter: it is certainly no alternative blindly to beat one's head against the wall of the universalising, and politically all-conquering, capitalist mode of production in an epoch of shaming socialist failure. There is also ideological relief to be gained on the ex-socialist left from acknowledging as obvious (and welcome) that the liberal-capitalist state's rights over its citizens rest, in essence and for the overwhelming majority, upon the assent of those citizens, freely and regularly given.

A second relief would come from owning up to what the left has also always known: that these same citizens' duties, disparaged and neglected as they are, are the duties not of the press-ganged serf – nor of the helot in the dicatorship of the proletariat – but of free individuals voluntarily resident in the (capitalist) territories they inhabit, and free to leave them. And having got thus far, yet another burden – all of them burdens of falsehood – could be lifted from the left's shoulders; it could actually admit freely that the great majority of the hundreds of millions now emerging from communist, state-socialist and even self-managing socialist thraldom seek to live in liberal-capitalist and parliamentary-democratic orders, with efficiently managed systems of environmental protection and public provision.

From such acceptance of the empirically evident, especially if it proved habit-forming, would flow many other ideological benefits. Among them would be the ending of decades of left hypocrisy, during which it has been crassly insisted that the separation of powers, executive accountability to parliament or even the rule of law were in effect no more than 'bourgeois' conundrums designed to deceive the oppressed 'proletariat'. This was always incantation. Now, with the socialist dictatorships exposed and in ruins, it rings hollower than ever.

Another benefit to be hoped for, a benefit of method, is that future left critiques of liberal-democratic institutions – a continuing necessity, not least in helping to refine our unfair electoral system – might come to rest exclusively upon empirical grounds, upon genuine inquiry, and upon the complexities of actual knowledge rather than (as now) upon propagandist assertion. It would also be a true intellectual freedom to be at least relieved of the classic mode of left argument: the abstract or metaphysical ideal of the socialist Utopia, now a busted flush, is held up against the imperfections of the actual circumstances around us, and the former absurdly given preference, *a priori*. The argument that 'Britain is not a democracy' derives precisely from this method.

Yet despite all these observations, the unregenerate socialist – and the socialist in me – retains the belief, or faith, that 'socialist' and 'citizen' could yet, in some world not so far created, be political synonyms. It is a Blakean dream, in which the lion lies down with the lamb, the shivering boy chimney-sweep is gathered into the arms of an all-loving (socialist) Father, and guileless egalitarians join hands around the Maypole of shared labour.

In this Arcadia, where rank is dissolved in fraternity, apple-cheeked benevolence displaces narrow-eyed competition, and decision is spontaneous, mutually agreeable and unclouded by self-interest, I too should like to live, just as I should like to go to heaven. But if neither exists, nor – more to the point – *can* exist; what then, comrades?

The response on the left to this kind of demand has hitherto been one of impatience and derision, or worse. Today, however, the boot is on the other foot. It is apologetics on behalf of socialism which have lost their meaning in a storm of jeering; even at its most fluent the cant of the left finds it difficult to avoid the facts of anti-socialist revolution, and the attempt in country after country to introduce a free-market order.

This is, of course, a dire outcome for past socialist endeavour, but an equally dire warning to those of the new generation setting off once more in pursuit of the socialist chimera, or fabulous unicorn of left-wing fancy. 'The idea of socialism,' Stefan Heym, the East German writer, told me in March 1990 on the eve of the free elections in the GDR, 'has suffered a tremendous defeat, which will postpone its further development for 30 to 50 years. What is going to come is an era of pragmatism, in which acting according to necessity takes precedence over ideology.

'The mistake we made on the left was not to have taken sufficient account of human nature. If you want to push the world forward, you have to know the people you are dealing with. I was a starry-eyed idealist in my youth, but you have to take the people as they are. We expected them to act in accord with some higher form of political consciousness or moral understanding, but instead they reacted to their immediate circumstances of existence. We socialists were fools not to have anticipated it. Now, the Cold War is over and 'really existing socialism' has failed. The people had become sick and tired of social experiments. They had had enough, and the corruption of the boys on top finished it.'

'They had had enough.' It is a terrible epitaph, but a true one. And whatever the further outcome of the liberal-democratic revolution in Eastern Europe, the new left should welcome the socialist debacle. To be 'progressive' demands it; honesty also.

'Even where the institutionalised lie holds sway,' Vaclav Havel has written, 'it is possible for citizens to speak the truth.' Socialism, in all but its most attenuated social-democratic forms, is such a lie, especially in its seductive and idyllic versions, conjuring up with its false hopes and comprehensive programmes a world unfit for real mortals to live in. But if it has always made many promises it knows it cannot keep, today – in the wake of the anti-socialist revolutions – it makes such false promises more knowingly than ever.

The prospectus for a 'socialist citizenship' in Britain is false in just this way, since it is founded on (among other things) a counterfeit premise which leads to a fearsome conclusion: that liberal democracy is 'not democracy', and therefore requires to be amended (or even, for some, overthrown) by the lights of some new, but as yet inchoate, version of the socialist schema.

There is, fortunately, no way forward for the left on the basis of such arguments. Instead, the philosophical assumptions of the liberal-democratic state, as well as the essential features of the capitalist economic relationships on which it rests, must be accepted if a progressive (and therefore non-socialist) utilitarianism of the left is to acquire political legitimacy and intellectual substance. Moreover, it is only on this basis, and on ground which must be shared with some of the right and the whole of the centre, that our understanding of the rights *and* duties of the citizen can be founded.

Part III – New Europeans

Europe is indeed a common home where geography and history have closely interwoven the destinies of dozens of countries and nations. Of course, each of them has its own problems, and each wants to live its own life, to follow its own traditions. Therefore ... one may say: the home is common, that is true, but each family has its own apartment, and there are different entrances too. But it is only together, collectively, and by following the sensible norms of co-existence that the Europeans can save their home, protect it against a conflagraton and other calamities, make it better and safer, and maintain it in proper order.

Mikhail Gorbachev, *Perestroika: New Thinking for our Country and the World*

Citizen Power in Prague

Jon Bloomfield

The Prague November commemorated the 200th anniversary of the French Revolution in the best possible way. In a classic revolution it took less than a fortnight of people's power to topple the old Stalinist tyranny, with its ruthless security apparatus. It was an extraordinary mass uprising, conducted with stunning discipline and calmness. The national flag was the movement's symbol but unlike elsewhere in Eastern Europe this movement was not driven by the uglier passions of nationalism. Fraternity was not forgotten in the quest for liberty and equality. At the demonstrations in Prague's Wenceslas Square before the Jakes regime fell, the people chanted 'Nemci, Nemci' – 'Germans, Germans' – in recognition of the example they were following, while on the six-month anniversary of the Tiananmen Square massacre the students held a commemorative rally.

In some ways the uprising echoed that of Paris in May 1968 with the calls for worker-student unity, the wall posters and even some of the slogans: 'Who? If not us! When? if not now!' But a key difference and the hallmark of this revolution was its absolute refusal to be provoked into any violence. This was a triumph of mass popular will, of sheer size and of national unity.

The students were the spark. Many of those who organised the 17 November demonstration, ostensibly called to mark the 50th anniversary of the death of student Jan Opletal at the hands of the Nazis, had been involved in earlier demonstrations. Student strike committee spokeswoman Monica Pajerova, for example, had been at the demonstrations marking the Soviet invasion and the death of Jan

Palach. She and her colleagues had become politically involved through their work on student magazines and newspapers, which were always operating on the margins of legality.

'Sometimes we were censored. If you try to tell the truth you inevitably get involved in politics here.' It was this group that formed the operating committee for the Opletal demonstration and by working through both the official structures and unofficial groups, got both permission for the march and an unprecedented unity. Pajerova was surprised at the huge turnout. After the students had marched to the cemetery 'we felt so strong that we decided to go to Wenceslas Square'.

Following the bloody suppression of that demonstration by the security police the students turned to strike action in an impressive display of organised unity. The 20 November strike was solid. Anger at the police brutality turned to energy. The students became the democratic movement's activists. They set up shrines where their colleagues had been beaten; produced and stuck up leaflets, broadsheets and posters, spread the strike to other universities, formed the early core of the protest demonstrations and put their case to workers in the factories and offices. Musicians, artists and many intellectuals gave immediate backing, while the Catholic church indicated its wish for dialogue.

Quickly, the ordinary citizens of Prague responded. As Libuse Silhanova, a communist expelled after 1968 and a former spokeswoman of Charter 77 explained, 'This was the moment when the experience of the mass rallies in Leipzig and Berlin linked up in our minds'. The rallies grew in size, confidence and determination during that week, culminating in the phenomenal rally of three quarters of a million on the Letna fields on Saturday 25 November.

During that week all sorts of workplaces held meetings. On the Tuesday, Prague's Metro construction workforce, over 5,000 strong, condemned the brutal attack on the demonstration, called for an independent commission to investigate it and demanded real dialogue with all groups in society. A big CKD engineering plant went further and called for free elections. All week support grew for a two-hour general strike which the students and Civic Forum had called for Monday 27 November. There were patches of resistance, most notably in the old industrialised region of Ostrava by the Polish border, but overall there was a phenomenal response to the call. The students' dream of worker-student unity was realised.

The motor co-ordinating and directing the movement was Civic Forum. Established just two days after the student demonstration at a meeting in a theatre, it brought together all the opposition forces under one umbrella with Vaclav Havel as its chairperson. Influenced by the egalitarian and tolerant approach of the underground movement, Civic Forum adopted a very open style of work. It always sought a consensus within its ranks and its demands gave clarity and focus to the movement.

Once the movement took off, the Jakes regime was helpless. Even the old social contract it had fostered with the industrial working class collapsed. They were no longer prepared to accept a decent standard of living in return for political servitude. The people no longer wanted to live a lie. All the regime had to rely on was the security apparatus. No Soviet tanks now stood behind them. The Jakes regime found that Talleyrand's maxim of 200 years earlier still held true: 'There are many things you can do with a bayonet, but not sit on one.'

The crisis of the stalinist regime had been ripening for a long time, but the tragic outcome of the Prague Spring bred a deep scepticism in much of the population about the prospects for political change. There was a respect for Charter 77 and the Chartists – but at a distance. Yet the Chartists' long, hard and often lonely struggle had paid off. Their stand over the last 13 years against abuse, lies and repression, their call for human, civic and democratic rights, has given them enormous moral authority, above all to Vaclav Havel.

But the Chartists also learned a new style of politics which has shaped the democratic revolution. Here Havel, with his skill in bringing together people with different opinions, has been crucial. Silhanova recalls how 'working under difficult conditions in flats and on the streets, we got to know each other as people, we helped out in family affairs, I learned about different ways people live and think. It was our first great school of tolerance.' This is an experience which has led many of the old Prague Spring communists to rethink their attitude towards party politics and to argue that some of the roots of Stalinism are to be found in the zeal and intolerance Lenin showed towards other socialist forces. They are also unhappy that, apart from the peace movement, most of the Western European Left showed little solidarity with their struggles.

The fruits of the egalitarian, tolerant style of Charter politics have been evident in November events. 'No violence' has been one of the most common slogans. The students met the riot police with flowers. It took real political vision for the Civic Forum to get a lieutenant in the riot police to address the crowd at Letna. He said they were only following orders but he apologised to the crowd, whereupon with a stunning absence of vindictiveness, they cheered him.

After 40 years of monolithic stalinist rule, interrupted only briefly by the Prague Spring, the democratic movement wants the new politics to be shaped by tolerance and reason. In this they are drawing both on the national traditions of Tomas Masaryk, the nation's founder, and some earlier Enlightenment traditions.

The influence of the Prague Spring communists on these developments is somewhat harder to gauge. As an older generation, they have been content with a more behind-the-scenes role. Some played key parts in the Charter movement. The club they formed – Obroda (Renewal) – was harassed by the security forces but has been important in fostering unity among the different opposition groups.

It was on their initiative that the Civic Forum was set up, following a meeting between Havel and Milos Hajek on 18 November, and when hardliners tried to provoke resistance to change in Ostrava, it was another Prague Spring leader, Venek Silhan, who was sent to sort it out. Effectively they have acted as a bridge to the older generations and here Alexander Dubcek has been the key figure. He has symbolised the links and continuity between 1968 and 1989. Many younger people know little about him or feel he is too old to lead them, although he is five years younger than President Mitterand. Yet there is a widespread affection for him, with posters all round central Prague and calls at the demonstrations for him to be president. This largely titular office may suit him best, for he himself remains undecided and ambivalent about his future political role.

The ideas of the Prague Spring remain influential in a broader sense. They cannot be picked up wholesale two decades later, for the world has moved on. Yet as Valtr Komarek, head of the very influential reformist Institute of Forecasting puts it, 'We are a reformist nation'.

Thus while the country faces some very severe structural problems – too much clapped-out heavy industry, too little modern technology, a weak service sector, a severely-polluted environment – the initial indications are that they will seek to carry out a progressive modernisation. Civic Forum's impressive seven-point programme, 'What We Want', calls for a democratic political system, a mixed economy, social justice and solidarity, protection of the environment, including 'a change in lifestyles', and the development of culture, science and education in ways which develop 'high moral responsibility'.

This is a broadly left-of-centre programme. Its most obvious omission from a West European viewpoint concerns women. The movement here is dominated by men, even among the students. Of the 42-strong central strike committee, only three are women. Pajerova herself admits that 'I have not been much interested in feminist ideas at all until now'. Asked why women have not been in the leadership, she replies, 'Many girls have been involved, typing, making food, things like that. Maybe it's in their nature. I don't know how to explain this.'

The political forces which will carry through this type of programme are inevitably unclear at this stage. The first free competitive elections since 1946 will be held during 1990. The jockeying for position has already begun, although Civic Forum is hoping to retain the unity of the democratic movements by itself participating in the elections.

Unlike in Poland, the Czechoslovak CP has been a real historical force. Yet its capacity to renew itself and win sufficient public confidence to play a part in a coalition government must be questioned. It is desperately cleaning up its act. The old leadership has been kicked out, 1968 reassessed, its own militia disarmed, although the first government announced by Prime Minister Adamec was a complete disaster. As in the 1960s, it does appear to have generated reformists in its ranks. The Democratic Forum of Communists wants to junk democratic centralism and present an entirely new policy programme. The Forum has already gained a significant rank-and-file following.

However, the problem for the Communist Party is not just shedding the past, but articulating its socialist vision of the future. Here the thinking of the Prague Spring communists speaks to the entire European left. One of their number, Rudolf Slansky, also a Chartist and engineer, puts it most clearly: 'For 40 years we had a great social experiment under way here. Now we can observe the results of the whole economy being under state and party control. If the state has the complete monopoly, then it has no reason to improve its functioning. Industry stagnates. That's why we think it is necessary for state enterprises to compete in the market.' It is this experience that has reshaped their thinking. The details of a new socialist system remain a question nobody can answer. 'But what we now understand by socialism is as much social justice as possible, the lowest unemployment, the best social security, the same opportunities for all, but not the system of wholesale state ownership. To be a socialist you don't have to support that.'

These values strike deep among the Czechoslovak people. The students finish their proclamations with the call for 'freedom, democracy and socialism.' Pajreova insists 'that the majority of us are still for socialism ... We want to keep the things that are good here ... though perhaps we are for socialism as we don't know anything else. Perhaps we mean like Sweden.'

It's the humanist and moral values, the strong collectivist traditions and sense of social justice and responsibility that appear to have deep roots here. These fuse aspects of the liberal and socialist traditions. But the Prague November has also indicated the new dimension of the environment, and most importantly it has shown a new culture of politics. The movement is still led by men – but without the usual tub-thumping machismo. It's the reassertion of the values of dialogue, reason and discussion as the motor of politics that are most impressive.

Here could be a new type of outcome to the unravelling of Stalinism and the cold war. Events here, as in the GDR, suggest that the new Eastern Europe need not automatically play to the Right. There are now huge opportunities for the left too. The vision with which END launched the 1980s – of a peaceful, non-nuclear and unified Europe – is no longer a dream. We start a new decade with new hopes and prospects. From across the Atlantic, Mr Fukuyama predicts the 'end of history'; here in the heart of Europe it feels more like a new beginning.

CIVIC FORUM: EIGHT RULES OF DIALOGUE

1 When searching for the truth together, your opponent must not be an enemy.

The aim of our discussion is the truth and not an intellectual competition. Participation in dialogue requires three types of respect: respect for the truth, respect for the other person and respect for yourself.

2 Try to understand the other person.

Unless you understand your opponents' ideas correctly, you can neither dispute nor concede their arguments. Try to think through their objections for yourself in order to be clear how they understand things.

3 A statement without proof is not an argument.

In such a case it is only your opinion, but the partner does not have to consider it a real argument.

4 Do not run away from the original subject.

Do not avoid unpleasant questions or arguments by changing the direction of a discussion.

5 Do not try to have the last word in the discussion at all costs.

The quantity of words does not compensate for missing the point. Hating the opponents does neither mean disapproving their points nor denying their ideas.

6 Do not threaten the dignity of your opponent.

Whoever attacks an opponent's personality, loses the right to take part in dialogue.

7 Do not forget that a dialogue requires discipline.

In the final analysis it is through reason not emotion that we form our own ideas (views) and judgements. Whoever is unable to control their feelings and is unable to express their opinions calmly, can never take part in a sensible dialogue with others.

8 Do not mistake dialogue for monologue.

Everyone has the same right to express themselves. Do not get carried away with secondary issues. Furthermore by saving time you are considerate to the others.

A Continent With an Identity Crisis

Martin Kettle

Half a century ago Neville Chamberlain famously described Czechoslovakia as a far away country of which the British knew little. It may have been a politically inept thing to say, but it was not untrue as a statement of fact. Today, we may not in fact know much more about Czechoslovakia than Chamberlain's generation did – we probably know rather less – but the idea of any European country as truly a faraway place would now strike most people as absurd. From Connemara to the Caucasus, we are all European now.

Internationalism has always enjoyed a prominent place in the left's pantheon, even if it has often been honoured in the breach. For many socialists, as also for a powerful liberal tradition, internationalism has been part of the moral bedrock of their view of the world. Yet the British left has tended historically to be isolationist, partly as a result of this country's imperial traditions. Hostility to the European Community, a hangover of those traditions, remained an article of faith on the 'old left' until well into the 1980s, and in some cases it still is.

Those certainties were swept away during the 1980s. Oddly, in view of Margaret Thatcher's own agnostic approach to Europe, this change was not provoked by any perceived need to accommodate to a Conservative-determined agenda. As a piece of political modernisation it was more genuinely autonomous and vernacular than the opinion poll-led changes of economic thinking. Initially, the reconciliation to Europe was more about reconciliation with the economic facts of British existence than it was about the courting of electoral favour. Yet Europe rapidly became a positive enthusiasm on the left, in ways which helped to redefine many of the political divisions of the early 1990s. As a result, great claims have been made about the new Europe as the embodiment of an important aspect of popular identity and sovereignty.

Many of today's swirling visions of the new integrated Europe are preposterous, vacuous and self-deluding stuff. Many will fail the tests of time and people. Some – like the briefly fashionable conceit of early 1990 that Europe was converging towards a new social-democratic settlement – have failed the test already. But the scale and framework of the British people's sense of Europe has undoubtedly changed, and this provides them with a much greater readiness to perceive the European dimension of their lives than was the case in the imperial phase of British history or before the era of electronic news gathering.

Nothing in European life, even in Albania, any longer retains the capacity to shock, even to shock people who have never left their home village in their lives. Europe is still a continent of separate localities and traditions, but it is infinitely more homogeneous than it was. Less than two centuries ago, when the English Romantics saw the Alps they could only stare with wild surmise. Until recently, more than 100 million Europeans invaded the Alpine ski-slopes each year, in the days when it used to snow.

It should not be underestimated how much this owes to the fact that, every year, more Europeans learn a little more about one another than their ancestors ever knew. Although the educated British may actually know rather less about Europe and speak fewer of its languages than their predecessors once did, the experience of Europe is becoming a relentless dimension of everyday life in myriad other respects. People take more foreign holidays. They make more business trips. It has become fashionable to go abroad for rock concerts and art exhibitions. In the last ten years the number of phone calls from Britain to other European countries has multiplied two and half times. The network of intercourse is unprecedented.

Of course, in an infinite number of places around Europe, people behave and think in ways which remain totally distinctive. Stand in a French village when the Tour de France goes by and you are participating in an event which is unambiguously and irreducibly French. Go to a provincial Italian opera house and you enter a quintessentially Italian world where the relationship between performers and audience is a private ritual. Talk to Lithuanian reformers about the political and economic crises of the Baltic and you will soon learn that they are literally obsessed with the situation in their own back yard.

Yet this does not mean in any sense that such encounters lack the European dimension. On the contrary, each of these random examples has an increasingly European context. The Tour de France is now broadcast daily into most European countries and you can find quite young children in London who will now argue the merits of Laurent Fignon, Pedro Delgado and Greg Lemond. Italian opera is beamed around the continent like never before; the first night of the La Scala season is on radio and television channels across Europe. And people of average political sensibility in many lands now routinely absorb good and up-to-the-minute knowledge of political events in places like Lithuania on a daily basis.

One of the results of this process in Britain has been the rapid growth of a very positive though extremely inchoate sense of Europeanism, especially among young people and the well-educated. At the level of the media and mass consumption, this phenomenon is extremely obvious. If an example is necessary, it is striking to compare the way that the BBC promoted the 1990 football World Cup highlighting the attractions of Italy and Italians to the accompaniment of Puccini, with the much more jingoistic, male and narrowly sport-obsessed way it promoted the World Cup in Spain only eight years previously.

This promotion of the new Euro-lifestyle is easy to parody. In this Europe there is a Benetton in every high street, Badoit and Czech Budweiser in every fridge, an Armani jacket in every wardrobe, Beaujolais Nouveau on every table, cable and satellite television channels in many languages in every living room, an Umberto Eco novel on every bookshelf, a Volvo in every garage, where CDs of the Orchestra of the Age of Enlightenment lie casually next to the Eurythmics, and where nipping across to Berlin to catch the Stone Roses tour is as natural as doing a day's business in London. It's an attractive vision, up to a point, and it does have a certain tangible reality, but it is basically an illusion. It cossets the complacent notion that Europe is now emerging into a wholly new identity, governed by peace not war, and by common aspirations rather than sectional concerns.

The illusion of European integration comes complete with a pedigree. There have been what Jacques Delors calls 'European projects' before. Some have been religious, mostly conceived by or on behalf of the Papacy, attempting to impose Catholic hegemony over schism, Protestantism, and even Judaism and Islam. Others have been ideological in other ways, on behalf of the French Revolution and the Rights of Man, or the power of reactionary princes in the age of Metternich.

Mostly they have been military, the attempt of one nation to subdue the rest. Philip II of Spain came close to achieving it, before he was defeated by, among others, half-naked English mercenary soldiers who 'for thieving and brawling had no equals' – the ancestors of the football fans whose violence is so depressingly notorious around Europe today. Louis XIV had a good try and Napoleon an even better one. For the first half of the last century, most European nations assumed that France would somehow try to repeat the project. After 1870, their attention switched to believing that Germany was a more dangerous antagonist, a belief which was borne out until 1945. Since then, and until very recently, Europe has been united against the fear, which would have seemed as absurd in previous centuries as it still does to many in the 1980s, of Russia.

And now? To hear some people talk, you would think such things are all in a jumbled undifferentiated past, much as Louis XIV's palace of Versailles with its real hall of mirrors now also houses Jacques-Louis David's massive celebrations of Napoleon and of the revolution which brought down the Bourbons who built it. The reality, today as before, is that Europe is one dimension of our identity – a growing and exciting dimension certainly, but still only a single dimension for all that.

That is one reason why enthusiasm for the different visions of Europe needs to be treated coolly and with care. European grand designs are seductive things, but they have rarely proved themselves to be either stable or wholly admirable settlements. One of the lessons of the brief survival of many European illusions amid the surging events of 1989-90 is surely that even the most historically durable European projects and institutions – the Papacy is the most obvious example –

have trouble sustaining their effort across so many different local cultures and circumstances.

So the British are not in any sense unique, though they may be an extreme example, in their preoccupation with themselves and their own ways. To expect Europe to become a single warm cultural bath is simply to mistake the nature of the European, and indeed any other, identity: to be European means utterly different things according to history and circumstance. In France it means to think globally about a French-led political Europe which will challenge the power of Japan and America. In Germany it is to commit yourself against nationalistic ambitions. But to be European in Lithuania or Scotland is to assert your nationality and the wish to get Moscow or London off your back. To be European in Italy is a logical extension of what is already assumed to be one's 'natural' multiple identity within a family, a city, a region and a nation. To be European in southern England, though, is to make a political statement against Thatcherism, philistinism and English insularity. We should beware, therefore, of projecting our own sense of Europeanism on to others whose sense, no less strong, is very different indeed.

Nor should Europe be treated as though it is a synonym for internationalism. The continent's own history is littered with fundamental reminders of conflict and prejudice, of course, but it is important to recognise that no grand design is going to prevent Poles hating Russians, Serbs hating Albanians, Ulstermen hating Irish Republicans, or even many French from hating Germans. All it can do is to mitigate the consequences of those continuing mistrusts and grievances.

Where, in any case, are the boundaries of Europe? Before people talk of Europe from the Atlantic to the Urals – as de Gaulle, Gorbachev and John Paul II have all done – it is important to look at the map and understand what this actually means. If you stand on the border of Hungary and the Soviet Union, you are nearer to Lisbon than to the Urals. If we truly share a common European home, then its logical capital is nearer to Kiev than to Brussels. The mental and emotional boundaries of Europe are even harder to draw. Europe is both a fact of geographical and commercial life and an aspiration. It is a place we live in and an ideal to which some aspire. But it is all too often regarded as a purely Caucasian ideal: nobody is more pro-European than M Le Pen. But what space is there here for Muslims? Precious little. There are Turks and Israelis who passionately consider themselves Europeans but there are also many Muslims and Jews for whom Europe is simply a hostile place where they try to survive, not always successfully.

Hardly a week goes by without some vivid piece of evidence somewhere of the difficulty which European society has and will continue to have in adjusting to modern Islam. Nowhere is this more vivid than in newly unified Germany. Here, the Great German dream could be the great nightmare for Germany's third-world population. But it is not just a question of Turks in Berlin or Turks in West Germany generally; for the Turks of Berlin read the Maghrebins of Marseille, the Pakistanis of Bradford, or the Somalis of Florence. The same issue exists in all the important societies of Europe. For such people the idea of a new European identity is as much a threat as a promise.

Even those who protest their especial commitment to Europe sometimes pollute the apparent purity of their intentions. No government has been more conscious of the need, as they perceive it, to build barriers protecting European civilisation against the dangers from American and Japanese audio-visual cultural imperialism than the French. It is a crusade which has rightly been admired around the continent and which the British in particular have notably failed to emulate. Yet it was also the French government which fought most ruthlessly, and successfully, to bring EuroDisneyland to Marne la Vallée in the early 1990s (despite the protests of young communists dressed in Disney character costumes).

The embodiment of the new Europe used to be said to be Mikhail Gorbachev. That claim looks much more tarnished in mid-1990, as he presides over a collapsing economy and a discredited political system. Looked at from the West, François Mitterrand or perhaps Karl-Otto Pöhl, president of the Bundesbank, might seem more appropriately technocratic candidates. But is there not a case for saying that we are currently witnessing the historic counter-attack of Christian Democracy, which has summoned up the traditions of Eastern Europe to redress the balance of the West? In that case, the most truly emblematic figure in the new Europe is actually Pope John Paul II and Gorbachev's visit to the Vatican in 1989 was the new Canossa. It was John Paul, after all, who said in April 1990 that 'a united Europe is no longer only a dream'.

All of this means that a certain caution is very much in order. The Europeanisation of British life may be a desirable thing, but it is still a fragile development. Important though it is, it is not yet based in any full hearted perception of a commitment to a continental destiny. The attractions of Europe often seem to rest as much upon wishful vagueness as upon proven knowledge. Two examples illustrate this problem. If any one event can be said to have changed the British left from agnostics over Europe into enthusiasts, then it was Jacques Delors' speech to the 1988 TUC Conference; and if any one development has oiled the wheels of that change it has been the Social Charter of Workers' Rights, which Delors has championed so strongly. The Social Charter focused the latent anti-Europeanism of the Thatcherites, culminating in the Bruges speech of September 1988, while also legitimating and stimulating the left's rapprochement with Europe.

The Charter rapidly became a convenient focus of international and domestic anti-Thatcherite feeling. Yet very few people, including those who so keenly support it, have actually read the Charter or even thought about its constitutional or economic implications. The Charter was a totemic political issue, not a substantive one. As a result, interest in the Charter was very vulnerable to new fashions and duly slumped during 1990, compared with what it had generated only a few months earlier. Whatever view one takes of the substance of the Charter, the whole episode has not elicited a particularly impressive response from British political institutions either to the European dimension or to the crucial industrial relations questions involved.

A similar problem has developed over federalism and political union. Rhetorically, the British left has gone a very long way down the road towards endorsing political union, even if it has stepped back from the brink of outright commitment. Nevertheless, the Labour group in the European Parliament has made much of the running on the question; and righting the so-called 'democratic deficit' in Europe is one of the main planks of any serious programme of constitutional reform which is put before the public. Once again, though, professional politicians' enthusiasm has tended to outstrip public interest and knowledge. Substantive questions about whether federalism is actually desirable have not been debated in any depth at all. It is hard to escape the feeling that the pro-European position is more enthusiastic than it is considered.

My own view is that the European dimension of British life has increased, that this is as desirable as it is a fact, and that it urgently needs to be legitimised by appropriate democratic institutions. But this is a pragmatic judgement, not an idealistic one: democracy and citizenship must be proportionate to the levels of decision-making power which exist in a society. That means there must be institutional modernisation to take account of the proliferation of European power which now applies to our lives. On the other hand, it is idle to forget history and naive to pretend that most peoples' identities in modern Europe are not predominantly defined by a sense of Europeanism but by many other factors, of which the single most important is their sense of nationality.

> A few years ago, many thoughtful men, in no way given to utopian ideas, had begun to hope that Western Europe would never again be the scene of the awful horrors of war. Everything seemed to favour that belief. Old feuds of race were diminishing, rivalries and prejudices were by degrees fading out. Such frequent and such intimate relations had thus been established between nations, that it seemed as if they must soon unite in one family, in one single federal state. No nation in Europe, had the question been fairly put to them, would have answered that they wished war.

A few months later, as Emile de Laveleye goes on to say in this essay of 1871, the Franco-Prussian war broke out, setting in motion the sequence of European conflicts which led, ultimately, to the obliteration of an earlier multi-cultural Europe in the wars of 1914–18 and 1939–45. It seems somehow presumptuous, still living in such a century, to believe that Europe has emerged into a cloudless world in which such things are now no longer possible.

Citizenship in the New Europe: A Last Chance for the Enlightenment?

Stephen Howe

There are no hierarchies, no infinite, no such many as mass, there are only
eyes in all heads,
to be looked out of

Charles Olson, The Maximus Poems, Letter 6

Mikhail Gorbachev's idea of the 'common European home' has become, throughout the continent, the most resonant political catchphrase of recent years. Yet the history, the ideologies, the geography, even the languages of Europe conspire to cloud its possible meanings. The French language does not have separate words for the related but crucially distinct English notions of 'house' and 'home'. '*Maison*' does service for both, as the 1989 Reith lecturer reminded us.[1] The same seems to be true of Russian. German, by contrast, has a cluster of emotionally charged terms: think of the different, almost dangerously burdened overtones which '*Heimat*' has accrued over the past decades. So is it a new structure, a set of common institutions, a 'house', whose construction is at stake; or a new sense of belonging, a new spirit, a 'home'? Can either the structure or the spirit be built at all; or are we moving into a new Dark Age of economic disintegration and national antagonism? The answers will depend mainly on what emerges from the revolutions of Central and Eastern Europe, the seismic shifts of power and alignment in the winter of 1989-90.

Communism in Eastern Europe was a child of two wildly incompatible ancestries. Both took their emblematic points of origin from 1789, but thereafter unbridgeable fissures opened both between and within them. On one side was the political rationalism of the Enlightenment, with its offshoots in citizen democracy and of a technologically, instrumentally defined concept of progress. On the other, a tradition of nationalist thought shading from notions of popular sovereignty, through elite-fostered forms of state creation and cultural homogenisation, to irrationalist cults of xenophobic and personalistic assertion, 'socialist' versions of the ideologies of *Volk, Reich und Führer*. Marxism in its original, Western forms derived overwhelmingly from the first, Enlightenment legacy. State socialism in the East, however, took on far more decisively the character of its other, darker lineage. Yet crucially, it continued to annex legitimation, self-justification and self-recognition from the rationalist tradition.

The consequences of those internal, ancestral fractures are urgently, even frighteningly present today as, by a genealogical paradox, the child has died leaving the parents to battle over the estate. They mean that the death of communism may be seen, and may profoundly, emotionally be experienced by its former victims, not as the failure of a particular mode of dictatorship, a specific form of social and economic organisation, a unique experiment in state formation, but as a failure of political modernism, of rationalism, of modernity itself. That may prove disastrous, and, in truth, is proving already so to be, in the myriad places where the slackening or destruction of totalitarian control has allowed ancient ethnic hatreds to resume the integrity of their quarrel. For, as arbitrarily, often brutally imposed forms of social bonding by state ideology collapse, the choice of alternative principles of community and identity east of the Elbe determines Europe's future.

Commentary from the West has customarily presented these choices in grossly simplified, wildly misleading terms. The winter revolutions of 1989-90 are proclaimed as the victory of the market principle, of the liberal centre, of democracy pure and simple. Some socialists in the West, wishfully and wistfully, talk of a revived, democratised socialism. Other commentators sniff the wind of nationalist reassertion with all the ugly consequences (above all, persecution of national minorities) which that has historically implied in eastern Europe. None of these observation is *ipso facto* mistaken; least of all, alas, the last. But they underrate, drastically, both the degree of *choice* available and its complexity.

The decisive question here, I would argue, is how well the new political systems of Eastern Europe can build on the strand of Enlightenment thought which enshrines the ideal of citizenship. Can a culture of citizen democracy, of individual rights, of a vigorous civil society form the new basis of social cohesion, both within individual states and transcending their boundaries? Can it shape the 'imagined communities' of nations and states in ways that develop also a genuine European imaginary, a viable common home of the civic, rationalist spirit beyond institutional structures? This hope of renewal has to contend with the possibility that the ousted dictatorships so mutilated the concepts and techniques of political modernity, in societies many of which had no pre-stalinist experience of a modern civic culture, that the atavistic return of earlier, exclusionary irrationalist modes of bonding cannot but triumph.

The latter outcome would be a bitterly ironic historical reversal, for the origin of the citizen ideal developed as the antithesis of monarchy: it envisaged a state which was not the personal property of an individual, of an aristocracy or a clique but in which government is the public business of all citizens and has as its aim the common good. This vision of government, encoding the liberty and cultivating the civic virtue of the citizens, found its origins, of course, in ancient Greece, and its supreme ideological statement in the Roman Republic. Modern republican thought, however, was born in medieval Florence, where Machiavelli and others drew on the classical inheritance to fashion a creed of the public good and participation in civic affairs.

At the core of the republican ethos is the vision of the active citizen who makes the concerns of the whole society his or her own, for whom political involvement is a positive good rather than an occasional necessity or the preserve of a minority, because it is in this involvement that we develop a sense of ourselves and of others as sharers in a community, a common humanity. In terms that would have been familiar to the classic republican thinkers, it is through politics that we learn to love one another; and this participation, through which the

125

citizens control the state, is the right of all. So far as is practically possible, everyone is involved in deciding all public matters: hierarchy, oligarchy, government secrecy, the concentration of power are all inimical to the republican vision.

From Renaissance Italy the citizen idea migrated to the Atlantic coasts of Europe, and from there to the New World. It helped inspire the English Revolution – the real one of 1642, not the fake which we celebrated in 1988 – though only a minority even of those who ordered the king's execution were fully convinced republicans. Ideas generated in England's turbulent 1640s and 1650s, driven underground at home, found new and more receptive resting-places in the New World colonies. They dictated the shape of the classic republican revolution, which brought the USA into being. If America's revolutions put ideals of citizenship back on the map, it was France which universalised them: 1789 remains the inescapable reference point for all subsequent thinking about citizenship. Indeed, as the legacy of 1917 is today divested of its contemporary relevance, its popular resonance, that of 1789 grows in importance. It provides the most telling common reference point for the European transformations of 1989-90.[2]

In its voyage westward from Italy through England to America and France, the republican idea underwent three great changes: of scale, of time and of attitudes to participation. Both ancient and medieval republicanism were affairs of city-states; it was thought this form of government could not work in larger units. The Dutch, the English and, far more decisively, the American and French revolutions burst the bounds of that limitation. The change in the sense of time was from a cyclical conception, in which a state of freedom would inevitably fall as it had risen, to a more optimistic one in which the extension of liberty was part of an ever-advancing march of human progress. This belief found perhaps its most potent, and sometimes destructive, modern expression in US self-images of national destiny; but it has fed in evident ways into most streams of liberalism and socialism. Its appropriation, together with the entire language of progress and liberation, by Soviet-model totalitarianism is now perhaps the greatest obstacle to a revived, and especially to an egalitarian, concept of citizenship in Eastern Europe.

The altered images of space and time induced a twofold change in the concept of representation. On the expanded scale of the nation state, the original republican idea of direct citizen participation in all political decisions had to be replaced by acceptance of a representative system. Attempts to reverse this trend and revive the participatory idea have recurred ever since Rousseau, and may receive new impetus both from the potential uses of information technology and from the environmentalist advocacy of return to smaller-scale social units. During the 1980s the recurrent dream of direct democracy found expression too in city after city as communist power cracked – in Civic Forum and Solidarity, Neues Forum and Ecoglasnost. Here for a moment seemed the renewal of what Hannah Arendt called 'the best in the revolutionary tradition – the council system, the always defeated but only authentic outgrowth of every revolution since the eighteenth century'.[3] But as in every previous revolution, their moment was brief indeed: the spontaneous, participatory organs of 'people power' generated in the moment of revolt splintered or faded, turned themselves (with very mixed success) into semi-conventional political parties contesting through the representative system, or simply disappeared into the maw of the big battalions of Christian and Social Democracy, resuscitated Peasant and hastily renamed Communist parties. The question remains whether the impulse behind them, which is the fragile soul of the citizen ideal, can survive and flourish through perhaps more alienated, but certainly more durable, political structures.

The eighteenth-century Enlightenment and 'Atlantic Republicanism' also saw a gradual widening of the scope of citizenship itself. Classical republicanism had always confined the rights of citizenship to minorities. After 1789 the idea that all men were or should be, citizens gained ground rapidly; and the first small voices, like pioneer feminist Mary Astell's, pressing the claims of women were raised. Yet almost nowhere, before the twentieth century, was the actual right to participate in government extended even to all men. Exclusions were justified on grounds of distinguishing between 'active' and 'passive' citizenship – as did the French Jacobins – or between overt and 'tacit' consent to government decisions, as did John Locke.

The underlying reason was, in most cases, fear of granting political power to the propertyless. The ghosts of these principles of exclusion continue to haunt contemporary debate on democracy even in an era of universal franchise; as does the exclusion of women from full political citizenship, which is far more than a ghost. They remind us that the question of citizenship is incalculably far from being resolved, in Eastern Europe as in the West, solely by the introduction of multiple parties, free elections, or liberty of expression. Feminist political theorist Carole Pateman argues rightly that the social contract which forms the founding myth of most political societies – and may in the framing of a republican constitution be, in a more limited sense, a real contract – rests on prior, concealed contracts of patriarchal domination and sometimes (as with the US Constitution) of slavery.

> Civil freedom depends on patriarchal right ... The original contract is merely a story, a political fiction, but the invention of the story was also a momentous intervention into the political world; the spell exerted by stories of political origins has to be broken if the fiction is to be rendered ineffective.[4]

The point is of imperative moment for democratic prospects in Eastern Europe, and not only because issues of women's rights have (with the conspicuous exception of East Germany) played sadly little role in the eruptions there. Just as most definitions of civil society are negative (defined by what the state is *not*), so conceptions of citizenship are as inescapably fictions, inventions, works of imagining as are those of nation. Neither nationhood nor citizenship is a *thing*; both are processes which involve, as Edmund Morgan says, inventing 'the People'.[5] The current transformation of Europe should surely demonstrate this if anything can, as not only constitutions and ideologies but state structures and national boundaries go into almost unprecedented flux. The seemingly solid dissolves into air, long submerged identities resurface, new ones are scratched on the backs of envelopes in smoke-filled assemblies. Some of those most centrally involved in the process of creation are even themselves creators of fictions in the more conventional sense – pre-eminently, of course, Vaclav Havel.

Yet the denial of this flux, the foreclosure of human choice can be encountered too in some of the most influential voices coming from Eastern Europe, including even some other great imaginers. There one finds a powerfully expressed vision of lost past and desired future, defining what it means to be European and thus to have the possibility of democratic citizenship through a very particular idea of culture that relies on fixed and inherited meanings. The *locus classicus* of this vision is Czech novelist Milan Kundera's much discussed essay on Central European identity.[6] It implies a species of cultural essentialism, and sharply delimits the possibilities of citizenship through a series of radical exclusions. The exclusions are not based this time on class or gender, or not overtly so. They flow from long historical tradition and are anchored by geography. The fatal consequence is that Russians simply cannot be democrats or citizens by the same token that they cannot be Europeans.

The origins of such a presumption are evident enough. We noted above the migration of the idea of citizenship across Western Europe and the Atlantic world. Its progress eastward was far less secure: it never found secure moorings, never won assent, outside very narrow circles of the intelligentsia, east of a certain line. The line itself has been variously drawn: at the limits of Western feudalism, of early mercantile capitalism, of Roman Christianity, of the Austro-Hungarian Empire, even (by those who have deplored or occasionally celebrated a supposedly intrinsic German distaste for freedom) at the Rhine. Whatever the precise boundary, beyond it civil society, democratic liberties and a culture of citizenship never existed.

As a historical sketch, all this has an obvious validity. But the point, and the flaw, of the argument Kundera and many others make is that a despotic history is claimed almost wholly to determine present events and future possibilities. With one breath they say that it is the civic ideal which distinguishes Europe and whose absence from Russian traditions has made communist rule such a disaster for Central and Eastern Europe. But then they turn and make a certain conception of culture – fixed by long history, bounded by elites, defined quasi-nationally, even semi-racially – the heart of the great divide. By this maneouvre Russia and Russians are placed forever beyond the pale: they had the wrong origins, and can never outgrow them, which is tough luck on them. The tragedy of totalitarianism after 1945, though, is according to this view not that of free citizens subjected to arbitrary power – power more absolute and more brutal over the peoples of the USSR than over its subjects further West. It is that 'oriental despotism', natural enough in

129

its own allotted sphere, was illegitimately extended too far west. The line was redrawn, at Yalta, in the wrong place.

Equally sweeping exclusions take place to the south and even to the west of the European heartland as to the east. The Arab, the Moslem and by evident extension the African and Asian worlds are barred as thoroughly as the Slavic from civic, from cultural, and implicitly, from human worth. The ethnocentrism of Jenö Szücs's otherwise profound essay 'Three Historical Regions of Europe' is breathtaking. Islam, in his view, simply 'expropriated the southern half' of the ancient world and thereafter disappears from the cultural map.[7] Kundera expels the USA too from his preferred world of the spirit.[8] And even within Central Europe whole peoples are subject to similar anathemas. For Mihály Vajda 'the Slovaks have never had true democratic traditions', unlike the Czechs.[9] Hungarians can be found arguing that Romanians are incapable of the democratic ethos; Bulgarians saying the same of their Turkish fellow-citizens; Poles denying Byelorussian potential for true civic consciousness; and, at any given moment, someone somewhere in Eastern Europe is saying it about the Jews. Claim and counter-claim about innate aptitudes for citizenship begin to replay old hatreds in modern democratic garb. The resultant carnage may yet give autocracy a last laugh from beyond the grave, enable it to proclaim that its version of forced-march political modernity, its police-state citizenship have proved after all to be the only viable ones for such societies. As the Soviet economy gridlocks and the Soviet empire unravels, it seems all too probable: in the USSR if nowhere else, autocracy might then not only laugh from the tomb but re-emerge from it, wearing who knows what clothes – an army uniform, the threadbare grey suit of a Yegor Ligachev, the gaudy national colours of Pamyat, or perhaps the billowing populist robes of a Boris Yeltsin.

Even where national and racial antipathy does not delimit and distort the new language of citizenship in the emergent European democracies, other threats to liberty may lie in wait within that language itself. The classical republican notion of citizenship always carried its own dangers; the Jacobin experience and the thinking of the greatest French republican theorist, Jean-Jacques Rousseau, show its dark side. The emphasis on solidarity can produce an enforced unity. The belief in participation can induce an undervaluing of the private sphere, even its attempted erasure – 'forcing people to be free'. The idea of community may be forged only by rallying people against internal dissidents or external enemies. A dictatorial, or even merely a charismatic, minority can convince itself that it incarnates the general will. Perhaps most menacing of all, the stress on citizen virtue can lead to the suppression of those deemed insufficiently virtuous. The primacy accorded to moral virtue in public affairs is the most problematic of all facets of the republican citizen tradition. It resonates throughout the events of the French Revolution, and the Russian too, especially in the chilling asceticism and moral fervour of Robespierre or Lenin.

Something of the same spirit moved in much of Eastern Europe: the masses of Romania and East Germany seem to have been revolted by their rulers' petty corruption at least as much as by their tyranny. It would be absurd, of course, to denigrate the desire for civic virtue. In Czechoslovakia, perhaps even more than elsewhere, it has been a vital part of the democratic and oppositional tradition, from Thomas Masaryk's wonderful injunction to the new state's citizens in 1918 – 'Don't be afraid; and don't steal!' – to his successor Vaclav Havel's credo of 'living in the truth'. Yet the history of every previous revolution, of almost every revolutionary in power, suggests surely that a puritan self-righteousness is at least as dangerous to liberty as any kind of greed or corruption. A modern politics of citizenship only holds out hope both to Eastern Europe and to us, in so far as it can free itself from that legacy.

Such admonitions from the West, and in particular from West European socialists, have been seen by some as the merest hypocrisy. Has not the history of Western socialists' attitudes to Eastern 'real socialism' been – as David Selbourne charges – that of 'a kind of intellectual treason … a betrayal not merely of the truth but of real people … a mixture of intellectual arrogance and foolish certitude, now defeated, yet unable to acknowledge its own dilemma'.[10] This is not the place to debate the record of Western socialism in giving or withholding sympathy, solidarity or practical aid to democratic oppositionists under communism: a dramatically uneven record which no global judgement could encapsulate. More to the present point is the Western left's success or failure in *understanding* Eastern Europe's communist past and probable democratic futures. Here two categorical judgements can, I believe, be justified.

First, those Western socialists who lament the expected rapid transition of many post-communist states from a stalinist command economy straight to a more or less unregulated market system, and who regard it, in Fred Halliday's words, as 'not an advance, but a recidivism of epochal proportions'[11] must acknowledge one basic fact. There may well prove to be much to regret in this sudden reversal: the economic future of many regions east of the Elbe under capitalism is likely to be at least as grim as their recent past has been under communism. The lot of the poorest in those societies will probably be, and in some cases already is, one of both relative and absolute immiseration. But the Western left has not produced, in theory or in practice, a single lucid, comprehensive model for an alternative socialism which combines economic viability, social justice and democratic legitimacy. There have been sketches, bright hypotheses, practical suggestions for specific reforms and utopian blueprints for general transformation. But all these added together are not enough to sustain negative judgement on anyone who, having lived under 'real socialism', concludes that the available range of humanly sustainable systems stretches only from the minimally fettered market to the welfarist mixed economy: roughly from Switzerland to Sweden. If we believe there is another kind of future, we must show one that works. We have never yet done so, and we certainly cannot expect the new democracies to be our laboratory rats in the experimental search for one.

Second, the Western left has, at least until very recently, shown an almost equal failure of the democratic imagination in relation to Eastern Europe. Marxist political theory, in particular, has remained in almost the underdeveloped state that it was left by Marx's own failure to write the book on politics (sequel to *Capital*) that he'd planned. Marxism can even be claimed to be *anti*-political in its vision of a classless society in which no political conflict would exist, in its utopian idea of an eventual withering away of the state, and in its reduction of all issues to expressions of economic interest. In fairness, Leninism rather than Marxism *tout court* might well be thought the real offender here. Nevertheless, a lack of interest in the political forms of socialist democracy has been general, and undoubtedly helped produce a dictatorial state socialism where politics is, according to definition, either stiflingly ubiquitous or aridly non-existent. In neat symmetry, it's not the state that's withered away, but civil society.

The writings of East European dissidents have been crucial in identifying these yawning gaps in socialist political thinking, and thus in reshaping Western socialists' views on democracy. The dominant theme of much recent radical thinking from the Soviet bloc, besides the obvious emphases on resistance to state repression and the need to keep independent, critical thought alive, has been to revive the classical distinction – first made by Hegel – between state and civil society. This underlines the importance to democracy of a rich, plural life of independent civil associations free from state control. These East European themes have struck immediate chords among Western socialists, not only because they raise issues almost entirely neglected by the Marxist tradition, but because many fear that civil society is under threat here too.

If new thinking from the East has been so obviously valuable to radicals in the West, the traffic in the opposite direction has been miserably sparse. In their reappraisal of citizenship, the republican tradition and the need for autonomous civil society, writers in the East either went back to Hegel and to Mill, to Adam Smith and Adam Ferguson, to the French and American revolutionaries, or they sought to systematise the dark insights of Orwell and Zemyatin. They found almost nothing helpful in the Western Marxist tradition. How could they? Almost the only major West European Marxist to debate these issues seriously was Antonio Gramsci, and even then his conclusion was to speak to the 'reabsorption of political society into civil society.'[12] Nothing could be further from the reality of what has happened in Eastern Europe. So even the most sophisticated, most developed Western socialist body of thought on the questions raised by democrats escaping from totalitarianism, reveals itself as almost valueless for understanding their societies. Having so utterly failed to provide a diagnosis of 'real socialism', how can Western socialists hope to be trusted to prescribe a cure?

Indeed the time is long past when 'we' could presume to be 'their' teachers. The learning and the building of a new European citizenship will be a task of equals, a task in common. It may not have much resemblance to what has been thought of as the traditional socialist project. Many, perhaps most, democrats in the East would reject it with scorn if it did. Still, democratic principles, the citizen ideal and the aspiration to a peacefully shared Europe provide more than enough common ground on which to work. And there is more than enough too to work *against*. One historic adversary, the great enemy whom too many on the Western left too long mistook for a friend, is dead; but there are other enemies, and they may be no less destructive to the democratic spirit than stalinism was. Although one twisted version of political modernism, the totalitarian 'engineer of human souls', has lost all appeal and almost all power, another seemingly less ideological variant lives and grows. What Habermas calls 'systems rationality', which recognises only quantitative and technical values and goals, threatens everywhere to annex both public and private spheres to itself. Creativity and community, autonomy and solidarity are not crushed beneath a stalinist iron heel, but more slowly, quietly have the life squeezed from them by the joint embrace of the bureaucrat and the image-maker.

Another older opponent of freedom is reviving all over Eastern Europe: irrationalist, essentialist nationalism, sometimes with fascist undertones; the ghoulish anti-Enlightenment feeding off the mummi- fied corpse of the pre-Enlightenment. This antagonist gains power from the accumulated resentments of 'real socialism', as well as the mass fears of bureaucratic rationality – identifying both great perversions of modernism with the Enlightenment legacy itself and damning all together.[13] Against it, radical democrats everywhere in Europe will either work together across national and ideological boundaries, or, each in their separate spheres, go down in defeat.

Notes

The general debts here to the thought of Benedict Anderson, Norberto Bobbio, Jürgen Habermas, John Keane and J.G.A. Pocock may be too obvious to require acknowledgement. The more direct aid of Geoff Andrews and Daphna Vardi, though, deserves and has my warmest thanks.

[1] Jacques Darras and Daniel Snowman, *Beyond the Tunnel of History*, Macmillan, London 1990, p74.
[2] See E.J. Hobsbawm's acute, concise dissection of the interpretive legacies of 1789

in *Echoes of the Marseillaise*, Verso, London 1990.
[3] Hannah Arendt, *Crises of the Republic*, Harcourt Brace Jovanovich, New York 1972, p124.
[4] Carole Pateman, *The Sexual Contract*, Polity, Cambridge 1988, p219.
[5] Edmund S. Morgan, *Inventing the People*, Norton, New York 1988.
[6] Milan Kundera, 'A Kidnapped West or Culture Bows Out' in *Granta*, no.11, 1984.
[7] Jenö Szücs, 'Three Historical Regions of Europe', in J. Keane (ed.), *Civil Society and the State*, Verso, London 1988, p291.
[8] Kundera, *op.cit.*, p112.
[9] Mihály Vajda, 'East-Central European Perspectives', in Keane (ed.), *op.cit.*, p355.
[10] David Selbourne, *Death of the Dark Hero*, Jonathan Cape, London 1990, xi-xii.
[11] Fred Halliday, 'The Ends of Cold War', in *New Left Review*, no.180, p22.
[12] Quoted in Norberto Bobbio, *Democracy and Dictatorship*, Polity, Cambridge 1989, p24.
[13] The emblematic intellectual representative of this kind of irrationalist anti-modernism is of course Martin Heidegger. Thinking through – and against – his influence will be as politically important for the 1990s as interrogating Lenin's was for the 1980s. See, to begin, Jürgen Habermas, *The Philosophical Discourse of Modernity*, Polity, Cambridge 1987; Luc Ferry and Alain Renaut, *Heidegger et les Modernes*, Grasset & Fasquelle, Paris 1988; Michael Zimmerman, *Heidegger's Confrontation with Modernity*, Indiana University Press, Bloomington 1990.

Claims of Rights

John Osmond

The Englishness of Charter 88

If the peoples of Britain and Northern Ireland are to free themselves from their monarchic, undemocratic, hierarchical, deferential and personally humiliating state structure, it will be the result of a co-operative endeavour. That is why I signed Charter 88.

The document declares that our freedoms are dependent upon sovereignty resting with the people, guaranteed by a written constitution. As an equally significant declaration, 'A Claim of Right for Scotland', also published in 1988, has it:

> The crucial questions are power and consent; making power accountable and setting limits to what can be done without general consent.
>
> These questions will not be adequately answered in the United Kingdom until the concentration of power that masquerades as 'the Crown in Parliament' has been broken up.[1]

Unlike 'A Claim of Right for Scotland', however, Charter 88 does not acknowledge that the United Kingdom is a multinational state, and this is a critical weakness. The Charter's aspirations are framed within a thoroughly English context. Thus, it calls for 'an equitable distribution of power between local, regional and national government', conveniently ignoring the national status, however ambiguous, of Wales and Scotland and the even more contested position of Northern Ireland.

Charter 88 is equally English in the stress it places on individual rights. This is not to deny their vital importance, but to assert at the same time that they can only be assured when due recognition is also paid to community rights which, in certain circumstances, take

136

priority. The linguistic rights of communities, for example, are a case in point and one to which we are sensitive in Wales.

The 'Englishness' of Charter 88 is indicative of the extent to which its authors are, themselves, victims of the cancer they are endeavouring to eradicate. The peculiarity of English nationalism, its abnormality in fact, is an underlying explanation of why sovereignty rests with that formulation 'Crown in Parliament' rather than the people.

Charter 88 wishes to change the institutional infrastructure of the British state so that sovereignty will rest with the people. Such a process would involve fundamental changes in the nature of English society. English nationalism would have to undergo a revolution in sensibility. The pursuit of democracy in England, such as that advocated by Charter 88, requires English nationalism to modernise and become more recognisable in world terms. It requires, most of all, a diminution of the role of the monarchy in the English imagination. All this is a formidable undertaking.

Most conventional nationalities the world over – and not least the Welsh, Scots and Irish – define their identity in terms of territory, language and a sense of the people as being the building blocks of the nation. The English, however, rely on none of these characteristics. Who can draw a map of England? England is a country of the mind, either smaller than its actual territory, focused around a 'Home Counties' rural arcadia, or larger: embracing the whole island of Britain (Northern Ireland is usually excluded) and formerly all those red bits on the map of the world, still sometimes retained in the form of the Commonwealth. The English language is regionalised into dialects and accents on the one hand, while on the other, Americanised into a world alternative to Esperanto. But most significant of all, for the argument being pursued here, there are no English *people* – only *subjects* under a Crown-Parliament hegemony established in 1688, long before democracy was heard of in its modern sense.

The Scots and the Welsh have a specific relationship with the idea of Britain. They see their British identity as something separate from being Scottish or Welsh. They have a dual identity, in fact, with each part of the whole being accentuated at different moments and in different circumstances. The English do not make the same distinction. For them England and Britain are the same. In the English mind there is a kind of fusion between the two, into an Anglo-British identity which is at the heart of the backward, undemocratic society that Charter 88 is trying to reform.

The project would be enormously reinforced if Charter 88 took seriously on board the multinational character of the British state, since it is in the outlying nations that the greatest energy for reform in a republican democratic direction lies. This is why the Celtic nationalisms that have been most responsible for forcing decentralisation/devolution on to the agenda of British politics are so distrusted, and even hated by the English/British 'Establishment' forces of both right and left. For example, in early February 1989, Mrs Thatcher, speaking in Glasgow, declared:

> Several countries in the European Community have separatist movements. If those movements were to succeed in their separatist ambitions, what would then be the position of the breakaway parts in relation to the Community?
>
> Fragment Europe and you destroy it. Not for us Fortress Europe closing inwards on itself against the rest of the world. We want Enterprise Europe, whose industry and commerce are efficient enough to prosper in fair competition.

Compare this statement with the one contained in her Bruges speech, some months earlier, in September 1988:

> To try to suppress nationhood and concentrate power at the centre of a European conglomerate would be highly damaging and would jeopardise the objectives we seek to achieve. Europe will be stronger because it has France as France, Spain as Spain, Britain as Britain, each with its own customs, tradition and identity. It would be folly to try and fit them into some sort of identikit European personality.

So suppressing the nationhood of Scotland or Wales is acceptable, but suppressing the nationhood of Britain/England is not. Mrs Thatcher, of course, in her Bruges speech was really referring to England. In the same breath she mentioned France and Spain. But Spain has a constitution which gives considerable autonomy to its constituent nations and regions, and even France is evolving more decentralised institutions; while West Germany, Italy and Belgium are already federal states with fully-fledged regional governments. In November

1988, the European Parliament passed by a majority of more than 100 a resolution calling for the European Regions to have the power to set up elected bodies with sufficient resources to manage their own affairs. Set against these realities within the other nation states of the European Community, Mrs Thatcher's Glasgow speech reveals more about the insecurity of the British governing class and its identity than a clearly thought-through policy position.

In the first of her statements quoted above, Mrs Thatcher was attacking the Scottish National Party policy of independence for Scotland within the European Community. She went on to accuse those who wanted greater self-government for Scotland within the United Kingdom (that is, devolution), of advocating 'yet another layer of government'. If anything, this assertion is more inaccurate than the first. In Scotland, and Wales, the extra layer of government, as Mrs Thatcher puts it, already exists – in the shape of the Scottish and Welsh Offices. The same argument was put, in slightly more measured but nonetheless breathtakingly inaccurate terms, a week earlier in an editorial in the *Spectator*:

> There is no doubt that regions further from London feel more neglected by it (although the facts of subsidy show almost the exact reverse). There is no doubt that the Celtic nations have never been as happy with the Union as have the dominant Anglo-Saxons. These are real problems. But it is only men crazed with politics who imagine that they would be solved by more layers of government.[2]

What are the 'facts of subsidy' claimed here? They can only be expenditure on social security payments and regional economic policy. But both are dwarfed by long-established government investment policies pursued as a form of positive discrimination in *favour* of the English south-east. This is quite simply the budget wielded by the Ministry of Defence. The equipment procurement budget alone of the Ministry of Defence amounted to some £8.3 billion in 1985-86 (spending on regional economic policy in the United Kingdom was halved between 1979 and 1986, cut by £1 billion, and was being halved again by 1990). The defence equipment budget accounts for about half the output of the aerospace and some 20 per cent of the electronics industries in Britain, and a large number of jobs, especially in research and development establishments.

It is, of course, the geographical spread of this defence spending that is the most sobering reality so far as Wales, Scotland, Northern Ireland and the outlying regions of England are concerned. England, south-east of a line drawn from the Severn to the Wash, accounted for 68 per cent of it in 1985-86; south-west English 11 per cent; East Anglia 3 per cent; and the south-east a staggering 54 per cent. In contrast northern England received 15 per cent; the Midlands 9 per cent; Scotland 6 per cent; and Northern Ireland and Wales came bottom of the pile with just 1 per cent each. The Ministry of Defence budget is, in practice, an unofficial regional economic policy, working to the advantage of the south-east of England.

What of the other claim, made in the *Spectator* editorial and repeated by Mrs Thatcher, that an Assembly for Wales or Scotland within the United Kingdom would be adding another 'layer of government'? Again, this assertion does not bear examination.

Take Wales: its population of just under three million people is administered by the Welsh Office with 2,300 civil servants wielding an annual budget of more than £3.5 billion, a figure representing some 80 per cent of Welsh public expenditure. Moreover, most of this money is not spent by the Welsh Office itself, but in conjunction with a panoply of quangos, from the eight Welsh health authorities to the Welsh Development Agency, Mid Wales Development, the Welsh Water Authority, the Wales Tourist Board, and the Welsh Arts Council – to name only thirteen. In a parliamentary reply in September, 1988, the Secretary of State for Wales, Peter Walker, revealed that he had made more than 270 appointments to 78 public bodies in Wales since taking office after the 1987 general election.

The Welsh Office is not comparable with other Whitehall departments. Like the Scottish and Northern Ireland Offices, it has responsibility for a whole range of functions – from developing the Welsh economy, to local government, health, education, roads, agriculture, housing, the environment and the arts. In Whitehall, each of these functions is the responsibility of a separate department monitored by select committees of the House of Commons, with 300 English backbench MPs ready to serve on them.

The Welsh Office has a select committee, too, but only around a dozen backbenchers available to serve on it, and an unscalable mountain of activities for it to monitor. The Conservatives typically have to import English MPs to administer Wales. Peter Walker is the outstanding example. In December 1988, the Minister of State at the Welsh Office, Wyn Roberts, chose an English backbencher, Derek Conway, MP for Shrewsbury, to be his parliamentary Private Secretary. In Scotland the position is worse. The Scottish Select Committee, for example, has been abandoned by the present Government because it simply does not have enough Scottish MPs to form a majority on it.

The fragility of the arguments brought by right-wing British/English political figures against decentralisation and effective democratic accountability for Wales and Scotland suggests that their opposition goes much deeper. What they fear is a people-centred democracy spreading from Wales and Scotland and undermining the Crown-centred oligarchy that presently runs Britain.

But if this is the real position of the British right it is not far from being the position of much of the traditionalist British left as well. The lack of a clear democratic vision at the centre of their politics goes a long way towards explaining their difficulty, even embarrassment, in embracing any uninhibited sense of patriotism.

If there is one area during the 1980s where the Labour Movement has been sidestepped at every point by the right, it is here. It is not just a question of the defence debate and the nuclear issue which in this arena have been merely symptomatic of a deeper underlying reality. The clearest indication was the way the Conservative Party in the 1980s managed to hijack the Union Jack. During this period it was impossible to imagine the Labour Party conference draped in the Union Jack and impossible to imagine the Conservative Party conference *not* draped in the Union Jack.

What the British left has consistently failed to see and imagine is that within the frame of the British state there exists a diversity of communities – Black British, Welsh British, Northern Ireland British, Scots British, and in various formations English British, whose Britishness exists only to provide them with a passport, but whose real community of identity is expressed through their sense of place, their distinctive cultures, their particular history, their social relationships and their feelings of responsibility arising from all these.

Taken together they provide the basis for a different, more human, radical and, most importantly, more democratic way of imagining Britain. A prime requirement in this project is the necessity for the English to think through the real meaning of being English, especially in the political context. The virtue of Charter 88, and why it deserves support despite its Anglo-centred shortcomings, is that it has provided an agenda and a route for this to happen.

Notes

This article was first published in *Planet*, no.75, June/July 1989.

[1] 'A Claim of Right for Scotland – Report of the Constitutional Steering Committee', Scottish Constitutional Convention, July 1988.
[2] *The Spectator*, 28 January 1989.

Reclaiming Scottish Sovereignty

Constitutional Conventions are set up only when the established form of government is perceived as having broken down, whether or not it is still formally operating. Our choice of weapons is simple. We have only one – the Convention. What matters is how the weapon is used.

(Jim Ross, who drafted the Campaign for a Scottish Assembly's Constitutional Steering Committee's report *A Claim of Right for Scotland*.)

At the end of the third meeting of the Scottish Convention in January, a cluster of journalists encircled an unhappy Donald Dewar, shadow Secretary of State for Scotland, and demanded: 'Well, what do *you* mean by Scottish sovereignty?'

The Convention, held in the ornate chambers of Glasgow City Hall, had been dominated by one Labour MP after another coming up to the rostrum and making a nationalist speech, to the embarrassment of a silent Donald Dewar sitting in the body of the hall.

In response to the journalists, Dewar, a tall, rather gangly but nonetheless shrewd and articulate Glasgow lawyer, pointed to the interim document the Convention had just approved. This states that a Scottish Parliament should be directly elected, with powers over matters such as health, economic development, education, housing, local government, the Scottish legal system and the police, but within the United Kingdom and with Westminster retaining control over defence, foreign affairs and 'central economic responsibilities'.

The line on a devolution package consistent with the continued integrity of a United Kingdom had been held, Donald Dewar was saying. Individual MPs were entitled to their views but a consensus was emerging that the Labour Party in London could live with.

Yet the fact that he had to explain the position in these terms, to Scottish political journalists who follow these affairs closely, but who nonetheless had been thrown into some confusion by the tone of the Convention's proceedings, was an indication of how far the debate on Scotland's future has progressed in the year since the Scottish Convention was inaugurated.

To a large extent this is a debate confined within the ranks of the Scottish Labour Party. Though the Convention is a cross-party body, with impressive support from a majority of Scottish MPs and MEPs, most regional and district authorities, the Scottish TUC and an array of other organisations, it has been boycotted by both the SNP and the Scottish Conservatives. Inevitably, the consequence has been that the Convention is very much a Labour-dominated affair, with a radical edge on constitutional questions supplied by the Scottish Liberal Democrats.

Thus Bob McCreadie, another Scots lawyer, chair of the Convention's working group on constitutional issues, is also vice-chairman of the Scottish Liberal Democrats. He told the Convention in January: 'There is no doubt that the belief in popular sovereignty is lodged within the Scottish consciousness.'

Arguing for collective rights to be entrenched in Scots law, and above the reach of the UK Parliament, he declared: 'It is the complete failure of the UK constitution – largely and dangerously expressed as unwritten conventions – to prevent governments of all political persuasions riding roughshod over fundamental rights, that constitutes the rotten core at the heart of British government.'

The issue of sovereignty was faced head on by Labour MP after Labour MP. Dennis Canavan, MP for Falkirk West, told the Convention:

The sovereignty of the Scottish people is inconsistent with the sovereignty of the United Kingdom Parliament and when we signed the Claim of Right for Scotland we were in effect challenging the sovereignty of Parliament.

So, if we were merely to hatch some scheme whereby the UK Parliament was to have any kind of veto on the powers and exercise of the powers of the Scottish Parliament, we would be denying the sovereignty of the people of Scotland and we would be falling into the trap of simply repeating the basic flaws in the 1978 Scotland Act.

What is now on the agenda in Scotland is a very different animal to the devolution measure that was attempted in the 1970s. George Galloway, MP for Glasgow Hillhead, quoted from an Enoch Powell speech made at Llwynypia, Cwm Rhondda in May, 1974, a time when the first modern Home Rule wave was crashing at the bastions of the British state: 'Devolution is not the same as the transfer of power,' Powell insisted. 'It is the opposite. Power devolved is power retained, and that retention is the very reason which makes devolution acceptable and possible.'

Labour in Scotland is desperately attempting to square the growing rejection within the Convention of this definition of the processes behind a Scottish Parliament, with the need to maintain at least the semblance of the integrity of a United Kingdom framework. And the effort is inexorably pushing it down a federalist road.

This was seen in January at a meeting of the Executive of the Scottish Labour Party, held a week before the Convention in an effort to set its agenda. Three key decisions were taken, all of which placed labour firmly on a federalist path.

First, the Executive decided to drop the word Assembly and use Parliament instead. 'There was no debate, it was just accepted,' said one member. In the 1970s, such a step would have been seen as an unacceptable concession to nationalism.

Secondly, the Executive agreed that the powers of the Scottish Parliament should be constitutionally guaranteed, or entrenched, so that they would not be just handed down from Westminster, but negotiated on the basis of equality.

Thirdly, it was agreed that whatever Home Rule scheme emerged should be seen as a forerunner for regional government throughout Britain. 'We have conceded federalism,' Donald Dewar is reported to have said.

However, an attempt to make the concession explicit, in the form of a resolution calling for a transfer of sovereignty from Westminster to Edinburgh – as opposed to a transfer of powers – was defeated by a three-to-one margin. If successful, this resolution would have made Scottish sovereignty totally transparent, by allowing a Scottish Parliament to reclaim all power and then decide what authority to transfer back to Westminster and Brussels.

The Executive decided against making this sovereignty move on the grounds that it would create division within the UK and cause a split within the party in Scotland. Mark Lazarowicz, chairman of the Labour Party in Scotland, said:

> We recognise that there is some feeling within the party that in the future we may wish to move to a situation where the UK adopts some kind of federalist structure.
>
> The relationship between a Scottish Parliament and Westminster might then have to be reconsidered in light of that. But the federal option should not be used to delay the establishment of a Scottish Parliament while similar systems were set up for Wales and the regions of England.

The first task of the Convention is to draw up a scheme for a parliament that can be agreed, not just by the various factions within the Labour Party, but by the wide range of other parties and interests represented. The signs are that this will happen within two more meetings, and certainly by the autumn of this year.

Leaving aside the argument about sovereignty, the main area of potential disagreement is over the system of elections to the Parliament once it is set up. The Liberal Democrats have declared that unless the principle of proportional representation is conceded, they would withdraw from the Convention.

However, there is growing acceptance that maintaining the first-past-the-post system would unjustifiably entrench the dominance both of the Labour party and of the Strathclyde region, Labour's heartland – in the 1987 general election Labour took 69 per cent of the Scottish seats with only 42 per cent of the vote.

Awareness of the innate injustice of such results (quite apart from the problems they raise of integrating outlying, largely rural areas of Scotland into a Scottish Parliament), is beginning to persuade influential sections of the Labour Movement in Scotland. For instance, on the same day that the Convention met in January, Scottish leaders of the Transport and General Workers Union resolved to back calls for proportional representation that will be made at the annual conference of the Scottish Labour Party in March. Following the same line being taken by other unions, including the National Union of Public Employees, this makes it now virtually certain that Labour will adopt proportional representation for a Scottish Parliament.

But achieving a consensus for a Parliament is only the first task of the Convention. Others, as laid down in the *Claim of Right* document that preceded the Convention's founding, are to mobilise Scottish public opinion behind an agreed scheme, and then deal with the London government in achieving its implementation. These, especially the last, will undoubtedly prove much more difficult.

If Labour wins the next election, the route forward is relatively easy. However, recent opinion polls suggest there could be a repeat version of what happened in 1987 – what is referred to in Scotland as the Doomsday Scenario Mark II. This is simply that while the Tories appear destined to lose in Scotland, even more heavily than last time, they may well win again in Britain as a whole, on the basis of their overwhelming strength in southern England.

The possibility was pointed up by a striking System 3 Poll published by the *Glasgow Herald* on the eve of the Convention meeting in January. This showed the Conservatives slumping disastrously in Scotland, from 21 points in November to just 16 per cent in late January, with Labour standing at 50 (compared with 49 in November), the Scottish Nationalists 21 (20), the Scottish Liberal Democrats 5 (5), the Greens 5 (4), and the SDP 1 (2).

In response to the prospect of another Doomsday, some of the boldest of the Convention's supporters have floated the idea of presenting a 'Dual Mandate' question to Scottish candidates at the next general election. Candidates would be asked to declare that, if the election did not produce a government prepared to legislate for a Scottish Parliament, they would hold themselves obliged to defy Westminster, set up a provisional Scottish Parliament, and take whatever action seemed necessary to bring Westminster to the negotiating table.

The idea of a general election result in Scotland being perceived, even potentially, as producing a separate mandate to that of the result in the United Kingdom as a whole, is another indication of the virus of federalism creeping into the thinking of Labour supporters campaigning for a Scottish Parliament. The dual mandate has been developed by the Labour Party pressure group, Scottish Labour Action. Now it has been taken up by the Transport and General Workers Union which has tabled a motion on the subject for the Scottish Labour conference in March. A similar motion at last year's conference was sidelined. It may be again this year but, if so, it is certain to be raised again, and more vehemently, at next year's conference in 1991.

What is emerging out of the debates taking place is that, as Jim Ross (a Labour Party member who was the civil servant in the Scottish Office responsible for the 1970s devolution legislation) has pointed out, the dual mandate was implicit in *A Claim of Right for Scotland*:

> That report took the Dual Mandate for granted by adopting the position that Scottish MPs have been elected to represent their constituents, and, if they cannot represent them effectively at Westminster, are not only entitled but obliged to find other ways of representing them. The gist of its argument was that only by a fluke would the British constitution accord justice to Scottish consitutional requirements, that this had been amply demonstrated, and that politics could not sensibly be based on waiting for a fluke.[1]

The extent to which Labour is wrestling with questions of Scottish sovereignty and principles of federalism is also a vindication of the Scottish Nationalists' controversial line in boycotting the Convention. If the SNP had taken part in its debates over the past year, it is fair to say that the Convention would have been much less likely to have moved so quickly and on such a broad front towards achieving a consensus around a scheme for a Scottish Parliament.

More than that, Labour itself would have been far less likely to have moved so far and so fast down the road of Scottish self-determination. This interpretation had been confirmed by a recent study of the Scottish Labour Party by two Glasgow-based academics, entitled 'Devolution and the Tartanisation of Labour'.[2] The authors focus on the idea of the Scottish mandate, originally a nationalist theme, but enthusiastically adopted and, as a result, legitimised by the Scottish Labour Party during the 1980s.

The study states, 'Labour politicians evidently feel increasingly comfortable with this idea, despite its nationalist origins and its profound constitutional implications'. The principal expression had been that the Tories had no mandate to run Scotland. Even the most senior party figures had fallen prey to the mandate theory, with Shadow Secretary of State for Scotland, Donald Dewar, claiming that an Assembly would have protected the Scottish people 'from much damaging legislation that does not reflect Scottish priorities'.

By stressing the negative consequences of rule from Westminster, while raising expectations about the power of a Scottish Assembly as an agent of social transformation, Labour was effectively undermining Parliament, and promoting the SNP case for greater independence.

In recent years there had been a constant move to adopt the 'standard stock-in-trade of traditional nationalists' with talk of interim Scottish Assemblies, extra-parliamentary action or disruption, and a referendum. Even the powers proposed by Labour for a Scottish Assembly (now significantly called a Parliament) were those the SNP put forward a decade ago.

Consequently, as the study states, 'The closing of ranks within Scotland on the necessity for an Assembly has produced signs of developing strain between the party nationally (sic), and the party in Scotland'. And it concludes that like Frankenstein, 'Labour politicians in Scotland have created a monster which now threatens to run completely out of control'.

Of course, it could also be concluded that, by grasping the Scottish thistle, Labour is ensuring that it will be able to outflank the Nationalists in the 1990s and convert itself, truly, into the national party of Scotland.

Notes

This article was first published in *Planet*, no.79, February/March 1990.

[1] Jim Ross, 'Towards a New Scotland – A Choice of Weapons', in *Cencrastus*, no.35, Winter 1989.
[2] Jack Geekie and Roger Levy, 'Devolution and the Tartanisation of Labour', in *Parliamentary Affairs*, vol.42, no.3.

Part IV – Citizenship and Non-Citizens

In an age of citizenship there are two types of non-citizens: those that have been exiled and those that have never been admitted.

Sarah Benton

Gender, Sexuality and Citizenship

Sarah Benton

When we read of Bulgarians and Hungarians in their first year of liberation eagerly buying the new wonders of pornography, we in the West were silent. Who are we to deny our brothers the freedom so long enjoyed on our side of the former Iron Curtain?

Yes, just who are we? First, from either side of the Iron Curtain, we are Easterners, or we are Westerners. Then when Gorbachev in 1989 called for us to assert the 'common brotherhood of Europe', we were all Europeans. Or were we? Can women be brothers? Can men be brothers to women, or only to each other?

There is no word to express a common bond between men and women in their (our) fight for liberty, equality and ...? Women can demand liberty, and fight for equality, turning them into points of contestation with men (more for us means less for you). But what do we do with fraternity? Do we destroy it or join it – thereby destroying its primary meaning anyway. So can women be sisters to men in the struggle for civic rights? The most sentimentally potent relationship is hymned in 'Bread and Roses', inspired by the American mill-girls' strike in 1913, when women's suffrage was the burning point in modern politics. Here the 'we' are women:

> As we come marching, marching, we battle too for men, for they are women's children and we mother them again.

In the new citizenry of Europe, are the men to be citizens and the women to be the strong and silent earth on which they dance? After the march for freedom, she returns to bake the fragrant bread, he sits down with a pornographic magazine showing another she who has stripped

151

herself naked and frozen in the pose that reflects his desire.

Each birth of each new citizenry in Eastern Europe, each struggle for democracy this last year, has adopted its own imagery for the destruction and creation of political society. The Chinese students spoke of martyrdom, of laying down their life for the cause, as testament to the truth of their beliefs, to avert further death. The Romanians spoke of revenge, of slaking that thirst for revenge through the killing of the Ceausescus, parents to a nation, and, through that final death, of foreswearing killing in order to usher in the new society. East Germans spoke of treachery and betrayal, Czechoslovaks of vindications and of finding their true voice. The Azerbaijanis, Armenians, Serbs, Kosovian Albanians spoke most often of brotherhoods, and mass killing and random rape were reported most often from their lands.

As euphoria faded in East Germany and the Baltic states, a language of land, soul, blood and soil emerged again. It is a language which, at best, treats women's sexuality as part of the common heritage of nationhood – the primal task of bearing sons. Where nationalism allies with the Catholic Church, as in Poland (and Ireland before), any struggle for sexual freedom as an equivalent 'birth-right' is smothered in silence. Some months before the inspiringly peace-loving Chinese students occupied Tiananmen Square, Chinese students had demonstrated against the presence of Africans who had had sex with ('raped', they claimed) 'their' women. Was *that* the birth of a national brotherhood, precursor of the assertion of civic life? Is the first step to common civil rights the nationalisation of women?

The moments of entry and exit from civic life are not like ordinary life. They excite a peculiar political awareness which, paradoxically, demands a language which goes beyond politics. Though such moments may be separated by centuries and thousands of miles, we nonetheless find people speaking of birth and death, killing and forgiving, belonging and betrayal, parenthood and abandonment as though only this language of existential fundamentals is adequate to the momentousness of the change. The very timelessness of these vocabularies, lying in the oblivion of our collective unconscious until we need them, gives high political moments their transcendent power.

People will also express these needs and desires through acts – pulling down statues and ripping open the rooms containing the secrets of their rulers. When the East Germans and Romanians burst open the offices, homes and locked cabinets of their rulers, they were symbolically destroying the power of the old citadel whose 'great business', records Lewis Mumford, was not communication but 'to keep the official secrets'. Going back 4,500 years, he writes:

> There is a bitter lament from Egypt's first great popular uprising that reveals the indignation of the upper classes because the lower orders had broken into their precincts, and not merely turned their wives into prostitutes, but, what seemed equally bad, captured knowledge that had been withheld from them.[1]

The control of sex and secrets is at the heart of political power. The French, marking the death of the Nazi regime and the inauguration of the new France, shaved the heads of women collaborators; a symbolic killing of women's sexuality which had betrayed their national resistance. Thus had Delila betrayed Samson ('At length to lay my head and hallow'd pledge/Of all my strength in the lascivious lap/Of a deceitful concubine who shore me ...'), causing him to betray 'the secret gift of God/To a deceitful Woman' and through her, to betray his countrymen. (No version of this manifold betrayal and Samson's subsequent 'life half dead, a living death' as an outcast is more bitter than Milton's *Samson Agonistes*, written after the cause of the New Commonwealth had failed.)[2]

The sexual imagery of these carnivals of joy or orgies of destruction is rarely far away. The most popular poster in the 1990 Hungarian elections showed a picture of a young couple absorbed in a kiss below a picture of Brezhnev and Honecker in the same embrace. The caption said 'now you can choose' – 'natural' (free) sex or 'unnatural' (tyrannical) embraces. Musing on the imagery of Havel in Czechoslovakia, the Hungarian George Konrad thought 'if it were summer and printed T-shirts were about, there would surely be girls with him on their bosom.'[3]

There are sexual acts also of revenge, punishment and death. Here is how Milan Kundera, the exiled Czech writer, described the moment when he knew he had been cast out of the citizenry: prohibited from working in his name, he was given work writing horoscopes by 'R', the young woman editor of a magazine that printed 'claptrap glorifying our brothers the Russians'. The secret police find out, she loses her job, and Kundera absorbs the horrible realisation that he has become the bearer of destruction to those he loves; he will have to leave his country. At this moment of realisation, he is possessed only by the

> monumental desire to rape that fine girl, my friend. The desire has remained with me, trapped like a bird in a pouch, a bird that wakes up now and then and flaps its wings.
>
> Perhaps that wild desire to rape R. was merely a desperate attempt to grab at something during the fall. Because from the day they excluded me from the circle, I have not stopped falling, I am still falling, all they have done is give me another push to make me fall farther, deeper, away from my country and into the void of a world resounding with the terrifying laughter of the angels that covers my every word with its din.[4]

In an age of citizenship, there are two sorts of non-citizen: those who have never been admitted, and those who are exiled. The distinction between citizens and non-citizens incarnates, like all fundamentalisms, man's splitting into good and bad, them and us, brothers and outsiders. (Kundera's account of his exclusion comes in his meditation on two sorts of laughter, that of angels and that of devils.) The traditional exclusion of women from political life hangs on just such a split. We are familiar with the argument that man splits womankind in two: mothers and whores, madonnas and sluts. We women must be either one or the other. But the first split, on which the city is founded, is the division made by men within themselves: each man is both pillar of the community and private pervert, good citizen and would-be rapist, minister of state and secret adulterer. Or so he fears.

Take, as an example, the founding father of progressive political thought, Jean-Jacques Rouseau. His objections to women taking their place as citizens in the ideal political body are well known; he discusses them in various places. The argument put forward in *Emile* is often quoted:

> Woman is made to give way to man, to put up even with injustice from him. You will never reduce young boys to the same condition, their inner feelings rise in revolt against injustice.[5]

Who then is the woman, and who the Jean-Jacques Rousseau, in this passage from his autobiography, *Confessions*?

> To fall on my knees before a masterful mistress, to obey her commands, to
> have to beg for her forgiveness, have been to me the most delicate of
> pleasures.[6]

His less delicate pleasure is to dream of being beaten by women and, he
says, this is the only sexual relationship he could imagine with a woman
for many years:

> In my crazy fantasies, my wild fits of eroticism, and in the strange
> behaviour which they sometimes drove me to, I always invoked,
> imaginatively, the aid of the opposite sex, without so much as dreaming that
> a woman could serve any other purpose than the one I lusted for.[7]

This self-rupture in man, doing – one imagines – such brutality to his
sense of self, is a driving force in the history of public life. St Augustine
argued that there are two cities: 'the one consists of those who live by
human standards, the other of those who live according to God's will.'[8]
This, he thinks, mirrors man's own evolution, 'inevitably evil and
carnal to begin with' and becoming spiritual, through rebirth in Christ.
Political man has reworked the division: with no city of God to be
accountable to, he owes his allegiance to king, to his brothers, to the
city they have made. He is accountable to them. He must, with them,
sacrifice his overpowering self-interest in the interest of creating the
city, and within that city he is 'public man'. Rousseau again.

> The problem is to find a form of association which will defend and protect
> with the whole common force the person and goods of each associate and in
> which each, while uniting himself with all, may still obey himself alone and
> remain as free as before. This is the fundamental problem of which the
> Social Contract provides the solution.[9]

He may, in some cities at some times, defend the public virtue of sexual
restraint, but this is not essential. Too many men have always been
aware of the potential hubris of this stance. For when he leaves his
public office to slip into something more comfortable, it is not
copulation for reproduction he dreams of. His wild fits of eroticism
may, like Rousseau's, stop at fantasies. (Here compare and contrast
President Carter's public confession to committing adultery 'in the
heart' to President Kennedy's wild, but secret, fornication.) He may
not actually consort with prostitutes, under-age girls or boys, other

men; may not beat or be beaten; or engage in any one of the 'perverted' acts of sex his public self denies. But the man who has no such dreams is even rarer than the man who forswears the public world all together.

For all the popular contempt for politics, man clings to public life. Cut adrift from it, with nothing to hold onto but his private perversions, he falls, falls and does not stop falling. Milan Kundera's man has known the transcendent joy of dancing in the circle of society, knows that if he steps outside it, refusing its uniform suppression of the truth, the circle will simply close up as though he had never been there. He will never get back in again. Public man is held in line by the greatest of his fears: that of exile. Exile is the death of public man.

Until last year, communist states routinely exiled those who did not owe allegiance to their city. Western societies no longer have these powers, yet the traces of exile are so strong in our culture that we easily recognise its meaning. We know Salman Rushdie's 'exile' from the Muslim community to be a form of living death. Exiled by Shakespeare's Richard II, the Duke of Norfolk protests:

> What is the sentence then but speechless death,
> Which robs my tongue from breathing native breath ...
> Then thus I turn me from my country's light
> To dwell in solemn shades of endless night.[10]

His punishment is on the (false) charges that he betrayed the king and that he killed the Duke of Gloucester, whose blood – 'like sacrificing Abel's' – cries out for justice. This coupling of crimes is a powerful reminder that fraticide and betrayal are the two most heinous crimes in public society; the punishment too is a reminder of the first exile. God banishes Cain for killing Abel.

> And Cain said unto the Lord, My punishment is greater than I can bear. Behold thou hast driven me from the face of the earth; and from thy face shall I be hid; and I shall be a fugitive and a vagabond in the earth; and it shall come to pass that every one that findeth me shall slay me.[11]

Cain ends his fugitive life by founding the first city. It is this that gives St Augustine the imagery of the city of man (Cain's) and the city of God (Abel's) to which the pilgrim is moving. Medina, the object of the great islamic pilgrimages, means 'the City' (and is where Mohammed formulated the legal and civic parts of the *Koran*). And it is to a city, in the popular civic metaphors of the rebellious seventeenth century, that John Bunyan's pilgrim is progressing.

Man's fear of exile, of the death of his civic self, causes him to guard with great jealousy his 'private' realm, even while he cannot publicly defend his knowledge that it is the domain of his perversity. Like mothers and the soil, his protectorate of wife, children, servant, exists out of time, and out of public life. It is enduring, it is safe, he can never be exiled from it as he can as a penalty for betraying the brotherhood of public life. Even if he damages and hurts those within his protectorate, this is never such a threat to public life as to cause his excommunication – unlike the great public crimes of fratricide and betrayal which the state must punish. Violence towards women was the accepted background clatter of all civic societies, just as women could be trusted to obey convention and keep the secrets of men's private life.

Public man is thus vulnerable; his status is not secure. Ever accountable to his fellow man for his acts and words, ever threatened by exclusion from the circle, the apolitical timelessness of his private life wherein he can be a sexual being is his guarantee of survival. Only his freedom in his private life is inalienable.

But even this safety is temporary and uncertain. This domain also includes those who might betray him – the objects of his erotic fantasies and acts which he cannot own, as he owns his family. Hence he must split the inhabitants of this domain, women and children, in two. On the one hand, there are the madonnas and mothers and innocent children whose sacred role in his life he must defend; these make up his protectorate. And, on the other hand, there are the whores and sluts, the (under-age) children of the devil, his brothers in perversity, who are the outcasts from the city. He needs them, cannot acknowledge he needs them, must keep them always close to him, but forever hidden.

Here the men are like Elias Canetti's persecuted crowd, which he likens to a 'besieged city'. Every city under siege, he says, gains new defenders but all of these bring 'the small invisible traitor' who 'quickly disappears into a cellar to join the traitor aready hidden there'. The traitors in the cellar are always more threatening than the besiegers outside. 'The activities of the enemy outside on the walls are open and can be watched; in the cellars they are hidden and insidious.'[12]

It is hardly surprising that the charge of treachery – the only crime still to carry the death penalty in most modern states – is so often associated with sexual perversity. An establishment which cultivates its all-male constitution, exists a skin's breadth away from the active homosexuality of the schools and clubs on which it feeds. It lives in constant terror of being betrayed by that homosexuality, so much so that the fear becomes self-fulfilling, in a figure like Guy Burgess. The claim that homosexuality meant treachery was once justified with the argument that homosexuals were liable to blackmail. Even now, when the gay movement has persuasively argued that in a tolerant society no homosexual should fear blackmail, the equation of treachery and homosexuality persists. There is no legal rationale. The fear expresses public man's anxiety that he will be betrayed by his private desires.

Down in Canetti's cellar too with male homosexuals are all sexual women. These are the prostitutes. Every civic society has them, and almost all outlaw them – though not the men who go to them. The more pressured a political society feels to create the irreproachable public man, the harsher its penalties against its own unacknowledged private desires. Gays and lesbians fear that the new Poland, dominated by a Catholic Solidarity, will not bring liberation for them but a reinforced exclusion.[13] The first target when a new public culture is being formed is usually prostitution. Britain's Contagious Diseases Acts, famously campaigned against by Josephine Butler, coincided with the period in which England invented its distinctive dominant culture. This, argues Philip Dodd, is the last quarter of the nineteenth century, when manliness was 'the core' of the curriculum in England's reconstituted public school system. He quotes from an 1872 journal, *The Dark Blue*: 'a nation of effeminate enfeebled bookworms scarcely forms the most effective bulwark of a nation's liberties.'[14]

In the summer of 1989, at the height of the passion to assert its political identity, fifteen prostitutes were condemned to death in Iran. The judge threw the first stone, and the crowd only stepped back from its storm of throwing when there was nothing left of the hooded women but a bloody pulp. Amongst the stone-throwers were, no doubt, men who satisfied their sexuality with prostitutes – perhaps the very ones whom they had just helped kill. Hypocrisy is a poor word for such violent vindictiveness towards the traitors in the cellar.

'Good' women cannot be admitted to political society for they, like nature itself, are outside political time. And 'bad' women cannot be admitted because man must keep his treacherous sexuality outside politics and public life. How are women to fight their way out from man's protectorate, and out from his cellars? If the very premise of citizenship has been the exclusion of women, how can women fight their way in to the city? And should they be changing its rules as they do?

Women have already begun to change the rules. As they have done so, they have thrown up some of the most intractable quandaries of modern political life. Above all, as women have gained political status, they have refused to keep men's secrets.

From at least the seventeenth century, men have defined the fundamental political problems as how to create a *common* wealth without the state taking too much of man's *individual* freedom. His battles have been both to direct the state, and to prevent its incursions into his private life. In this regard, he has gradually codified classical civil liberties. The Leveller leader, John Lilburne, wrote in 1653: 'the first fundamental right that I contended for ... was for the freedom of men's persons against arbitrary and illegal imprisonment' and in staking his claim, he refers back to the Magna Carta. Placing themselves in this tradition, picketing miners in 1984-5 expressed their outrage at their subjection to arbitrary arrest.

Yet arbitrary arrest has (with the significant exception of prostitutes) rarely been at the forefront of women's grievances. After all, if women are excluded from political society, their activities rarely constitute a menace against it. Only at the moments of women's mass protest – the suffrage battle, Greenham Common – have women experienced the same outrage. But more common has been women's need for the state to step forward *into* private life in order to free them from its tyrannies. Over the last twenty years, it has been state intervention in childcare, state provision for abortion and contraception, state intervention in domestic violence, in child abuse, even state action against pornography and sex shops, which some women have demanded. At the peak of fear about the Yorkshire Ripper, in the late 1970s, when police advised women not to go out alone at night, some feminists proposed a state-imposed curfew on men.

Women and men constitute continuous threats against each other's freedoms. Like Milton's Samson, men traditionally speak of being 'snared' by women, of having to forsake their freedom to fuck and to play because of domestic demands. If men often portray mothers as saints and martyrs, their hostility to maternal tyranny is expressed over and over in their mother-in-law jokes. But these restrictions on freedom are not equal in scope or kind. By dividing womankind into saints and sluts, men create a domain of women over which they have command, and free access to women's sexuality. A prostitute can't say no. Legally, a wife can't either; but if this were not a contested area, men would not have to talk of their conjugal rights.

The original, and compelling, argument of Carole Pateman in *The Sexual Contract* is that in establishing their civic brotherhood, men also establish their 'sex-right' over women.

> The brothers make a sexual contract. They establish a law which confirms masculine sex-right and ensures that there is an orderly access by each man to a woman. Patriarchal sex-right ceases to be the right of one man, the father, and becomes a 'universal' right. The law of male sex-right extends to all men, to all members of the fraternity.[15]

I think this is by far the most interesting theory which incorporates sex into hypotheses of the social contract. But for us, today, it has two problems. Firstly, the idea that the distinction between man and woman has the same universal meaning has a psychoanalytic (as well as physical) truth. Pateman buttresses her argument with quotations from Freud on brothers committing parricide. Yet psychoanalysis and politics are not the same discourse. Each may illuminate, sometimes mirror, the other; but they also have their own rules, and the universalities of psychoanalysis are constantly disrupted and re-ordered by politics. The term brotherhood therefore has never been used to mean all men. It was and is used to denote an exclusive society of men, a club, band or indeed fraternity. It exists to assert its solidarity against other men, as well as to exclude all women. The brotherhood of trade unions asserts their solidarity against the employers and in contrast to the non-union workers. Even Gorbachev's open-armed embrace of 'a common brotherhood of Europe' excludes all non-Europeans. Only an extra-terrestrial being could create a universal brotherhood. If we women regard all men as linked in a unitary brotherhood, we are creating another fundamentalist dichotomy.

This points to the second problem. In the evolution to political society, the links with family remain vibrant, and then replicate themselves in clans, tribes and wider bondings. The brotherhoods of blood have a different relation to sexuality than modern ones constructed for more instrumental reasons. Male bonding is not constant in form through time. It may appropriate women's sexuality most actively at times when men most aggressively assert the identity of their nation, clan or tribe, as in Iran today. It may, as with the Mafia, function as an essential anti-political brotherhood. In other words, brotherhood as such can be a paradigm for male political egalitarianism and for the secret undermining of political rules; one form of brotherhood can buttress despotisms while another can overthrow it. In short, without the qualification of how brotherhood is linked to family and sex and land, we cannot know how it is linked to politics.

Lastly, there is the problem of 'rights'. What do we mean by men's 'sex-rights'? Should women be pressing for their place in political society by demanding rights? In the last article she wrote before she died, Simone Weil disparaged the whole tradition of rights.

> The notion of rights is linked with the notion of sharing out, of exchange, of measured quantity. It has a commercial flavour, essentially evocative of legal claims and arguments. Rights are always asserted in a tone of contention; and when this tone is adopted, it must rely upon force in the background or else it will be laughed at.[16]

It is true that we only use the language of rights when the question of power is in contention. It is our word for disputing power that is exercised over us – 'You can't do that, you've got no right; I can do that, I've got the right'. We don't use the word 'right' when power is not in contention. So we should be wary of assuming that the term 'conjugal rights' meant that men exercised an uncontested sexual power over women. According to Thomas Paine in *The Rights of Man*, the Magna Carta was a *reclamation* of rights, and almost invariably when people talk of rights they invoke a sense of a birthright – something they once enjoyed, that was inherent in nature, but which was taken away from them. The language of rights is still a language of reclaiming power.

161

The problem for women is how far our own originary mythology suggests we enjoyed the command over our own lives which something, or someone, has since taken away. Feminism has attempted at times to create the myth of matriarchy, a time when women were, above all, in command of their own sexuality and through this could exercise public power. But there is little in our cultural heritage to give this myth resonance. More potent is the knowledge that the societies we know developed out of societies in which slave-owning and woman-oppression were the order of the day. The mythology of historical victimisation exercises a far more powerful hold over women's imagination and has proved more intractable.

Nevertheless, the very carnality of sexuality means it is easier for us to see it as a quality that belongs to us. If we feel dispossessed of our sexuality, as so many women do, then the notion of reclaiming it does have some meaning. All the same, I think it very doubtful that, in the move towards a fuller female citizenship and women's possession of their own sexuality, a language of rights is adequate. Certainly when contesting issues like abortion, contraception, rape and 'conjugal rights', we cannot escape from the idea of rights. Moreover, when it suits women to claim the same freedoms as men the language of equal rights is potent. Mary Wollstonecraft called her book *A Vindication of the Rights of Women* in deliberate evocation of Paine's *Rights of Man*, despite the fact that she rarely used the word 'rights' in her argument, preferring a more emotional, moral and humanistic language.

We have been dispossessed of this second language, in the era of professional politics, as surely as women feel dispossessed of their sexuality. Although the pioneers of women's liberation rapidly learned the language of rights, it was not of rights we talked in the early women's groups, and the pioneers of new 'authentic' forms of women's politics, like the women at Greenham Common or those pursuing 101 forms of holistic enterprise, have largely discarded the language of rights except when they are in confrontation with the state.

The obstacle posed by the notion of a brotherhood united in its exercise of sex-right over us is that it creates the sort of suspicion and denial which makes reclaiming sexuality impossible. If the consequence of seeing all men as sexual predators were to make women into joyfully active lesbians, perhaps the only ones to suffer would be heterosexual men. But that is not the consequence, as we know. What has happened today, as happened to the first suffragette movement, is that women create a fundamentalism which castigates male sexuality as rapacious and disease-bearing. (The peak of the suffragette movement, in 1913-14, coincided with the peak of hysteria about syphilis destroying women, children and the body politic.) In this fundamentalism, sex itself becomes repugnant and oppressive and women's 'sex-right' is reduced to the mere right to say no. In the journey to full possession of our humanity – which is surely the oldest and most compelling story of all – women risk accepting the death of their sexuality before they begin. A politics of citizenship founded on liberty, equality and above all *fraternity*, offers little of value to members of the sorority.

Notes

I would like to thank Sally Alexander and Anne Phillips for their helpful and perceptive comments on this article.

[1] Lewis Mumford, *The City in History*, Peregrine Books, London 1987, p120.
[2] John Milton, *The Complete Poems*, Dent Dutton, London 1980, pp454, 447.
[3] *The Guardian*, 'Review' section, 4 April 1990.
[4] Milan Kundera, *The Book of Laughter and Forgetting*, Penguin Books, Harmondsworth 1981, p76.
[5] Jean-Jacques Rousseau, *Emile*, Basic Books, New York 1979.
[6] Jean-Jacques Rousseau, *Confessions*, Penguin Books, Harmondsworth 1953, p28.
[7] *Ibid.*, p27.
[8] St Augustine, *The City of God*, Penguin Books, Harmondsworth 1984, p595.
[9] Jean-Jacques Rousseau, *The Social Contract*, Everyman (Dent), London 1973, p12.
[10] William Shakespeare, *Richard II*, The Complete Pelican Shakespeare, *The Histories and Non-Dramatic Poetry*, Penguin Books, Harmondsworth 1981, p216.
[11] Genesis 4, *The Bible*, Authorised Version.
[12] Elias Canetti, *Crowds and Power*, Penguin, Harmondsworth 1973, p25.
[13] See the report by 'Out on Tuesday', broadcast on Channel 4, 26 March 1990.
[14] Robert Colls and Philip Dodd (eds), *Englishness: Politics and Culture 1880-1920*, Croom Helm, London 1986, p5.
[15] Carole Pateman, *The Sexual Contract*, Polity Press, Cambridge 1988, p109-10.
[16] Simone Weil, 'Human Personality', in Sian Miles (ed.), *Simone Weil: an Anthology*, Virago Press, London 1986, p81.

Citizenship in the Age of AIDS

Simon Watney

One of the major characteristics of Thatcherism has been the great confidence with which the government speaks and legislates in the name of 'traditional' moral values, in areas which all previous postwar administrations have regarded as highly sensitive and complex. Of these, the question of sexuality and 'the family' has been especially important: much of the government's popularity has resided in its successful presentation of 'the family' as uniquely threatened and vulnerable, and therefore in need of stringent defensive measures, mainly from lesbians and gay men who have consistently been presented as one of the gravest threats to this fantasy of uniform 'family life'. In Mrs Thatcher's personal rhetoric, 'family' and 'nation' have long been presented as mutually interchangeable terms in such a way that imagined challenges to the former can also be presented as deeply dangerous for the latter. Again it comes as no surprise to learn that the Prime Minister was the driving force behind Clause 28 of the 1988 Local Government Bill which sought to prevent 'the promotion of homosexuality' by local authorities. The widespread acceptance of legislation against such imaginary offences, not least by the Labour front bench, is indicative of the sophistication of Thatcherism's ideological strategies, drawing on a real if regrettable legacy of anti-gay prejudice in British legal and popular culture. From the field of sex education to domestic video use, Thatcherism has sought to abolish former distinctions between the public and the private, in the name of the 'family values' that supposedly transcend all other estimations of individual and collective rights.

Yet AIDS confronts the government with a complex reality that cannot easily be disposed of in such over-simplified terms. We are not dealing with a single epidemic, but with a series of unfolding and overlapping epidemics within and between different population groups, determined by the modes of transmission of HIV in the decade or more before its existence was realised. The result has been a significant tension between conflicting imperatives. On the one hand ministers such as David Mellor congratulate organisations such as the Terrence Higgins Trust in the voluntary sector, whilst on the other, hard-line back-benchers continue to make political capital out of the crudest forms of prejudice, aided and abetted by the ever-dependable services of large sections of the British press. One consequence of this tension has been a bizarre compromise between the government's official moral ideology and the need for effective health education, which seriously suggests that recommending monogamy or celibacy is the best 'solution' to the issue of HIV infection. It is as if the actual complexity and diversity of human sexuality is as much of a problem for the government as the epidemic.

Direct censorship of health education projects produced by the government's own Health Education Authority provides shocking evidence of Thatcherism's unwavering reliance on moral homilies, which are policed at entirely unaccountable levels of executive government. An overriding commitment to a politically expedient vision of 'family values' is being sustained indefinitely, at the direct expense of effective health education strategies. This can only serve to guarantee the increased transmission of HIV, especially among heterosexuals who have been comfortably cocooned in the potentially deadly delusion that they are not really at risk since the beginning of the epidemic. Given the average of ten years between HIV infection and diagnosable symptoms of AIDS, the government's direct legacy of preventable AIDS cases will not be fully apparent until the late 1990s.

The opposition parties have failed to challenge the validity of the picture of British social life depicted by Thatcherite fundamentalism, or to question the government's long-term failure to acknowledge the actual complexity of the population that it claims to represent. Even political parties in opposition to Thatcherism seem uniformly unable to grasp the political dimensions of the HIV epidemic. The left has only

165

been able to register AIDS against the criteria of pre-existing policies and priorities. In practice, this has guaranteed an almost total silence on the entire subject. It would not be correct to conclude that the Labour NEC has simply buckled under the pressure of external anti-gay prejudice, real as this is. On the contrary, it has been fully prepared to exploit that prejudice to its own imagined electoral advantage. AIDS may be privately described as a 'disaster' or even a 'tragedy', but it is *never* publicly identified as an epidemic which in almost every respect has been, and continues to be *allowed to happen*.[1]

Since the early years of the epidemic, lesbians and gay men have been at the forefront of attempts to produce effective health education materials, for all sections of the population. Unfortunately this work has been hampered both by lack of funds, and archaic indecency and obscenity legislation. The Thatcherite model of business sponsorship for private charities has proved a disastrous failure, even for the government's own National AIDS Trust (NAT) which has failed to raise funds from the City or other commercial sources. We now face a situation in which the consequences of a decade of inadequate medical reporting in the British press has led to widespread ignorance of boredom with the whole subject of AIDS, reinforced by the government's attempts to perpetrate its values on the epidemic through its own 'official' advertising campaigns, which are based on a heady brew of sexual puritanism and scare-mongering.

This is exemplified by the typically individualistic approach of the work of the Health Education Authority (HEA), whose adverts share a common by-line 'AIDS: You're as safe as you want to be'. The situation is further complicated by the fact that the HEA itself has long been under attack from the radical Right, which wishes to present AIDS as a form of direct retribution against those who wantonly fail to live lives of exclusively monogamous heterosexuality. The prevalence of this retributive view is most tragically apparent in the widespread acceptance of the belief that the success of Safer Sex campaigns amongst gay men may safely be disregarded by the rest of the population because of our 'exceptional' status. The exceptionalist argument holds that gay men constitute 'a community' which adopted Safer Sex only when we saw our friends dying around us. This is untrue and dangerously misleading, since until very recently indeed it was statistically most unlikely that most gay men had any direct experience of either HIV infection or AIDS in their immediate friendship circles. Yet Safer Sex was indeed taken up by most gay men in Britain in the mid-1980s, as official epidemiology makes perfectly plain. It is only possible to understand this refusal to learn from the demonstrably proven effectiveness of Safer Sex education amongst gay men in terms of a larger and prior inability to regard lesbians and gay men as fundamentally ordinary and intrinsically unremarkable members of British society. For that reason anti-gay prejudice continues to make heterosexuals increasingly vulnerable to HIV.

At the same time we should notice the extreme levels of prejudice and ignorance concerning the position of the thousands of gay men living with HIV or AIDS in Britain, in order to understand the full significance of the 'moral standards' that have dominated British public life in the 1980s. If there has been a dramatic resurgence of gay political activity in this period, it is hardly surprising since it has become so painfully clear that our very existence is widely regarded as regrettable. It is important to consider the full significance of the government's continuing failure to support community-based health education among the social groups most severely affected by HIV disease since 1981. We read and hear about how well 'the gay community' has done in cutting back the rate of new cases of infection, yet in reality the social relations of gay men in Britain are fragile, and the absence of a powerful model of civil rights politics has tended to undermine the emergence of a confident gay culture in Britain.

In these circumstances, community development is much the most important strategy in HIV/AIDS education, since it is based on the development and reinforcement of the sense of individual and collective worth and responsibility. HIV education among gay men has emphasised the importance of Safer Sex for all men having sex with men, regardless of their known or perceived antibody status, as opposed to official messages which continue to demonise people living with HIV.[2] A special irony of the current situation is that Section 28 has brought gay men and lesbians together as never before, in opposition to frankly anti-gay legislation, and this in itself has stimulated a strengthening of gay community values. Yet through all this, I am not aware of a single statement either from the Prime Minister or the Leader of her Majesty's Opposition that draws attention to the tragedy of an epidemic that has already affected tens of thousands throughout the UK. This resounding silence demonstrates with frightening clarity the full extent of the divorce between British parliamentary politics, and the lives of the actual subjects of Britain.

This grim separation of political priorities from the field of everyday life is still more apparent at the level of biomedical research. In the United States there are currently over 200 ongoing clinical trials of possible new treatment drugs against HIV, and the wide range of opportunistic conditions that collectively make up the Acquired Immune Deficiency Syndrome. In Britain there are only two clinical trials, which largely duplicate American research. The Medical Research Council (MRC) has established a directed programme of research, which its Director has described as having 'the aim of developing vaccines for the prevention, and drugs for the treatment, of HIV infection and AIDS'.[3] Yet if one turns to the back of the MRC's guide to its *AIDS Directed Programme*, one finds committees supervising vaccine trials and the ethical aspects of vaccine research, but there is no committee supervising treatment research or the medical ethics of treatment-related clinical trials, for the simple reason that treatment research is *not* taking place. The entire bulk of more than £40 million at the MRC's disposal for HIV/AIDS research has been dedicated to the search for a vaccine for the *un*infected: people living with HIV disease have been written off in their entirety. Whilst there are excellent reasons for British scientists to wish to build on previous expertise in the field of vaccine research, it is chilling that this has been posed as an alternative to treatment research. In this context we might consider the statement by one leading MRC microbiologist that treatment research raises 'a moral dilemma', since it would 'run the risk of prolonging the lives of people who would be infectious in the community'.[4] It should be perfectly clear that the lives of people living with HIV disease, and their immediate communities are held very cheap both by official HIV education and the top levels of the MRC.

In the United States there have been more than 100,000 diagnosed cases of AIDS since 1981, of whom more than 60,000 are already dead. The Centers for Disease Control (CDC) in Atlanta, Georgia estimate that there are at least 1.5 million people infected by HIV in the USA.

Moreover, both HIV and AIDS statistics faithfully duplicate pre-existing patterns of health-care provision, economic inequalities and prejudice. For example, only 9 per cent of children with AIDS in New York are white. It was not until Thanksgiving, 1987 that the then President Reagan found himself able to utter the word 'AIDS', at a time when 25,644 people had *already* died. He announced that he had asked

the Department of Health and Human Services to determine as soon as possible the extent to which the AIDS virus has penetrated our society.[5]

Earlier in the year a group of activists had formed the 'AIDS Coalition To Unleash Power' (ACT UP) in New York, to draw attention to the scandalous government failure to respond to the needs of the epidemic, and to put pressure on all the leading institutions managing the course of the epidemic – from the Food and Drug Administration, which directs biomedical research, to the private sector multinational pharmaceutical industry, and the mass media. ACT UP has become one of the most remarkable and successful political forces in modern America, drawing on a long tradition of carefully organised civil disobedience, to which it adds the skills and techniques of modern advertising and video technology.[6] It has also drawn together the various constituencies of race, class and sexuality affected by the epidemic, into the new social identity of the committed AIDS activist. ACT UP was able to draw on an extraordinary flourishing of networks of medical and welfare-related information that had emerged in the mid-1980s, providing gay men in particular with details concerning all aspects of the epidemic that they were systematically denied from other sources. Most remarkable of these has been the continuing literature concerning biomedical research and the ethics of clinical trials, in relation both to private medicine and the state. From very early on it was recognised in the USA that AIDS is through and through a *political* issue, and that no major decisions are made about any aspect of the epidemic that are not informed by economic and ideological priorities, rather than the health and welfare of people with HIV.

Given the close links between British and American gay culture, it is surprising that such understandings have been far less developed in the UK, or elsewhere in Europe. This confirms the point that throughout the EC, people with HIV in countries with socialised medicine tend to have a far less critical attitude to their doctors, and have much greater faith that the overall goals of medical research will not conflict with their own personal interests. In a European context, the demands of ACT UP that people with HIV should be consulted at every stage in the design of protocols for clinical trials implies a much more active model of involvement in the power of relations of medicine, and a more immediately political perception of those same relations. The insistence that clinical trials of new drugs should be regarded as forms of treatment is a radical threat to the traditional divisions between 'pure' researchers and primary care physicians. This has been most marked in the emergence of Community Research Initiatives (CRI), which have mushroomed in the United States in recent years, though not without considerable resistance from the medical establishment. The CRI movement insists that biomedical research should take place in the community, with general practitioners providing counselling, support and constant monitoring for those who have volunteered to take part in such experimental trials. This has had the great advantage of permitting large numbers of fast, clinical trials in an emergency situation, and has gone some way to challenge the standard procedural use of placebos which, it is objected, literally *require* that many people will sicken and die in the course of 'successful' experiments. This new focus on medical ethics on the part of the communities affected by AIDS marks a profound break in the history of modern pathological medicine, and it is significant that it has been the gay community which *forced* such major innovations.

Unfortunately the situation in Britain is unlikely to produce such dramatic and far-reaching changes in the practice of medicine, if only because gay men here have largely lacked the support of strong advocacy organisations like the American Civil Liberties Union (ACLU) and others, which have played an important role at all levels of the US epidemic, from fighting direct discrimination through the courts, to championing patients' rights in relation to biomedical research. Furthermore, the British left which might have been expected to take an active interest in the epidemic has on the contrary largely ignored it. Sadly, we suffer from the long legacy of a tradition of ultra-leftism that seems trapped in its own estimations of radicalism that rarely exceed the field of class-related politics, which is hopelessly inadequate to the complexities of power in the modern world. This is not of course to deny the centrality of class in British society, but to point out the impossibility of trying to understand or intervene in the political struggles around AIDS in class terms alone. Moreover, the left generally chooses to interpret its refusal or inability to work with other groups and lobbies as evidence of its own purity and correctness, rather than of the bankruptcy of its own self-styled radicalism. A similar puritanical separatism also afflicts many sections of the British women's movement, which has still hardly begun to grasp the wider political significance of AIDS, in relation to longstanding concerns about the management of sexuality and sexual reproduction. At a further extreme, 'revolutionary' feminists have long seen AIDS in terms that differ little from those of *The Sun* or *The News of the World*: as a condition that only affects 'the enemy', that is men, and women who collude with them.

The history of the British AIDS epidemic demonstrates with disturbing clarity that lesbians and gay men are still far from widely recognised as a legitimate social consituency within British society, or that we continue to face a health crisis unparalleled in modern times. When Health Minister David Mellor observed that perhaps 25 per cent of gay men in London may already be infected, his only comment was that 'people must not breathe a sigh of relief and think it will soon blow over'.[7] Such statements betray a shocking indifference to the actual scale of suffering caused by HIV – shocking, but hardly surprising given the generally abysmal record of British journalism outside the gay press since the very beginning of the epidemic. The mass media continue to pump out prejudice and misinformation that either confuses and alarms readers, or simply denies any possibilty of risk to 'decent' people. We may fairly detect two consistent characteristics of such attitudes. On the one hand, the presentation of AIDS as a 'gay plague' continues to articulate deep anxieties about homosexuality. The epidemic thus becomes the viral projection of an unconscious desire to kill gay men, and these unconscious attitudes should never be discounted or underestimated.[8] On the other hand, the 'homosexualising' of AIDS, and the denial of HIV transmission among heterosexuals offers a semi-magical delusion of intrinsic safety which is as potentially threatening to heterosexuals, as their homophobia is to gay men.[9]

In all this, it should be apparent that fundamental questions about the meaning of democracy in modern Britain are at stake. We should not have to struggle against the odds to establish effective health education which rejects scare-mongering, victim-blaming, and irrational sexual puritanism. Effective health education should be a basic and indisputable right, and never more so than during an epidemic. At the same time, standards of health-care provision and medical research should never be dependent upon the individual's sexuality, class, race or ethnicity. The political management of the British AIDS epidemic demonstrates repeatedly and at all levels that there are many higher priorities than either preventive medicine or the saving of lives. It is therefore critically important that we should be able to identify the leading institutions responsible for deciding and directing social policies in relation to HIV disease, from individual departments of government, to the mass media, regional and district health authorities, the Health Education Authority, the General Medical Council and so on, in order to lobby them effectively. If such institutions fail to respond, civil disobedience may well prove necessary, and ACT UP (London), which was formed early in 1989, has already organised a number of well-targeted demonstrations in relation to the cut-backs in social security and other issues.

Unfortunately, ACT UP faces formidable problems in Britain. Firstly, there are the difficulties of 'band-waggoning' and attempts to hijack the emergent AIDS activist movement by far-left 'interventionists'. Secondly, there is no sustained tradition of civil disobedience politics in Britain, and British police definitely do not recognise lesbians and gay men as a legitimate social constituency, unlike many other European countries. Similarly there is no local tradition of training in non-violent civil disobedience, or of the organisation of 'affinity groups' which has been so successful in ACT UP (New York) – establishing small, close networks of people who have prepared before a given action to work as a team. Thirdly, there is little sense in Britain of the possible role of a cultural politics concerned with images and symbols, such as exists in the USA, where the famous 'Silence = Death' poster from 1986 opened the way for a whole flood of incisive and stylish political posters, T-shirts, badges, which provide AIDS activists with a strong cultural identity, and which in turn have raised vital issues of information in the public spaces of New York. Lastly, the absence of the sense of constitutional rights that so shapes American oppositional politics makes demonstrators very vulnerable to arbitrary arrest and violence, and means that there is not a large and 'ready-made' culture of direct political interventionism on which to draw. This was reflected in the early decision by the 'Frontliners' organisation, which works on behalf of people with AIDS, to dissociate totally itself from ACT UP (London), on the bizarre grounds that:

> Certain extreme elements ... have called for demonstrations which would result in people with AIDS/ARC and people with disabilities being arrested.[10]

Clearly the author of that comment could not imagine a situation in which people with AIDS might decide for themselves whether or not they wanted to take part in organised civil disobedience. Nor do British AIDS service organisations appreciate the full extent to which the influence of ACT UP (New York) and other AIDS activist groups such as AIDS Action Now (Toronto) is *already* being felt in UK. For example, the Bristol-Myers corporation has announced plans to make the anti-HIV drug DDI available on the grounds of 'compassionate usage' largely as a result of North American activist pressure. Bristol-Myers have also been careful to include members of AIDS service organisations and the gay press at planning and information meetings, which is unheard of in the field of British pharmaceutical industry behaviour.

It is clear then that AIDS can generate political identities which did not precede the epidemic, and draw together groups such as lesbians and gay men, together with black people and the disabled in ways that could not have been anticipated before the AIDS crisis. Such identities and alliances are not natural or inevitable, but have to be forged in collective experience and in shared aims and objectives. For those like myself, who have had direct long-term experience of the American HIV epidemic, personal loss has been a major motivating factor in our personal involvement. But this is clearly not the case for most lesbians and gay men in the UK, who are still statistically unlikely to have knowingly had much direct experiences of HIV disease, especially outside London. At the same time it is abundantly clear from the consistently low rates of new cases of HIV infection among gay men since 1984 that it has *not* been direct experience of AIDS that has determined the success of the Safer Sex revolution in our lives, or the extraordinary growth of non-governmental AIDS service organisations all round the country. On the contrary, it has been the strength of gay culture – from the gay press to theatre and independent film, but most of all in our everyday lives and friendships.

Yet it is precisely gay culture that the present government has consistently targetted, and that the opposition seems unwilling or unable to defend. We constantly hear that straight society has nothing to learn from us, that we are an 'exceptional' case, that we only took up Safer Sex when we literally saw our friends and lovers dying in front of our very eyes. Such an interpretation is not only ignorant and insulting, it is also profoundly tragic, for it strongly suggests that anti-gay prejudice will continue to prevent many heterosexuals from even trying to learn from our collective cultural experience. This is why the question of entitlement to effective community-based health education and health-care provision, especially in the form of community medicine, is so apparent to so many lesbians and gay men, especially since we are rarely, if ever, identified as a community of need by the National Health Service and other state institutions, regardless of the specific needs relating to AIDS.

There is thus all the more reason that the debate about citizenship should be firmly grounded in the concrete circumstances of individual and collective social life, and in concrete questions of entitlement in contemporary Britain. The experience of lesbians and gay men in relations to AIDS in the 1980s provides just such an example. A written parliamentary answer in January 1989 revealed that no less than 35 gay men aged 16 to 21 were criminalised by the courts in Britain for consensual sexual relations above the age of consent that obtains for heterosexuals. I am not aware of a single comment on this disgraceful situation outside the gay press, which might as well be written, printed and distributed on Mars as far as the vast majority of professional commentators and politicians are concerned. Nor is the gay press's unparalleled long-term record in AIDS journalism ever acknowledged in other publications. The decision of the 1989 Labour conference to throw out the National Executive Committee's rejection of calls for a single age of consent for everyone in Britain, including gay men, strongly suggests that political debates founded upon the ethical principle of entitlements can prevail over the stubbornly entrenched prejudice and tactical electoral calculations that result in the defence of fundamentally unjust and undemocratic legal double-standards.[11]

In the short term it is increasingly important for lesbians and gay men to develop effective lobbying organisations at Westminster and Brussels. It is also vital that we should continue to build on the new solidarity that we have forged in resistance to Clause 28, throughout the UK. Yet our resources are very limited, and the many tasks of HIV/AIDS work, from distracting fund-raising to direct service provision, are often all but overwhelming (even though these are still the early years of the British epidemic). The experience of AIDS has raised fundamental questions for lesbians and gay men alike concerning the workings of British politics: it is far from clear that we can ever expect British parliamentarianism to recognise our demands for civil rights across a wide range of institutions from the age of consent laws, to health care and education at all levels, and to party politics themselves. At a time when any mention of advocacy for gay people is dismissed as an electoral 'liability', it is hard not to conclude that we ourselves are regarded in a similar light. For it is precisely the fossilised forms and unquestioned values of parliamentary procedure and tradition that have guaranteed many aspects of otherwise wholly avoidable suffering and stress for people with HIV, their families and communities. In housing, social security provision, life insurance, health promotion, treatment research and direct health-care provision, it is painfully apparent that we are not regarded as political subjects with the same rights as other holders of British passports, even in the circumstances of a health crisis that has affected us far more seriously than any other section of the overall population.

The long domination of the United Kingdom by England and effectively Westminster has meant that we have never established the range of progressive, federalised national or state identities that have proved so important as the prerequisite for gay political and cultural recognition in countries such as Canada, Australia, the USA, or in the Scandinavian League. Instead we are stuck with relatively conservative nationalist movements and parties that are generally insensitive to feminism and sexual politics. In these circumstances we cannot rely on the assumption that lesbians and gay men will be able to establish autonomous 'gay rights' in advance of other major *constitutional* reforms that are essential for any enlargement of British working democracy and democratic pluralism. At a time when pluralism is itself such a distinctly unfashionable concept, on the grounds of its 'moral relativism', it is worth considering Josef Brodsky's timely reminder that 'moral absolutism is not so hot either'.[12] This suggests a shift away from a sexual politics founded on the theory of discrete 'minorities', each with an attached bundle of specific rights, towards a far more adventurous vision of democratic politics – the wider context of full citizenship, guaranteed by a bill of rights. This involves a direct refusal of the status of subjecthood and the subjectivities it produces, as well as the entire political culture of parliamentary hierarchy and deference that leaves us all subject to the whim of any government that has managed to achieve the absolute power of a parliamentary majority.

Substantial numbers of British lesbians and gay men who have hitherto lacked much sense of a collective identity are now waking up to the direct realities of discrimination and culturally sanctioned prejudice. The deeply engrained sexual conservatism of the labour movement in Britain has effectively abandoned radical sexual politics to the far left and the women's movement, neither of which have any direct relation to the lives of most gay men. This in effect means that many lesbians and gay men tend to associate the very notion of 'rights' with larger political programmes with which they have little sympathy. At the same time, an articulate but numerically tiny core of professional lobbyists continues a politics in and around the palace of Westminster that has hardly changed since the long years of lobbying that preceded and followed the publication of the Wolfenden Report on homosexual law reform in 1957 – in many cases they are the same people. But the assimilationist approach offers few if any real opportunities for the establishment of a broadly-based and effective gay politics in the foreseeable future, for the obvious reason that such an approach is so deeply committed to the parliamentary status quo.

The recently formed lobbying organisation for lesbian and gay rights, the Stonewall Group, has shown considerable imagination in the drafting of a possible Homosexual Equality Bill. This proposes specific legislation to protect lesbians and gay men against discrimination based on sexual orientation, together with the legal recognition of 'domestic partnerships' between same-sex couples, the lowering of the age of consent for gay men to 16, and the criminalisation of incitements to violence on the grounds of sexual orientation. Such measures would bring Britain in line with existing laws in many other European countries, and in relation to 'hate crimes', with the USA. Furthermore, they would exemplify the general principle that sexual rights should be above parliamentary party politics. They would also go some way towards the establishment of a *culture of citizenship* among lesbians and gay men, as a constant reminder of constitutional rights, founded upon ethical principles.

We urgently need to establish a far more ethically grounded politics of gender and sexuality, in order to realise what Michel Foucault described in one of his final interviews as 'practices of freedom': 'For what', he asked 'is morality, if not the practice of liberty, the deliberate practice of liberty?'[13] Rather than assuming a natural, inevitable unity among gay men, or between gay men and lesbians, such an approach grounds our experience, in all its diversity and complexity, within a wider *ethical* context. We need to ensure, constitutionally, that no other social constituencies will ever have to endure what gay men have been through in increasing numbers throughout the course of the 1980s, as if *our* health and *our* lives are not as irreducibly valuable as those of other sections of society. The concept and practice of citizenship is one powerful means to this end precisely because citizenship not only involves a discourse of rights, but also of *responsibilities*. Without such a double emphasis, pluralism quickly descends into a free-for-all competition between rival and conflicting definitions of rights, and difference becomes an identity to be defended by a siege mentality that obscures shared patterns of oppression. AIDS has demonstrated with frightening clarity that lesbians and gay men are not just under-represented within the existing framework of British politics, but are positively excluded from the most basic processes and practices of democracy. This sordid reality has been tacitly or 'tactically' accepted for far too long.

Subjecthood remains the dominant British political identity, founded in the constitutional settlement of 1688. As such, it has protected British politics from what has long been regarded by Westminster as the threat of federalism. It is the ideological cement that holds together the fragile unity of the United Kingdom, but is increasingly vulnerable to the critiques both of competing nationalisms, and the more general cultural pressures that lie behind the emergence of the 'new social movements' of feminism, black politics, environmentalism and gay liberation. Over time, subjecthood has also served to defend the claims and privileges of parliamentarianism, providing a transcendent national political identity, united in allegiance to the Crown-in-parliament, over and above the divisions of class and all other structures of social difference. Furthermore, it encourages the belief that any criticism of either parliamentarianism or the monarchy itself are somehow 'unpatriotic' and anti-democratic. Subjecthood is thus intimately connected to the wider patterns of cultural and class-based deference that are so characteristic of British politics and civil society, by comparison with other European nations.

A whole bundle of major constitutional reforms have recently come under discussion in the wake of the publication of Charter 88. These include electoral reform, freedom of information legislation, the formal incorporation into British law of the European Convention for the Protection of Human Rights and Fundamental Freedoms, a bill of rights, the reform of the judiciary and so on. What is now needed is an energetic *ideological* initiative, to recruit support for these concrete issues of entitlements and responsibilities as they arise for different social constituencies. In its current formulation, the movement for constitutional change in Britain retains the primacy of political and legal institutions which would be empowered to endow or deny rights with the same impunity as the parliamentary traditions that Charter 88 seems unwilling to challenge adequately. This explains the importance of emphasising the *ethical* dimensions of political and legal reform programmes, and of holding on to questions of power in relation to identity, which is especially important if we accept that identity is not a simple, unitary, and uniformly consistent entity, given from birth. The political culture of subjecthood involves a clear ranking of priorities within our individual and collective identities, a *subjection* to political, juridical and regal authority in our sense of who we are. Citizenship, however, at least offers the potential for very different processes of identification with one another, founded upon ethical considerations that should always be understood to have precedence and priority over the domain of the legal and the political.

Citizenship emerges as one strategy in what Foucault described as the 'political technology of individuals',[14] who may be brought to recognise and identify themselves through many different aspects and arenas of the social formation, whether through gender, nationalism, religion, health issues, regionalism, race and so on. In one of his later lectures Foucault described his aim to

> show people that a lot of things that are a part of their landscape – that people think are universal – are the result of some very precise historical changes. All my analyses are against the idea of universal necessities in human existence. They show the arbitrariness of institutions and show which space of freedom we can still enjoy and how many changes can still be made.[15]

This is especially obvious in his work concerning the conditions of emergence of the modern categories and identities of sexuality. Much of Foucault's later work was taken up with questions of how such historical understanding might be practically applied, and their ethical implications for the constitution of the sense of self. From this perspective, citizenship also offers a concrete alternative to the type of humanism

> that presents a certain form of ethics as a universal model for any kind of freedom. I think there are more secrets, more possible freedoms, and more inventions in our future than we can imagine in humanism as it is dogmatically represented in every side of the political rainbow.[16]

This is in itself hardly surprising, since humanism has a prior interest in arguing that identity precedes social and political structures, which are seen to work in a purely external way upon a pre-formed rational 'human' subject, which is incompatible with Foucault's contention that:

> In effect, we live in a legal, social, and institutional world where the only relations possible are extremely few, extremely simplified, and extremely poor ... Society and the institutions that frame it have limited the possibility of relationships because a rich relational world would be very complex to manage. We should fight against this shrinking of the relational fabric.[17]

The concept of citizenship naturally develops from his interest in the notion of relational rights that might supplant both the given power relations of sexuality and gender relations, and the excessive claims made by the modern state over our affectional lives. His argument lends great weight to our contemporary need to find ways to acknowledge personal relations beyond the current cultural validation of marriage and the family, as if these exhausted the possibilities of legitimate social and sexual choice.

One great weakness in the discourse of civil rights in Britain has been its long association with minorities, as if rights were not fundamental for the entire population. Entitlements have similarly been widely regarded primarily as *exemptions*, such as council housing, free prescriptions, or free school meals, thus limiting the concept to the weak and the disadvantaged. An ethically grounded practice of citizenship has the great initial advantage of being posed to, and on behalf of, the entire population – no longer pictured in crude parliamentary terms as a majority surrounded on all sides by distinct and possibly threatening minorities, but rather as a complex unity of many overlapping and interrelated groups and identities. Citizenship invites such a politics that proceeds from the recognition that our identities are multiply formed and positioned, rather than fixed rigidly in mechanical dualistic polarities.

Ten long years of Thatcherism have brought home to many the full significance of Foucault's stark observation that:

> the search for a form of morality that would be acceptable for everyone – in the sense that everyone would have to submit to it – strikes me as catastrophic.[18]

It is precisely from our close understanding of the catastrophe to which such a search has led us that the recognition of the need for a common goal of ethical citizenship emerges, and with it the conditions for the emergence of new political identities and forms of social solidarity. In this respect, ethical citizenship anticipates Hannah Arendt's political vision of *the republic*, dedicated to the overriding principle of *freedom*, that is quite distinct from familiar notions of popular sovereignty. For Arendt, freedom is incompatible with the democratic politics of majority rule, which ensure that minorities are inevitably oppressed. In her political vision, modern western democracies are at best a 'very imperfect realisation' of the ideal of the free commonwealth, embodied readily in the corresponding concept of *citizenship*.[19] The political history of the AIDS epidemic strongly supports Arendt's explanation of the origins of totalitarianism, which insists that totalising state power starts

> with *the story of the pariah*, and therefore with the 'exception', with the 'politically anomolous' which is then used to explain the rest of society, rather than the other way round.[20]

The experience of countries such as France, West Germany and the United States demonstrates that the status of legal citizenship does not of itself automatically curb excessive state power or the oppression of minorities. But such countries do enjoy the benefits of the *culture of citizenship* that are almost entirely absent from the UK, where the concept of national sovereignty so frequently steamrollers any respect for cultural diversity within the nation. In this light, citizenship emerges not simply as a political goal, but both as an ethical necessity, in defence of old liberties and as a means for the active encouragement of new practices of freedom, on which the very possibility of a future for Britain as a fully European democracy currently depend.

Notes

This is a revised version of a piece which appeared in Jonathan Rutherford (ed), *Identity: Community, Culture, Difference*, Lawrence & Wishart, London 1990.

[1] Douglas Crimp, 'Mourning and Militancy', *October*, MIT Press, Cambridge, Mass. 1990.
[2] See Simon Watney, 'Introduction', in Erica Carter and Simon Watney (eds), *Taking Liberties: AIDS and Cultural Politics*, Serpent's Tail, London 1989.
[3] Medical Research Council, *AIDS Directed Programme: Programme Plan and Research Opportunities*, London, July 1988.
[4] See Simon Watney, 'Tasks in AIDS Research', *Gay Times*, May 1989.
[5] Quoted in Douglas Crimp, 'AIDS: Cultural Analysis/Cultural Activism' in Douglas Crimp (ed), *AIDS: Cultural Analysis/Cultural Activism*, MIT Press, Cambridge Mass. 1988, p11.
[6] See Simon Watney, 'Representing AIDS' in Tessa Boffin and Sunil Gupta (eds), *Ecstatic Antibodies*, Arts Council/Rivers Oram Press, London 1990.
[7] *Daily Mirror*, 4 October 1988.

[8] See Simon Watney, 'The Possibilities of Permutation: Pleasure, Proliferation and the Politics of Gay Identity in the Age of AIDS' in James Miller (ed), *AIDS: Crisis and Criticism*, University of Toronto Press, Toronto 1990.

[9] See Simon Watney, 'Safer Sex as Community Practice' in Peter Aggleton *et al* (eds), *AIDS: Individual, Cultural and Policy Dimensions*, Falmer Press, Lewes 1990.

[10] 'Frontliners disassociation from ACT UP', *Frontiers*, no 4, 1 June 1989.

[11] John Jackson, 'Age of Consent', *The Guardian*, 4 October 1989.

[12] Josef Brodsky, 'Isaiah Berlin at Eighty', *The New York Review of Books*, 17 August 1989.

[13] Michel Foucault, 'The Ethic of Care for the Self as a Practice of Freedom' in James Bernauer and David Rasmussen (eds), *The Final Foucault*, MIT Press, Cambridge Mass. 1988, p4.

[14] Michel Foucault, 'Truth, Power, Self: An Interview' in Martin L. Luther *et al* (eds), *Technologies of the Self: A Seminar with Michel Foucault*, Tavistock, London 1988.

[15] *Ibid.*, p11.

[16] *Ibid.*, p15.

[17] Michel Foucault, 'The Social Triumph of the Sexual Will', *Christopher Street*, Issue 64, vol 6, no 4, New York 1982, p38.

[18] Michel Foucault, 'The Return of Morality' in Sylvère Lotringer (ed), *Foucault Live*, Semiotext(e), New York 1989, p330.

[19] Agnes Heller and Ferenc Feher, *The Postmodern Political Condition*, Polity Press, London 1989, p97.

[20] *Ibid.*, p89.

British Citizenship and Cultural Difference

Bhikhu Parekh

It has become commonplace to refer to modern Britain by such allegedly synonymous terms as a multi-racial, multi-ethnic or multi-cultural society. It might be argued that it does not matter what words we use. I'm afraid it does, for words are never mere words. They embody concepts, are charged with historical memories and associations, and shape our understanding of, and approach to, the world. Linguistic sloppiness is both a product and a cause of confused thinking and leads to confused and sometimes dangerous practice.[1]

Of the three currently fashionable terms, the term multi-racial is the least satisfactory. The term race is a product of the deeply misguided anthropology of the eighteenth and nineteenth centuries. As we know from past experience and on the basis of research evidence, mankind cannot be neatly divided into races. And even if that had once been possible, it is no longer so in a world which has seen so much cultural and biological intermingling between the 'races'. We well know, too, that race does not determine the psychological and moral constitution of an individual or a society. It has, therefore, neither a taxonomic nor an explanatory value. Furthermore, the term race creates the illusion that the undoubted differences between different communities and forms of life are grounded in nature, deeper than they really are, and cannot be overcome without doing violence to the integrity of the relevant communities.

The term multi-cultural society is better, but it does not quite capture

183

the social specificity of contemporary Britain. The term culture is used today in the loose sense of covering almost everything that is not natural, and includes beliefs, practices and institutions that owe their origins to human choices. Since human beings rarely make identical choices and lead identical lives, almost every society today is in that wide sense multi-cultural. More importantly the term multi-cultural does not adequately express, and even seems to obscure, the kinds of differences that obtain between different communities in modern Britain. The cultural differences between the Afro-Caribbeans and whites are not like those between, say, middle- and working-class whites or between heterosexuals and gays. The Afro-Caribbean culture has a distinct bearer, namely, the Afro-Caribbean people, and a distinct social basis and geographical origin. It is a product of their unique history and experiences of oppression and struggle; and it is embodied in their literature, myths, songs, rituals, signs and gestures. In other words the Afro-Caribbean culture is not the culture of a collection of men who, independent of each other , happen to have made common choices, but the culture of a distinct and cohesive community. And it is not a matter of choice but one into which its adherents are born. That is, it is a community culture, an ethnic culture. What is true of the Afro-Caribbeans is also true of the Asians and the Jews and the Gypsies.

It would therefore seem more correct to describe contemporary Britain as a society consisting of ethnic communities, each with its distinct culture or ways of thought and life. They are not just cultural groups but communities, and they are not ordinary communities but *ethnic* communities. They are not communities in the same sense in which, say, miners are a community. The miners are brought together by a common occupation around which they have woven a fascinating pattern of social organisation. By contrast, the Asian and Afro-Caribbean communities are ethnic in nature, that is, physically distinguishable, bonded by social ties arising out of shared customs, language and practice of inter-marriage, and having their distinct history, collective memories, geographical origins, views on life and modes of social organisation. The House of Lords in *Mandla v Dowell Lee* in 1983 listed seven characteristics, two of them 'essential' and the rest desirable, which a group must meet before it could be classified as ethnic. Although their 'definition' is not perfect, it is adequate for practical purposes, and that is all that one can hope for in social and political concepts. The ethnic communities that migrated to Britain were already communities before their migration. Their pattern of migration and the fact that they tended to be drawn from the same region, island, caste or religion and shared significant post-migration experiences intensified their sense of community.

It is a little misleading to call them ethnic *minorities*. The terms minority and majority are numerical concepts, and individualistic in their orientation and implications. Strictly speaking they apply to individuals, not to organised groups and communities. The term ethnic minority implies that it is a minority like the gays, bearded men or bachelors, subject to fluctuation and a contingent collection of otherwise unrelated individuals. It thus de-ethnicises or de-communalises ethnic communities, and implies that they are chance collections of isolated individuals. As we saw, this is not the case. We should therefore call them minority communities, or simply ethnic communities, but not ethnic minorities. In so far as contemporary Britain consists of such tenacious communities, it is a multi-communal or *plural* society.

Sometimes two objections are raised against such a description of Britain. First, it is argued that the ethnic communities constitute just over four per cent of the population, and that this no more makes Britain a multi-ethnic society than a similar percentage of gays and farmers makes it a homosexual or agricultural society. This is a strange argument. A society is multi-ethnic when it contains more than one community. The size of the communities involved is no more relevant than the size of an individual in deciding whether or not he is a man. The analogy with the homosexual is absurd because four per cent blacks do not make Britain a black society, only a society composed of different communities.

Second, it is argued that Britain has always been a multi-ethnic society and that there is nothing new about postwar immigration. This is only half-true. It is true that Britain has long consisted of such ethnic communities as the Scots, the Welsh, the Irish and the English. However, they differ from immigrant communities in at least two important respects: unlike the latter they are not defined or separated from each other by differences of colour, religion and the history of colonial occupation (as different from political subjugation); and they have distinct geographical bases, remain more or less where they have always been and, with the qualified exception of the Irish, are not immigrants. The presence of black and Asian communities therefore make Britain multi-ethnic in a rather special way. If we so prefer, we might call it a multi-cultural society, provided we bear in mind that the cultures involved have an ethnic basis and constitute the historical forms of life of specific communities. In this paper I shall use the term multi-cultural in this specific and limited sense.

Many commentators have attempted to draw unwarranted practical conclusions from its multi-cultural character. For example, the massive Swann Report pleads for multi-cultural education on the ground that *since* Britain is a multi-cultural society, it needs multi-cultural education. This is obviously a *non sequitur* and involves a naturalistic fallacy. We may accept the fact that Britain is a multi-cultural society, but go on to argue that it should not be one, that it destroys national unity and cohesion, and that the minority communities should thoroughly assimilate themselves into British society. In other words no normative conclusion can be drawn from the fact that Britain is a multi-cultural society. The British people have to *decide* how to respond to this fact, bearing in mind their own history, systems of values and aspirations as well as the likely reactions of the ethnic communities. They could rejoice in its multi-cultural nature, or reluctantly acquiesce in it, or quietly try to undermine it, or openly declare a war on it. Such decisions necessarily presuppose a vision, a broad conception, of the kind of society they would like Britain to be and the place of minority communities within it.

When the Afro-Caribbean, and later Asians, first began to arrive, Britain knew that it was recruiting people of different 'races' and 'colours' whose presence was likely to cause a measure of social tension. Since it desperately needed their labour, it had no choice but to admit them. Thanks to the domination of liberal historicism, it was convinced that such cultural differences as the blacks and browns brought with them would disappear, automatically and inexorably, under the impact of a 'superior' secular worldview, at least so far as their progeny was concerned. After all, Britain's colonial policy and history were based on the belief that their cultures were 'backward', ill-suited to the modern age and incapable of resisting its momentum. And if they did show tenacity in the new environment, it only had to resume its earlier 'civilising' policy with increased vigour. The immigrants were not going to create economic problems, because jobs were available in plenty, and in any case they were only going to take those in which the whites were uninterested. The only problems likely to arise related to such matters as housing and good neighbourly relations, and these were deemed to be easily surmountable.

This optimistic analysis proved incorrect. As the Asian immigrants came to be joined by their wives and families and later by their fellow-Asians, most of whom came from the same region, caste or religion, they formed communities with their own distinct lifestyles. Worries about the unity of their families and inter-generational continuity gave culture an added importance. In the late 1960s and early 1970s the self-confident East African Asians brought with them common memories of oppression and expulsion, well-developed and homogeneous communities, skills in building and sustaining communities in an alien environment, and new economic energies. Since family unity, caste network, religious and social cohesion and the ethic of mutual help were all necessary for Asian social stability, self-respect and, above all, economic success, maintenance of shared ethnic and cultural identity became an *economic* necessity. Their sense of community thus acquired an additional economic legitimation and support. The economically far more disadvantaged Afro-Caribbeans, exposed by their choice of occupation to great racial discrimination, and culturally less well cushioned against it, had to wage *political* struggles, and found in their shared ethnic and cultural identity the necessary basis of their *political* unity. For the bulk of Asians ethnicity and culture were directly related to the economy; for most Afro-Caribbeans they were politically mediated. Not surprisingly their attitudes to politics, ethnicity, and the economic and political role of culture varied greatly.

For their own different reasons the Asians and Afro-Caribbeans therefore began to stress and cherish their ethnicity and culture. Britain found itself confronted with an unusual and wholly unexpected situation. It now discovered that it had in its midst, not collections of

187

black and brown individuals, not just economically disadvantaged and racially discriminated groups whose problems would hopefully disappear with the eradication of racism, but self-conscious, assertive and fairly cohesive minority communities. Though they were so far mutually indifferent and even at times hostile, they were capable of forming an alliance and even a single political bloc. As so often in its history, Britain found that a good deal was happening behind its back which it had failed to notice in its now notorious feats of absent-mindedness. The discovery of ethnic communities and their potential political significance in the late 1960s made them a *political* issue. What was hitherto seen as a source of social and economic problems now became a political threat. Not surprisingly it changed the political landscape and gave rise to a new political vocabulary and new concerns. Enoch Powell, the Columbus who made his discovery, articulated it with characteristic precision. His diagnosis was correct, namely that Britain now had in its midst strong, proud, cohesive and potentially powerful communities, but his solution was utterly unrealistic and irresponsible.

Once Britain realised what had happened, and was happening, it knew that it needed to work out a coherent response. Thanks to Enoch Powell's highly influential formulation of the problem, the response was grounded in the following crucial assumptions more or less uncritically taken for granted. First, Britain was a cohesive and unified society, a 'nation', held together not only by allegiance to a common authority but also by common commitment to a shared body of values and a shared way of life. Second, the ethnic communities represented different and incompatible ways of life and could not be integrated into British society at all or without radically altering its character. Third, so long as they remained cohesive they were not only internally oppressive but remained 'alien islands' at its geographical and cultural heart, and posed a grave cultural and political danger. Fourth, if Britain was not willing to repatriate the new immigrants, it should at least as a matter of urgency break up the communities and set about 'Britishising' their decommunalised members. It could not remain cohesive without fully integrating them, and it could not integrate them without dismantling their internal bonds. That was indeed how, historically, it had itself become a 'nation' in the first instance. It had loosened or broken up traditional communities, and then reintegrated their atomised members within the modern state. The disintegration of the immigrant communities was the *sine qua non* of the integration of British society, and their extinction a necessary basis of its continuing survival.

Within this deeply flawed but widely and uncritically accepted theoretical framework, only two responses were possible to the minority communities, namely the assimilationist or nationalist and the integrationist or liberal. We shall examine each in turn.

The assimilationist approach consisted in ensuring that minority communities became British in all respects save religion, to which everyone had a right in a liberal society, and colour, about which no society could do much. Some did urge greater racial intermingling, but they were few in numbers and not sure how to achieve it. The assimilationist pressure was exerted in all areas of British life including education, health and social services, and took the form of insisting on uniformity of treatment, castigating any recognition of special needs or circumstances as privileging and even amounting to positive discrimination in favour of minority communities. In addition to the usual methods of moral blackmail and the organised pressure of public opinion exerted both locally and nationally, the assimilationist relied on two major instruments of cultural engineering. First, immigration policy, which was now used not just to reduce 'number' or primary immigration but as a tool of restructuring the minority communities. Highly restrictive and morally dubious immigration laws and administrative rules, applied in a discretionary manner by officers functioning within the framework of assumptions listed earlier, were used to frustrate movements of elderly parents and relatives and, above all, to prevent Asian boys and girls from choosing these spouses within the Indian subcontinent. It was feared that such 'imported' spouses reinforced the Asians' cultural identity and strengthened their ties with their countries of origin. Given the unfavourable sex ratio in some Asian communities, the latter began to show signs of strain and slow disintegration.

Education was the second major instrument of cultural engineering. The minority communities' languages, religions, cultures, history and so on were denied place on the curriculum; requests to celebrate or give symbolic recognition to their new year days or major festivals were contemptuously dismissed; the schools were urged to use their enormous power to anglicise them; and even such simple demands as the exemption of Muslim girls from mixed sports, wearing shorts or swimming, or provision of *halal, kosher* or non-beef meat were vigorously resisted. The Education Reform Act is a logical culmination of the assmilationist approach. The state now decides what subjects to teach in schools, how, and what books to require pupils to read in each subject. It has paid particular attention to the teaching of history, the most political and ideologically charged of all subjects, and seeks to ensure that all children from now onwards will share an identical and state-endorsed view of British history and national identity. The Government and its academic sympathisers have repeatedly complained that teachers are seduced by Marxist and other types of 'dangerous propaganda' and cannot be trusted to exercise their own judgment. It would seem that pupils are now to be protected against their benighted teachers, and the latter against the hidden enemies of Britain. A Government that places so much value on choice is evidently unwilling to trust the academic choices of its own grown up and professionally trained teachers. The Education Reform Act rests on a policy of cultural protection and political engineering, and represents an attempt by the state to cast British society into a homogeneous and nationalist mould.[2]

The liberal or integrationist response was quite different in nature. It welcomed cultural differences and diversity and acknowledged that they enriched British society. It recognised that equality did not mean uniformity, and that it allowed differential treatment based on recognition of the special needs and circumstances of ethnic communities. It was clearly formulated by Roy Jenkins in 1975:

> Integration is perhaps a rather loose word. I do not regard it as meaning the loss, by immigrants, of their own national characteristics and culture. I do not think we need in this country a melting pot, which will turn everybody out in a common mould, as one of a series of carbon copies of someone's misplaced vision of the stereotyped Englishman ... I define integration, therefore, not as a flattening process of assimilation but as equal opportunity, coupled with cultural diversity, in an atmosphere of mutual tolerance.

Alhough the liberal spokesmen talked about integration, cultural diversity, equal opportunity and mutual tolerance, they neither clearly defined these terms nor worked out the relations between them. The liberal model of integration remained vague and was not clearly distinguished from its assimilationist rival; it welcomed diversity, but neither specified its range nor explained how it was to be related to, and accommodated, within the integrationist framework. Since the liberals tended to think that cultural diversity might militate against equal opportunity, their advocacy of it was often half-hearted and had a touch of nervousness about it.

By and large the liberals relied on education and the law to realise their model of an integrated Britain. Education was expected to foster a climate of better understanding and mutual tolerance, and anti-discrimination legislation to create equal opportunities in major areas of life. Schools were to welcome and encourage cultural diversity by such means as multi-faith school assemblies, broad-based curricula, celebration of ethnic festivals, provision of minority languages and books, recognition of minority preferences in diet, dress and sports, and the disciplining of racist behaviour. As for anti-discrimination legislation, it was to rely on combating direct and indirect forms of racism by means of a complex strategy involving prosecution, public exposure, formal investigations and quiet persuasion, as laid down in the Race Relations Act 1976.

So far, successive governments and local authorities have relied on a mixture of the assimilationist and integrationist approaches. Each political party contains factions championing both, and tends to swing from one extreme to the other. When the political climate is relaxed, the liberal tendency gains ascendancy; when it is tense, as in the aftermath of the Rushdie Affair, all political parties gravitate toward the assimilationist approach. Even Roy Jenkins, the most articulate spokesman of the liberal tendency, panicked earlier this year and gestured towards assimilationism.

I submit that both approaches are ill-thought-out and fraught with danger. As for the assimilationist approach, it is oppressive, intolerant and denies the ethnic community's universally recognised right to preserve its cultural identity. It is also counterproductive. As we have witnessed in recent months, the greater its fear of losing its identity under the assimilationist pressure, the greater is the minority community's tendency to arrest the inescapable internal process of change and turn fundamentalist. The assimilationist response is also self-contradictory. By and large its advocates have commended the Asian community for its enterprise, hard work, family life, respect for law, the will to succeed, the spirit of self-help and peaceful conduct – all made possible by the cultural resources, cohesiveness and the communal spirit of the Asian community. One cannot cherish its strengths and at the same time undermine the very conditions that make them possible. Once its distinctive identity and communal basis are undermined or rudely shaken, as they would be under the assimilationist pressure, its widely admired virtues could hardly be expected to last. Indeed, there is ample evidence to show that many Asian children growing up in non-Asian areas, or taught in overzealous assimilationist schools, are deeply confused, insecure, tense, anxious, emotionally hollow, ashamed of their past including their parents, lack resilience and self-confidence, and display disturbing disorders in their thoughts, feelings and behaviour. Many of them are beginning to show poor academic results, or pay an unacceptably high moral and emotional price for their achievements. Indeed if we are not careful, the Asian bubble might soon burst.

Let us now turn to the liberal response. While it avoids some of the dangers of the assimilationist response, it does not go far enough and runs into predictable difficulties. While it welcomes cultural differences, it does not appreciate the conditions under which alone they can flourish or even survive. It is not easy to bear the burden of difference, especially for the young. Difference draws attention to oneself, intensifies self-consciousness, singles one out as an outsider, and denies one the instinctive trust and loyalty extended to those perceived to be 'one of us'. One therefore tends to take the easy option of merging into the crowd, or playing dumb, or excelling at things the majority values, thus deflecting attention from oneself to one's achievements. The single-minded, almost obsessive, Asian preoc-cupation with academic success springs from, among other things, their desperate concern both to cushion themselves against, and to overcome, racial hostility. Racism has different effects on and evokes different responses from different individuals and communities. Some may disintegrate under its impact, whereas others become obsessively achievement-oriented. Far from signifying either the absence of white racism towards them or their lack of sensitivity to it, as many including the Swann report have suggested, the academically high-achieving and economically successful Asians often demonstrate the opposite. Their cultural self-esteem is not as high as is often suggested, which is why they generally base it not on their own cultural norms but on their perception of what *white society* values and respects.

While the liberals rightly cherish cultural differences, they do not appreciate that cultures lose their vitality and self-regenerative power when they are not given public and institutional status and accepted as a natural and integral part of mainstream society. Unless he feels that the majority community values his heritage and differences, a minority child feels nervous and diffident. Even if he has to pay a heavy price – including the risk of alienation from his community, relations, friends and parents – he would struggle to master white society's values and even be ashamed to admit that he lives differently or speaks a different language at home. As the older generation of Jews have reminded us, many of them used to feel deeply embarrassed in the 1930s when their parents spoke in Yiddish in public or could not reply in English. The sad phenomenon is still pervasive as many Asian parents and their children will testify. A couple of years ago when I was travelling by train from London to Hull, I was sitting opposite an elderly Pakistani couple and next to their adolescent daughter. When the crowded train pulled out of King's Cross, the parents began to talk in Urdu. The girl, who was sitting next to me, began to feel restless and nervous and started making strange signals to them. As they carried on their conversation for a few more minutes, she angrily leaned over the table and asked them to shut up. When the confused mother asked her for an explanation, the girl shot back: 'Just as you do not expose your private parts in public, you do not speak in *that* language in public'. Though no one had presumably taught that to her, she knew that the public realm belonged to the whites, that only *their* language and customs were legitimate within it, and that ethnic identities were to be confined to the private realm. In a society dominated by one culture, pluralism requires more than mere tolerance.

The liberal response also runs into other difficulties. It looks at cultural differences almost entirely from the standpoint of the minorities, and asks how the majority can show its respect for them. While this is commendable, it runs the risk of alienating the majority by appearing to pamper and privilege the minorities. By not convincing the majority that minority cultures enrich it and are a valuable resource, and that their preservation is in its interest, the liberal response encourages it to think that it is bearing the moral burden of tolerance as an earnest of its generosity towards them, thereby paving the way for an unhealthy and inherently contentious relationship between the two. The liberal response suffers from the further handicap of taking the majority culture as more or less given, and not opening it up to creative contributions by minority communities. In the ultimate analysis it is therefore compelled to rest on a flawed, bipartite strategy. It confines minority cultures to the private realm and hands over the public realm of common culture to the majority. The minorities are free to cherish their differences, but as far as the shared public realm is concerned they are required to accept, and become integrated into, the common culture more or less as it is. The liberal response thus does little more than carve out a precarious area of diversity on the margins of a predominantly assimilationist structure.

I should like to outline a different vision of Britain and propose a different model of national integration. In opposition to the Powellite or at least Powellish assumptions undergirding the assimilationist and liberal approaches, I submit the following.[3] First, cultural differences are a valuable national asset. Second, since they are ethnically grounded and remain fragile and fragmented outside their basis in the ethnic communities, they cannot be preserved without preserving the latter. Third, the communities not only do not threaten Britain's social cohesion but positively strengthen and nurture it. Fourth, the widespread belief that British society is made up of, and only values, self-determining individuals and cannot tolerate self-conscious communities is fundamentally mistaken. It is widely conceded that the growing social, moral and economic problems, including those created by a sizeable and increasing underclass, cannot be solved by benign neglect or by throwing more money at them, but only by creating lively, responsible and self-disciplinary communities. It is absurd to seek to create such communities while destroying those that already exist. The ethnic communities do, of course, run the risk of becoming internally oppressive and reactionary, but that requires their constant, internal self-regeneration, not extinction. Finally, the minority communities are an integral part of British society and entitled to have a say in shaping its shared public culture. They are unlikely to develop an attachment and allegiance to the common culture if they feel it as an imposition. It is therefore vital for them to be involved as full and conscious citizens in determining the kind of society Britain should become and their own place in it. Just as they must adjust to British society, it should in turn accommodate their legitimate cultural needs and aspirations. Integration requires movement on both sides, otherwise it is an imposition.

Ethnically grounded cultural differences are a positive asset to British society and deserve to be preserved and encouraged, not just in the interest of the minorities but also its own. They widen the range of lifestyles open to all its citizens, enabling them to borrow from others what attracts them and to enrich their way of life. They also bring different traditions into a mutually beneficial dialogue and stimulate new ideas and experiments. A creative interplay between the Asian or Afro-Caribbean musical, culinary, literary and artistic traditions on the one hand, and British traditions on the other, has already resulted in several exciting developments and opened up many new areas of exploration and research. Take, for example, the English language. Over the centuries it has greatly benefited from the contributions of writers who have drawn upon the resources of their native tongues and introduced new metaphors, images, idioms and forms of writing. By stretching it to accommodate new sensitivities, they have helped it to become genuinely universal, not merely in its geographical spread but in its ability to express an unusually wide range of human emotions and experiences.

In this context Rushdie's *The Satanic Verses* is a truly remarkable work. Unlike almost all other foreign-born writers, he has tried to force open the English language, changing its rules of grammar, syntax, vocabulary and even spelling in order to bring it into harmony with, and to reflect accurately, the way an Indian thinks, talks and feels. Rushdie is not content to say what the English language allows him to say. Instead, he bends it to his will, asserts his equality with it, introduces Indian words and literary mannerisms, and genuinely

195

Indianises it. In the process he both enriches it and affirms the integrity of the Indian sensibility. At a different level he probes the English psyche from the perspective of an immigrant and uncovers its deepest tensions: its capacity for self-deception, its vulnerability, its tenderness as well as its toughness, and the fascinating interplay between its kind and cruel and generous and mean impulses. As an outsider he sees things in the English character and society that the English cannot, and enriches their self-understanding.[4] Thanks to their diffidence, sense of insecurity and the obvious pressures of the literary establishment, many ethnic community writers have largely written about their own community. Once they begn to feel relaxed and self-confident, one would expect them to turn their skills to the exploration of British society, hold a mirror to it, and offer it the supreme gifts of self-knowledge and critical understanding.

What creative writers do at a sophisticated level, ordinary men and women do in their daily encounters. An Indian taking invasive pictures at a religious ceremony was gently asked by an English friend if that was a common practice in India and did not offend the feelings of the gathering. The Indian and his friends got the message and behaved better on future occasions. When a white colleague died, an Afro-Caribbean asked their common white friend to join him in calling on the widow. His friend reluctantly agreed, and was pleasantly surprised by her welcome and warmth, appreciating that the common and largely unquestioned practice of leaving the bereaved alone could do with a change. In short, communities educate and even 'civilise' each other in subtle and elusive ways, provided, of course, that none is too overbearing and self-righteous to welcome a dialogue.

At a less exalted level, the minority communities bring with them new talents, skills and sensitivities, different kinds of imagination, new ways of looking at things, new forms of social organisation, new ideas and interests, a different sense of humour and new psychological and moral resources. All these represent a most valuable human resource which can be fruitfully harnessed in such different areas of life as sport, business, management, industry and government. One need hardly emphasise the contributions of Afro-Caribbean footballers, boxers, cricketers, sprinters and long- and short-distance runners not just to their respective sports, but also to the ways in which sport is organised and viewed in Britain, and at a yet deeper level both to the culture of sport and the place of sport in British culture. At a different level, the Asian corner shop has changed not only the very concept of such shops, but also British shopping culture. It has humanised the inner city, familialised the shop, redrawn the family-civil society distinction, introduced new items on our menu, and made shops an integral part of the local community.

The minority communities, then, represent a most valuable asset. They were recruited because of their cheap labour. They have provided that aplenty, and additionally given Britain an unexpected bonus in the form of new sources of energy and vitality, new forms of self-consciousness and new opportunities for its economic and cultural regeneration. Even if there were no assimilationist pressure, their self-interest and vulnerability as well as the sheer moral and cultural weight of British society would ensure that the communities would disappear within a generation or two, leaving behind rootless, feeble and fragile black and brown atoms tracelessly submerged in British society and periodically resorting to panicky and mindless forms of fundamentalist self-assertion. If we are happy with such an outome, we should continue with the present policy. If not, we need to explore a more imaginative and pluralist vision of Britain, and develop a new social and cultural policy capable of nurturing ethnic identities within a shared cultural framework. A politics of citizenship which both promotes the *rights* of communities with regard to each other, as well as the *obligations* of communities to each other is an essential precondition of this pluralist vision.

First, cultural diversity should be given public status and dignity, so that minority communities are able to accept their identity without a sense of embarrassment or unease. Schools play a crucial role in the process and should become places where cultural differences are accepted as a matter of course, protected and nurtured. Bilingual education, teaching minority languages, recognising minority customs in matters of dress, diet, sports and music, celebrating minority festivals, genuinely multi-cultural curricula, involvement of parent governors from minority communities, recruitment and promotion of suitably qualified minority teachers and so on, ought to become an integral part of our educational system. If the fairly secure British identity needs government protection – as is evident from the Education Reform Act – the insecure ethnic identity needs it even more. The recent Canadian, Australian and American initiatives suggest how this might be done.

Second, minorities can hardly expect to be taken seriously and play their part unless they accept the full obligations of British citizenship. this involves allegiance and loyalty to British society, and sensitivity to its values, fears and dilemmas. It also implies that they must master English and acquire detailed knowledge of British history, society, traditions, customs, and political and economic systems. Unless they do so, they risk behaving and talking in an unacceptable and counter-productive manner, as some of the Muslim reaction to *The Satanic Verses* showed, thereby deeply alienating the majority community whose partnership and goodwill they desperately need.

Third, the minority communities must be allowed to develop at their own pace and in a direction of their own choosing. Those minority practices and values that offend the basic values of British society must obviously be changed; and if they do not do so voluntarily, the law may need to intervene. Beyond that point they should be left alone to decide for themselves how to change themselves, and to do so by mobilising their own regenerative resources. Basic social reforms cannot be dictated from outside, at least in a liberal society, and the communities cannot be harried or blackmailed into making them. Contrary to popular impression, great changes are afoot within ethnic communities, and every family has become a terrain of subdued or explosive struggles. In every family, husband and wife, parents and children, brothers and sisters are having to renegotiate and redefine their patterns of relationship in a manner that takes account both of their traditional values and those characteristic of their adopted country. Different families reach their own inherently tentative conclusions, exchange ideas and experiences, learn from each other's failures and successes, and grow at their own pace. The minority communities are not all new to this; some have already undergone the adjustment once and well know what it entails.

The minority communities include intelligent and wise men and women, most of them heirs to old civilisations, and familiar with the art of making changes. They love their children, are deeply concerned about their well-being, and know better than anyone else that their future is tied up with British society, which they must therefore understand and to which they must adapt, however painful the process. For years the Asians tended to bring in spouses for their children from the Indian subcontinent. Thanks to their painful experiences, widely reported and discussed within the community, the practice is very much on the decline. Their attitudes to women and children, dress and food, and the tendency to wasteful and conspicuous consumption are also undergoing changes. If the state tried to build protective walls around minority communities, or engaged in an interventionist programme of social and cultural engineering, it would not only impede but distort the process.

Fourth, like individuals, communities can only flourish under propitious conditions. They need a sense of their own worth, role models, the confidence that the wider society is not hostile to them, the feeling of being socially valued and welcomed, and opportunities to gain positions commensurate with their abilities and to play their part in the decision-making process at all levels. If the state wants them to flourish and make their full contribution, it should create these conditions. It should ensure, as of right, equality of opportunity and promote a programme of affirmative action designed to raise the disadvantaged and the weak to a point where they are able to compete as equals and take full advantage of the available opportunities. It should enact stronger anti-discrimination laws than exist at present, and make a determined attempt to eliminate the racism that still stifles the potential of thousands of men and women. Its economic policies should release large sections of ethnic communities from the cumulative cycle of deprivation by drawing on *their own* strengths and skills and strengthening their *communal* basis. The state and other public agencies should encourage and, where necessary, give a helping hand to minority communities to enter the public realm of the media, the political parties, the civil service and Parliament. Their visible and audible presence here can go a long way toward increasing their sense of collective integration, self-esteem and power and the majority community's acceptance of them as their rightful fellow citizens.

Fifth, the distinct character of ethnic communities needs to be recognised by our legal system. Contrary to the demands of some

Muslim spokesmen, Britain cannot allow separate legal systems for different communities without violating the fundamental principles of common citizenship and equality before the law. However it can and should accommodate acceptable cultural differences without violating these principles. Despite its conservative tendency, and sometimes strange judgments, the judiciary has shown how to pluralise the interpretation and application of the law without compromising the unitary character of the legal system.[5]

In *R v Bibi* (1980) the Court of Appeal reduced the imprisonment of a Muslim widow, found guilty of importing cannabis, from three years to six months on the grounds that, among other things, she was totally dependent on her brother-in-law and was socialised by her religion into subservience to the male members of her household. In *R v Bailey* and *R v Byfield* the moral codes of men brought up in the West Indies were taken into consideration in sentencing them for having sexual intercourse with girls under 16. In *R v Abesanya* the Nigerian mother who had scarred the cheeks of her fourteen and nine year old sons in accordance with tribal custom was convicted, but granted an absolute discharge. Her children had been willing parties, the cuts had been made in a ceremonial atmosphere and were unlikely to leave permanent marks, and the mother did not know that her conduct was contrary to English laws. In *Malik v British Home Stores* (1980) it was decided that in appropriate circumstances Asian women may wear trousers at work but not white women. In *Dawkins v Crown Supplies* (1989) it was decided that a Rastafarian cannot be refused employment merely because he is unwilling to cut off his dreadlocks. In all these cases a person's cultural background made a difference to his or her treatment by the courts. The law was pluralised and departures from the norm of formal equality were made in different ways and guises, showing how to reconcile the apparently conflicting demands of uniformity and diversity.

Parliament too had recognised that the general principle of the uniformity of law should give way to important cultural and religious values in furtherance of the principles of individual liberty, religious tolerance and promotion of social harmony. Under the Shops Act 1950, Jews may open their shops on Sunday without being in breach of the Sunday trading laws, provided that they register with the local authority. Under the Slaughter of Poultry Act 1967 and the Slaughterhouses Act 1979, Jews and Muslims may slaughter poultry and animals in abattoirs according to their traditional methods. Under the Motor-cycle Crash-helmets Act 1976, the Sikhs are excused from wearing crash helmets provided they are wearing turbans. The law on carrying knives in public places contained in the Criminal Justice Act 1988 exempts those carrying them for religious reasons.

In none of these cases was it felt that equality under the law was violated. Jews are hardly offered real equality under the Sunday trading laws, as otherwise they would be reduced to opening their shops on only five days a week when others have the advantage of an extra day. Under certain circumstances, equality rules out uniformity and requires differential treatment. Such treatment neither confers privileges on those involved, nor amounts to reverse discrimination. Difficult questions do, of course, arise. The proposal to exempt Rastafarians from the Misuse of Drugs Act 1971 and to allow them use of cannabis or marijuana has never been taken seriously. Although it bears some resemblance to the Sikh exemption from not carrying knives, it raises different kinds of problems. The Rastafarians cannot be easily isolated from the rest of the community, there is always the risk of large-scale traffic in these drugs, and the likely health risk to them cannot be ignored by the state.

Parliament and the courts have also indicated several broad principles for deciding which ethnic practices are unacceptable. The Female Circumcision Act 1985 bans all forms of female circumcision. Polygamy constitutes the crime of bigamy under the Offences Against the Person Act 1961. In *R v Derrivierre* (1969) a West Indian father was found guilty of assault in inflicting excessive and overzealous corporal punishment on his son. In a number of cases in which the question of respect for minority cultural practices has been specifically raised, English judges have appealed to notions of reasonableness, public policy, principles of humanity, Britain's commitment to international conventions on human rights, and repugnance to the conscience of the court.

The courts are located at the point of intersection between the state and society as well as between the law and the individual. The state appears there in the form of a law; and the individual to whom the law is applied brings with him his social values, customs, practices and special circumstances. The courts confront one with the other and decide how best the *general* intentions of the law can be realised and justice done as well as seen to be done in a specific and *unique* case. In so doing, they both individualise the law and generalise the individual, and tease out the limits of diversity and tolerance. Such problems and dilemmas as they throw up become a subject of public, and eventually parliamentary debate and find their resolution in a better informed law. The British courts have played a limited but most valuable role in negotiating the moral and cultural differences between the majority and minority communities, and have both reaffirmed and revised the contents and parameters of the shared culture. This would appear to offer encouragement to those concerned about the judicial interpretation of a written constitution or bill of rights vis-à-vis community relations.

Finally, we should take a plural view of British identity. British identity has evolved over time in response to, among other things, the presence of new migrants. The British are not the same people today as they were 100 years ago and, thanks to the momentous change after 1992, they will not be the same 50 years hence. National identity is necessarily dynamic, requiring cultural negotiation between the constituent communities and subject to a periodically redefined consensus. Within the framework of a shared body of values, to the definition of which minorities should have an opportunity to contribute, one can be British in several different and equally legitimate ways. So-called 'Britishness' is the core which different individuals and groups appropriate differently, and around which they frame their different identities. It is not an abstract but a concrete and internally differentiated universal. It is not something all Britons *possess*, but rather a milieu, a self-renewing process in which they *participate*. Even as we all speak English but in our own different ways and accents, the Indians, the Pakistanis, the Afro-Caribbeans, the Scots, the English and the rest can all be British in their own unique ways. They speak the same cultural language but in different though mutually intelligible accents and idioms, and use it to say different things.

Being British is not a matter of sharing a body of *values*, for no values are common to all Britons, not even monogamy, which is accepted largely becuse it is enforced by the law, and is circumvented in practice in all too familiar ways. Nor is it a matter of sharing a *common view of British history*, for here again there are great differences. Nor is it a matter of accepting *parliamentary democracy*, for many a Briton prefers a more participatory and less centralised form of government; and in any case no form of government can be regarded as sacrosanct and beyond criticism and change. Nor is it a matter of *obeying laws*, for even foreigners on British soil are bound by them. Nor is being British a matter of *loving* British society, for a communist or an anarchist who ardently wishes to change it is no less loyal than its enthusiastic defenders. Britain represents a specific form of life, that is, a specific way of talking about and conducting common affairs. Being British therefore means learning the grammar, vocabulary and syntax of the prevailing form of life and knowing how to participate in its ongoing dialogue intelligently and intelligibly. It is, as observed earlier, a matter of acquiring conceptual competence in handling the prevailing cultural language, and has only a limited substantive content.

The cultural language is not static. It has undergone great changes in the past and is undergoing even greater changes today. The Asians, the Afro-Caribbeans and even such long-established communities as the Scots and the Jews have 'pluralised', and speak the prevailing cultural language of Britain in different accents and idioms. Since the British way of life is conducted in a *common* language spoken in *different* accents, to be British is to be able to understand and handle the prevailing variety of accents. A white Briton who does not understand the cultural accents of his Muslim or Afro-Caribbean fellow-citizens is just as incompletely British as the Indian ignorant of the way his white fellow-citizens speak. In other words none of us *is* fully British. We are all constantly trying to *become* one, each in his own way and at his own pace. Only he *is* fully British who can honestly say that no British citizen, black or white, Christian or Hindu, is a cultural stranger to him. Those generally regarded as quintessentially British are in some ways the least British.

What we need in contemporary Britain then is a new spirit of partnership, a spirit of what the Romans called civic friendship, between the majority and minority communities. The majority must accept the minority communities as rightful members of British society, create spaces for their growth, cherish their heritage just as much as they do, and establish the economic, educational, social and political conditions under which alone they can remain vibrant, proud, self-confident and self-critical. For their part the minorities must pledge their loyalty to Britain, accept and cherish its great historical heritage as their own, and make room for themselves without subverting its basic character. The Rushdie affair has taught us two important lessons. We *have* made some progress toward civic friendship, which is why the Muslim protests and white society's deep anger and unease did not get out of control and lead to bloodshed as they might have easily done. It also showed that we still have a *long way* to go, which is why both the protests and white society's reactions were so very uncivil, and the two communities so often talked past each other. The two lessons should respectively *reassure* and *caution* us in our progress toward a properly pluralist civic culture and a genuinely multi-communal Britain.

Notes

I should like to thank my good friends Michael Day, Peter Sanders, Richard Fries and Anthony Rampton for many long discussions on the subject. This paper is based on my Alan Little memorial lecture delivered at Goldsmith's College, London in November 1989.

[1] For a further discussion, see the postscript in Bhikhu Parekh (ed), *Colour, Culture and Consciousness*, Allen and Unwin, London 1974.
[2] This is not to deny that in several other respects, the Education Reform Act is progressive and welcome.
[3] For a good critique of some Powellite assumptions, see John Plamenatz's short but perceptive article in *Colour, Culture and Consciousness, op.cit.*
[4] For yet another critically sympathetic immigrant perspective on English character, see my 'The Spectre of Self-Consciousness' in *Colour, Culture and Consciousness, op.cit.*
[5] For an excellent discussion to which I am indebted, see Sebastian Poulter, 'The significance of ethnic minority customs and traditions in English criminal law,' *New Community*, vol 16 no 1, October 1989. See also E. Ellis Cashmore, 'The Dawkins case: unofficial ethnic status for Rastas', *ibid.*

Part V – Beyond Charter 88

A constitution is not a thing in name only, but in fact. It has not an ideal, but a real existence; and wherever it cannot be produced in a visible form, there is none. The constitution ... is the body of elements, to which you can refer, and quote article by article; and which contains the principles on which the government shall be established, the manner in which it shall be organised, the powers it shall have, the mode of elections, the duration of parliaments, or by what other name such bodies may be called; the powers which the executive part of the government shall have; and, in fine, everything that relates to the complete organisation of a civil government, and the principles on which it shall act, and by which it shall be bound.

Thomas Paine, *Rights of Man*

As long as we keep up a double set of institutions – one dignified and intended to impress the many, the other efficient and intended to govern the many – we should take care that the two match nicely, and hide where the one begins and where the other ends ... In truth, the deferential instinct secures both.

Walter Bagehot, *The English Constitution*

The British constitution is not worth the paper it isn't written on.

David Steel

Charter 88

We have been brought up in Britain to believe that we are free: that our Parliament is the mother of democracy; that our liberty is the envy of the world; that our system of justice is always fair; that the guardians of our safety, the police and security services, are subject to democratic, legal control; that our civil service is impartial; that our cities and communities maintain a proud identity; that our press is brave and honest. Today such beliefs are increasingly implausible. The gap between reality and the received ideas of Britain's 'unwritten constitution' has widened to a degree that many find hard to endure. Yet this year we are invited to celebrate the third centenary of the 'Glorious Revolution' of 1688, which established what was to become the United Kingdom's sovereign formula. In the name of freedom, our political, human and social rights are being curtailed while the powers of the executive have increased, are increasing and ought to be diminished.

A process is underway which endangers many of the freedoms we have had. Only in part deliberate, it began before 1979 and is now gathering momentum. Scotland is governed like a province from Whitehall. More generally, the government has eroded a number of important civil freedoms: for example, the universal rights to habeas corpus, to peaceful assembly, to freedom of information, to freedom of expression, to membership of a trade union, to local government, to freedom of movement, even to the birthright itself. By taking these rights from some, the government puts them at risk for all.

A traditional British belief in the benign nature of the country's institutions encouraged an unsystematic perception of these grave matters; each becomes an 'issue' considered in isolation from the rest. Being unwritten the constitution also encourages a piecemeal approach to politics; an approach that gives little protection against a determined, authoritarian state. For the events of 1688 only shifted the absolute power of the monarch into the hands of the parliamentary oligarchy.

The current administration is not an un-English interruption in the country's way of life. But while the government calls upon aspirations of liberty, it also exploits the dark side of a constitutional settlement which was always deficient in democracy.

The 1688 settlement had a positive side. In its time the Glorious Revolution was a historic victory over royal tyranny. Britain was spared the rigours of dictatorship. A working compromise between many different interests was made possible at home, even if, from Ireland to India, quite different standards were imposed by Empire abroad. No criticism of contemporary development in Britain should deny the significance of past democratic achievements, most dramatically illuminated in May 1940 when Britain defied the fascist domination of Europe.

But the eventual victory that liberated Western Europe preserved the paternalist attitudes and institutions of the United Kingdom. These incorporated the popular desire for work and welfare into a post-war national consensus. Now this has broken down. So, too, have its conventions of compromise and tolerance: essential components of a free society. Instead, the inbuilt powers of the 1688 settlement have enabled the government to discipline British society to its ends: to impose its values on the civil service; to menace the independence of broadcasting; to threaten academic freedom in universities and schools; to tolerate abuses committed in the name of national security. The break with the immediate past shows how vulnerable Britain has always been to elective dictatorship. The consequence is that today the British have fewer legal rights and less democracy than many other West Europeans.

The intensification of authoritarian rule in the United Kingdom has only recently begun. The time to reverse the process is now, but it cannot be reversed by an appeal to the past. Three hundred years of unwritten rule from above are enough. Britain needs a democratic programme that will end unfettered control by the executive of the day. It needs to reform a Parliament in which domination of the lower house can be decided by fewer than 40 per cent of the population; a Parliament in which a majority of the upper house is still determined by inheritance.

We have had less freedom than we believed. That which we have enjoyed has been too dependent on the benevolence of our rulers. Our freedoms have remained their possession, rationed out to us as subjects rather than being our own inalienable possession as citizens. To make real the freedoms we once took for granted means for the first time to take them for ourselves.

The time has come to demand political, civil and human rights in the United Kingdom. The first step is to establish them in constitutional form, so that they are no longer subject to the arbitrary diktat of Westminster and Whitehall.

We call, therefore, for a new constitutional settlement which would:

Enshrine, by means of a bill of rights, such civil liberties as the right to peaceful assembly, to freedom of association, to freedom from discrimination, to freedom from detention without trial, to trial by jury, to privacy and to freedom of expression.

Subject executive powers and prerogatives, by whomsoever exercised, to the rule of law.

Establish freedom of information and open government.

Create a fair electoral system of proportional representation.

Reform the upper house to establish a democratic, non-hereditary second chamber.

Place the executive under the power of a democratically renewed parliament and all agencies of the state under the rule of law.

Ensure the independence of a reformed judiciary.

Provide legal remedies for all abuses of power by the state and the officials of central and local government.

Guarantee an equitable distribution of power between local, regional and national government.

Draw up a written constitution, anchored in the idea of universal citizenship, that incorporates these reforms.

Our central concern is the law. No country can be considered free in which the government is above the law. No democracy can be considered safe whose freedoms are not encoded in a basic constitution.

We, the undersigned, have called this document Charter 88. First, to mark our rejection of the complacency with which the tercentenary of the Revolution of 1688 has been celebrated. Second, to reassert a tradition of demands for constitutional rights in Britain, which stretches from the barons who forced the Magna Carta on King John, to the working men who drew up the People's Charter in 1838, to the women at the beginning of this century who demanded universal suffrage. Third, to salute the courage of those in Eastern Europe who still fight for their fundamental freedoms.

Like the Czech and Slovak signatories of Charter 77, we are an informal, open community of people of different opinion, faiths and professions, united by the will to strive, individually and collectively, for the respect of civil and human rights in our own country and throughout the world. Charter 77 welcomed the ratification by Czechoslovakia of the UN International Covenant on Political and Civil Rights, but noted that it 'serves as a reminder of the extent to which basic human rights in our country exist, regrettably, on paper only'.

Conditions here are so much better than in Eastern Europe as to bear no comparison. But our rights in the United Kingdom remain unformulated, conditional upon the goodwill of the government and the compassion of bureaucrats. To create a democratic constitution at the end of the twentieth century, however, may extend the concept of liberty, especially with respect to the rights of women and the place of minorities. It will not be a simple matter: part of British sovereignty is shared with Europe; and the extension of social rights in a modern economy is a matter of debate everywhere. We cannot foretell the choices a free people may make. We are united in one opinion only, that British society stands in need of a constitution which protects individual rights and of the institutions of a modern and pluralist democracy.

CHARTER 88

The inscription of laws does not guarantee their realisation. Only people themselves can ensure freedom, democracy and equality before the law. Nonetheless, such ends can be far better demanded, and more effectively obtained and guarded, once they **belong to everyone by inalienable right**.

Universal Principles

Geoff Andrews

I have always held the suspicion, or the prejudice, that politics is the enemy of the imagination ...

I have marched and talked for CND, but I have never joined it. I have voted Labour, and even canvassed in some general elections, but I have never joined the Party. Likewise, I have voted and spoken for the Greens, but never joined ... And yet, I am a committed, paid-up supporter, council member and speaker for Charter 88.[1]

Ian McEwan

I have never written a novel, but I have been to enough political meetings over the last decade to share McEwan's view that Charter 88 is a very different political phenomenon from what has gone before. For one thing the Charter, which has its origins in the magazine *New Statesman & Society*, is not inhibited by the traditional structures of the left. Its leaders (or 'spokespeople') are not held accountable to the grassroots membership ('signatories') for their actions. There are no delegates, mandated by constituencies to annual conferences. There are no annual conferences.

The Charter exudes a very different culture. There is a sense of amateurism about its approach to politics. Its lack of an internal democratic structure, you feel, is probably because they haven't had time to get round to it, what with moving offices and keeping up with Labour's ideological gymnastics on constitutional reform. It only recently held its first public event, which took place on Bastille Day to commemorate the modern origins of citizenship, two hundred and one years after the French Revolution.

The Charter certainly has an imaginative and attractive way of denouncing the government and expressing its beliefs. Charter signatories do not 'struggle' for their demands, by going on demonstrations. They hold 'vigils', regularly attended by the rich and famous, and lead delegations and petitions to Whitehall and Westminster. Politics is fun with the Charter, as the shining faces of Prunella Scales, Bamber Gascoigne, Timothy West and Billy Bragg remind us, 'parading [as the recent Charter mailing puts it] the demands on the steps of St Martin in the Fields'.

The Charter's appeal is not to a mass culture, but to an informed public opinion, the sort that watches (and appears) on 'The Late Show', or read and write for the *New Statesman & Society* and *Marxism Today*. It has a large number of lawyers and academics among its leading spokespeople. You won't come across many local Charter groups in Lancashire, but you will find two in Oxford, which supplies almost a third of the Charter's Council.

The Charter is an attempt to 'break the mould of British politics'. And like the SDP, the Charter seeks the moral high ground in order to do so. Moreover, it has what the SDP lacked, a Big Idea – 'universal citizenship'.

Chartists are very self-assured in their condemnation of what's wrong: we know where we stand with the Charter; we are all in the same boat; we are subjects in search of 'inalienable' rights and freedoms that would be guaranteed by a written constitution and a bill of rights.

But even more striking than the different culture and style of protest is the actual politics. The Charter is a celebration of the individual: it is individual freedom not the collective will of the proletariat that forms the driving force behind the Charter's demands – 'We Charter signatories are indignant at government interference with journalistic freedom, shocked at unrestrained police powers, incensed that the state can tap our telephones'.

The Charter's concern with the individual has been instrumental in forcing the left to start reclaiming the idea of liberty from its long identification with the economic freedoms of Thatcherism. Roy Hattersley has made this a personal crusade: his latest charter of rights being a more flexible (he argues) alternative to a formal bill of rights. In this discussion of rights it is political and civil rights that take precedent: social rights have moved backstage. In the Charter's long list of 'inalienable rights', entitlement to welfare or a minimum wage are not among them.

So, are we Charter signatories all 'born-again liberals'? This would seem to be the case. Indeed, with its omission of social rights and its preference for the claims of the individual rather than the welfare of the community, the Charter has more in common with nineteenth- than twentieth-century liberalism. Above all, the Charter promotes the rules of law: 'Our central concern is the law. No country can be considered free in which the government is above the law.'

The Charter may be a liberal document, but it is far from spineless in its demands. Despite its tactical agnosticism on the question of social rights, in the political sphere it does not believe in tinkering with the system; nor does it mince its words.

> Three hundred years of unwritten rule from above are enough ... [The freedom] which we have enjoyed has been too dependent on the benevolence of our rulers. Our freedoms have remained their possession, rationed out to us as subjects rather than being our own inalienable possession as citizens. To make real the freedoms we once took for granted means for the first time to take them for ourselves ... The time has come to demand political, civil and human rights in the United Kingdom.[2]

The cause of our 'subjecthood' is therefore made quite explicit by the Charter: without a written constitution we have no guaranteed freedom; we have no defence against authoritarian governments which are able to enforce regular curtailments of civil liberties. Sovereignty – ultimate power – is not our possession, residing instead in our paternalist parliamentary system. Consequently, according to the Charter, our status as citizens will only be realised by a new constitutional settlement.

However, despite the promise of a new political culture and its enhancement of democratic goals – I have, on reflection, two disputes with the Charter. My first problem is that Charter 88 only tells us part of the story of citizenship. It expects too much from its constitutionalism. Of the core citizenship values the Charter lays great emphasis on rights, but does not talk of duties, the other side to the citizenship equation. The significance of citizenship duty is not merely obedience to the state, but as a comment on the extent of social cohesion that exists among individuals in their different communities. In a period in which the crime rate reaches a new peak, intolerance towards the gay community grows in the wake of the moral panic over Aids, divisions between the white and muslim communities deepen in

214

the aftermath of the Rushdie affair, and the critical future of the planet requires more than ever an ethic of solidarity, there is an urgent need to rebuild a sense of *community*. The crucial importance of duty in this context is that it implies a commitment, an obligation, for individuals themselves to solve the problems within their communities. It puts the local, and now the global, well-being at the centre of citizens concerns, above that of self-interest.

If this is not the purpose of the Charter, then why the claim to 'universal citizenship'? In fact, leading Charter spokespeople *have* entered the debate on citizenship duty, though they have done so on negative grounds, joining with others in denouncing the idea of the 'active citizenship' concept – that creature of Douglas Hurd's.

The purpose behind the 'active citizen' idea is clear enough: the Conservatives were coming to be seen, in a period of declining support, as the party of social division and heartless individualism. This was not helped by Mrs Thatcher's silly proposition that 'there is no such thing as society'. Douglas Hurd's active citizen was an attempt, from one of the few remaining 'patrician' Tory ministers, to show that Conservatives do see individuals as part of a community, with voluntary obligations through charity-giving and other good works to help the less well-off, but also with a duty to uphold the principles of the enterprise culture – the sole guarantor of freedoms – by following your own initiative and standing on your own two feet.

Hurd's intervention prompted a wider debate on the responsibilities of the citizen, which was taken up both by the Speaker's Commission on Citizenship, in its investigation of how an ethic of civic virtue could be promoted in schools and community groups, and by the Prince Charles volunteer army scheme, formed with the purpose of creating self-respect and greater opportunities for disaffected, working-class youth.

In Charter 88's response in the pages of the *New Statesman & Society*, Anthony Barnett, the Charter's co-ordinator, derided the active citizen as a conscript to the state, or 'vigilante', constructed by the Government to divert attention from 'real' citizenship demands (in other words, those concerning constitutional reform). The concept of the active citizen was a spoiling operation, to make sure that the more fundamental concepts of citizenship are displaced ... Active citizenship is not simply an evasion of the undemocratic realities of today, it is a provocation: an attempt to seize the initiative on citizenship so that citizenship can burn.[3]

The problem with the outright dismissal of the active citizen is that with no alternative discussion of civic duty proposed, the Charter, which sees itself as the voice of the liberal-left on citizenship, is in danger of disengaging itself from the essential discussion of why divisions exist within communities and the processes through which people learn to accommodate and respect each other.

In a letter in the *New Statesman & Society* advertising the Charter's latest Teachers 'vigil', Anthony Barnett even took issue with the proposed appearance of citizenship on the national curriculum: '... how are teachers supposed to do this (ie, teach citizenship) if their pupils are to remain subjects?'

Here, I have to declare an interest, as I currently teach something called 'citizenship' as part of the politics 'A' level syllabus. However, the problem is not that my teaching is impaired by lack of a constitution, but it is because 'citizenship' as it appears on the syllabus is confined – as it is with the Charter – to constitutional issues. I feel much happier teaching citizenship (though it is not described as such) to my other sixteen-year-old sociology students, where we talk about the future of the planet, gender, class and racial divisions and different cultural identities.

In setting themselves up as the 'true' representatives of citizenship in its limited constitutional form, the Charter has placed constraints on the debate itself. Subjecthood is not only a lack of rights but a condition of individual, national or cultural exclusion. While a bill of rights can outlaw discrimination, it cannot legislate against the kind of prejudice that continues to divide many communities. In fact it is outside the Charter's terrain, and that of the wider left, that we find rumblings of the need to foster a sense of community if social divisions are to be ended and global catastrophes avoided. This was germinated by the experience of Live Aid, Comic Relief and One World week, all of which have hinted at a popular citizen culture which goes beyond the narrow concerns of the Charter.

Likewise Prince Charles has raised a concern about the breakdown of the community which the left's politics of citizenship has largely failed to address. His volunteer community army, aimed directly at working-class youngsters, is intended to bring back a sense of self-esteem to disaffected youth. Most of the left's response to this is to see it as cheap labour – a palliative for structural problems whose only remedy is real jobs. But in a society in which only twelve per cent of school-leavers go on to higher education, young people desire and deserve more than the prospect of a secure dead-end job.

Charles's concern about the waste of human resources and potential highlighted in 'One World week' has thrust him forward as the New Model Citizen. As Dick Hebdige put it, in his stimulating profile of Charles, 'the champion of the underdog' 'feels personally responsible for 'what's gone wrong' – 'He is tormented by the spectacle of social division, the waste of human and natural resources'. Citizen Charles 'in his expression, gestures and vocal intonations ... sometimes seems literally to embody the submerged crisis of values which gives the lie to Thatcher's tired miracle'.[4]

My second problem (which relates to the first) is that despite the historic compromise between liberalism and socialism apparent in the politics of the Charter, and beneath the attraction of a new kind of political activity, there is a sense of déjà vu in the priorities of its leadership. It is easy to get the impression that the Charter is serving a more direct function as a focus for socialist renewal. The Charter has recently formed alliances with END and the Socialist Society to promote the European Citizens' Assembly. Lord Scarman, stalwart of liberal civil rights may have emerged as a leading Charter advocate, but the Liberal Party's longstanding tradition of local community politics is conspicuous by its absence from the language and culture of the Charter.

It is the language that is the most strikingly déjà vu element of the Charter: fewer people have signed the Charter than buy the *New Statesman & Society* every week, yet it still projects itself as a 'citizens' movement'. Why not, as most commentators refer to it, 'a pressure group for constitutional reform'? After all, the Charter performs the essential functions of a pressure group: it seeks to lobby parties and MPs; it asks for signatures to a petition; it attempts (recently with considerable success) to influence political debate rather than gain political power. In common with other pressure groups, its Council and Executive members are not elected.

However, a pressure group is a single-issue concern, which does not fit with the universal, all-embracing ambition of the Charter. This universalism identifies the enemy as the constitutional (rather than capitalist) system; the solution, undiluted, uncompromising citizenship – not 'active citizenship', or Labour's half-baked list of constitutional reforms (in fact the most significant proposals put forward by any party for over a century), but 'real' or 'full' citizenship. According to the Charter, any talk of citizenship without a written constitution is pernicious nonsense. The alternative contention that forms of *subjection* might co-exist with a new constitutional settlement is never considered by the Charter. And how can it be, when its case for 'universal citizenship' begins and ends with constitutionalism?

Some absurd consequences arise from the Charter's universalism: one is the contention that the Oxford University student and the Brixton teenager will acquire, through a written constitution, the same relationship to the state and the same status as empowered equals in a fully-fledged citizenry. On the contrary, although it is obvious that we will have a much improved democratic and civil libertarian political system if the Charter's proposals become reality, it is equally certain that we will still have major social divisions.

There is also, of course, for socialist Chartists (myself included) an irony in this undiluted, uncompromising idea. The 'good society' which previously depended upon social and economic transformation, is now to be achieved through the extension of civil liberties.

Notes

I am grateful to Martin Jacques for his comments on earlier drafts of this article.

[1] Ian McEwan, 'A New Licence For Liberty', *The Guardian*, 30 April 1990.
[2] Charter 88, see p207.
[3] Anthony Barnett, 'Charlie's Army', *New Statesman & Society*, 22 September 89.
[4] Dick Hebdige, 'Designs for Living', *Marxism Today*, October 1989.

Charter 88: Wrongs and Rights

Stephen Sedley

In my area cinema-goers on their way to see anti-apartheid films are sometimes asked for money by people with collecting tins marked 'Fight Apartheid'. After donating on several occasions, it occurred to me to ask one of them who they represented. They turned out to be members of a small but pure revolutionary organisation which was opposed, among many other things, to apartheid. When I declined to contribute any more to their funds it was suggested to me that I must be a supporter of apartheid. It is a familiar technique of evangelisms of all sorts to insist that failure to support their version of virtue is support for vice.

The protagonists of Charter 88 are above this kind of doorstep guilt-tripping, but the Charter's demands inescapably have a similar effect on people, myself included, who are worried about both the historic deficiency and the present slippage in democracy in the United Kingdom. We feel that not to express our support for democratisation and accountability is to be against them. I want to suggest that reflection shows the choice to be a different one; and, indeed, that one of the problems about Charter 88 is the way it envisages and poses the choices.

Like virtue, most of the ten main demands of Charter 88 contain little that can be objected to except on factual and practical grounds. In other words, the argument which it invites is not about whether we *ought to* support freedom of information, open government, remedies against abuses of state power and the other good things on the list, but about whether and to what extent we already have them. This raises subsequent questions about whether and to what extent it may be necessary to restrict them, and whether and to what extent some of them would in any case have the desired effect. The last of these arguments chiefly affects the proposal of proportional representation (a topic on which the veneer of principle tends to come away pretty quickly from the old timber of political self-interest), the reform of the House of Lords and the demands for a written constitution enshrining a bill of rights. It is on the last of these that I want to concentrate, both because it is the vehicle for the other reforms and because it crystallises the key problem: whether to achieve such a new constitutional settlement would significantly alter the maldistribution and abuse of power in our society. I regard this as the big problem because, as I hope to show, unless power in our society is radically redistributed it will frustrate or skew the realisation of constitutional rights.

Only the most naive legitimist would suppose that simply by changing the rules you can change a society. But it's also important to see *how* false the notion is, and why, because its converse is nearer the truth: a society can change radically without changing its rules. Britain in the 1980s is not a bad example, but a sharper one still is the corruption of the Soviet Union by Stalin's terror under a succession of constitutions which set out shining rows of civic rights and constitutional norms. An equally harsh contrast has been the intermittent but long and shameful history of denial of human rights by the executive and the courts under the US constitution.

To record this is far from saying that such norms and written rights are unimportant. On the contrary, they are a key source of legitimacy for those who contest the denial of rights and liberties by the state and its courts. Not only has the Soviet popular opposition now been vindicated in its pressure to make a reality of the fine words of the constitution; in the USA, the constitution has in this century provided both a rhetorical and a legal underpinning of the major struggles for free speech and racial equality. But in neither case, nor in any other that history throws up, has the constitutional instrument been the engine of radical change: its value is as fuel in a motor with a great many moving parts.

Does it then follow that a constitution along Charter 88's lines would give that motive power to the movements for a more equitable society?

Charter 88, the case goes, cannot itself procure a redistribution of social power, but it can legitimise and promote movements which seek to do so. In some cases, there would be specific legal rights which citizens could claim through the courts. In others, the restructuring of parts of the state would facilitate the access of people to the levers of power. I do not contest these propositions in themselves, but I believe that they are partial and that a fuller view suggests that they may be misleading.

While developing this view in the debate about Charter 88 (and in the years of discussion about a bill of rights which preceded it), it is important to remember that there is a left conservatism which tends to cling to traditional oppositional forms. On the hard left it is argued, in support of this habit, that because nothing fundamental in western capitalist society has changed this century, no fundamental change ought to be made in the organised labour movement's strategy and mode of opposition. I do not believe the premise of this argument, and even if I did, I would not accept the conclusion. There is also in parts of the left an unarticulated urge to cling to the wreckage of familiar forms in the belief that they will at least keep you afloat, whereas if you try to reach land you may drown. I recognise this political psychology in some of the opposition to Charter 88, not only on the hard left but on the traditionalist right of the labour movement. Indeed, one of the big attractions of Charter 88 is that it is opposed not only by Thatcher and Tebbit but by Kinnock and Hattersley. But the real problem is distinct from both the inherited inhibitions and the venal self-interest of current political alignments and organisations.

Rights by themselves are empty vessels. Their significance depends on what is poured into them, and this in turn depends on who has access to them. Entrenched freedom of expression may be of some value to everyone as a minimum restraint on state power; but it is of disproportionate value to the few people who can amplify their own voices a millionfold. This much is commonplace, but it is only the start. If a state bound by an entrenched bill of rights attempts to protect people from the abuse of free expression by powerful corporations, for example by banning tobacco promotion or by enforcing a right of reply, it will be met with a constitutional lawsuit to prevent it interfering with what is presented and argued as the pure principle of free expression but is in reality the monopolistic use of it by a body wealthy enough to stand up for *its* rights. Then to give the judiciary the final word on the balance between free speech and social policy is to abdicate the central democratic function.

This is not because judges have no proper role in the interpretation and application of rights: it is because the simplistic view of rights as inherently egalitarian has a number of consequences which tend to be overlooked. First, it leads to an assumption that you can deal with complex problems of private power to do public harm by simply analysing them in terms of value-free rights, without regard to the location and capacity of power to make use of the right or to resist its use. If the use and enforcement of rights in an unequal society tends to be proportionate to the distribution of power, simply to accord neutrally stated rights to everyone will tend to vest more power in those who already have power. Secondly, the simple view overlooks the fact that rights are not historically fixed, and that new and emergent rights will be suppressed in the name of either accepted traditional rights or (worse) particular rights or exceptions enshrined through political pressure at the moment of constitutional reform. Thirdly and consequently, it ignores the need (or rather, the right) of citizens to be protected by government from the abuse of private power, which requires a separation of the democratic from the judicial process.

It is also extremely risky to assume that the enforcement and use of rights is necessarily a good thing, and I am not speaking of outcomes which you or I may simply disagree with. It may well be a good thing in the long run, for fairly obvious reasons, that due process sometimes results in the acquittal of guilty people – however angry you or I may be at a particular acquittal. But is it in any politically responsible sense a good thing if an entrenched right to free expression permits the tobacco corporations to compel television companies and newspapers to accept cigarette commercials and advertisements designed to place pressure on young people? I choose these examples because they are exactly what the entrenchment of the right has led to in the USA and is being used for in Canada. It takes not a longsighted but a myopic point of view to see this as an ultimate good. What it represents is the use of rights to enable those with power to consolidate and extend their power. Citizens have no countervailing right, in the classic liberal paradigm adopted by Charter 88, to protection from the exercise of irresponsible

CHARTER 88: WRONGS AND RIGHTS

commercial persuasion, let alone to an unpolluted environment. Yet the articulation and eventual acceptance and entrenchment of such rights is high on the contemporary political agenda. What thought has been given to the risk of entrenching currently conventional rights which will be deployed by powerful interests to stifle the growth of new and countervailing rights?

None of this is merely theory. In 1982 Canada enacted a Charter of Rights and Freedoms, giving its courts the power to enforce them 'subject only to such reasonable limits prescribed by law as can be demonstrably justified in a free and democratic society'. There was practically no opposition to its contents at the time: it seemed to embody all political virtue. In less than a decade the Charter has vested a large tranche of sovereignty in the judiciary. The latter have built up a jurisprudence of rights which has its own dynamic and a certain autonomy but which has ultimately replicated the grossly unequal distribution of power in Canadian society.

The Charter, for instance, guarantees freedom of conscience and religion. A supermarket chain has used the guarantee to strike down a law which forbade Sunday trading on religious grounds. It was held not to be an obstacle that a corporation can have no religion, nor that its purpose was not to defend the conscience of others but to enhance its own profits. And the countervailing need of its workers for a day of rest did not rank as a Charter right, because economic and social rights are deliberately excluded.

The Canadian women's movement fought successfully for an equality section to be included in the Charter. It reads:

> Every individual is equal before and under the law and has the right to equal protection and equal benefit of the law without discrimination ... based on sex.

It goes on to give specific exemption to affirmative action – laws and programmes aiming to redress historic sexual disadvantage. But the outcome has been that for every successful claim brought by a woman under the equality section, ten have been brought by men. The results have damaged legislative attempts to redress the gross imbalance of social and economic power between men and women. Charter lawsuits have been used by men to challenge a variety of welfare provisions

223

which recognise that the social burden of childcare ordinarily falls upon women. They have also been used in the name of due process and formal equality before the law to challenge protections for rape survivors who give evidence in court, a process assisted by the statutory revision of sexual offences into 'gender-neutral' crimes so as not to offend against the equality clause. None of these are easy problems in any society or system, but the use of entrenched power to the powerless, has served to concentrate power in places where it already resides.

How *does* Charter 88 then envisage the actual protection and enforcement of substantive human rights in the face of the social distribution of power? It hopes, if it does not believe, that the best vehicle for its programme will be a minimum consensus, which therefore omits these prickly issues, and a judiciary which will have the will and the power to give it effect. The problems confronting this position loom like mountain tops receding into the distance. In this landscape, Charter 88 itself appears trapped in a time-warp.

It may be that some of the difficulties I have touched on can be grasped and dealt with in the UK as part of Charter's 88's project. It is certainly a prime requirement, for example, that only individuals should rank as beneficiaries of civil liberties and human rights. Private corporations as well as public ones are artificial creations of statute law, and it typifies the inappropriate approach of the common law that Canada's judges, like Britain's, treat a limited company as a legal person for all possible purposes (except going to gaol). In Canada, as in the USA, this has included the entitlement to claim constitutional rights. Charter 88 proposes to 'ensure the independence of a reformed judiciary'. I assume that this has inadvertently been put the wrong way round, but I do not believe that even the reform of an independent judiciary is any guarantee that we would escape the historic nonsense of corporate legal personality. This is one of many issues that requires specific and judge-proof laws, not broadly stated good intentions.

But the corporation problem only begins here. The conventional liberal paradigm of rights, which Charter 88 adopts, poses the state as the enemy of individual liberties. Even if you eliminate artificial persons from the category of individuals, the question still remains whether it is simply the state that the individual needs to be protected against. Certainly in the USA and Canada, and increasingly in the UK, citizens look to the state to protect them against the effects of corporate activity. The relevant paradigm of rights in the coming period needs not simply to deny corporations constitutional personality but to recognise them as a creation and a responsibility of the state and to accord citizens both the state's and the law's protection against them. And further, it needs to assert the fundamental right of citizens to general vigilance and protection on the part of the state.

Charter 88, however, skirts the question: *what* rights? Its short list does not purport to be exhaustive, but it is the characteristic list of traditional liberal philosophy. Certainly, by omitting economic and social rights – to a home, a job, welfare, education – it follows the international human rights instruments. The Canadian Charter did the same, thereby avoiding a minefield of difficulties for government regulation of the economy, for the judiciary and for itself. But there are two reasons why Charter 88 may not be able to afford the same luxury of self-denial. One is that these are among the rights that matter most to most people, and which both the state and private enterprise fail to deliver equitably or, sometimes, at all. The other is that this terrain is going to be contested whether we like it or not. There is a significant Conservative lobby in favour of a bill of rights, and what it wants to see entrenched are rights to private education, private medicine, unlimited property, unfettered freedom of contract and so forth. If the Charter 88 project wins the influence it hopes for, it is going to have to respond to these demands. If it does so defensively on the minimalist ground that there is no consensus about them, it will have to endure the shame of saying the same about housing, work, welfare and education. The only alternative will be to take sides, in which case it ought to start thinking about where it stands now.

Beyond these rights lies a whole new generation of coming rights: the rights of peoples to economic as well as political self-determination; the right to a wholesome environment and to an unviolated global home. They may command wide assent as slogans or goals, but turning them into real rights presents formidable problems of enforcement and of conflict with more traditional rights, and indeed with each other. Nevertheless, it is the struggle to turn these into enforceable rights and to secure a political balance among them and with other, received rights that is the critical constitutional agenda for the next century. The present movement for entrenched rights, by way of salute to Czechoslovakia's Charter 77, has chosen to locate itself by reference to the year 1988. Its critics may ask whether the year 1688 is not a more accurate location for some of its thinking.

None of this is intended to dismiss or marginalise Charter 88. Every movement which enhances and propagates awareness of the gulf between the complacent rhetoric and the unprepossessing reality of our society, and of our constitutional poverty as its citizens, is important. My argument is that this is a long and difficult road down which it is not decently possible to travel only the first straightforward mile as Charter 88 wishes to do. At some point down the road travellers are going to encounter the fundamental issues of the nature, location and uses of power, and they are going to need the equipment to deal with these issues if they are to reach a destination where the benefit of acknowledged rights depends not on power but on citizenship itself.

This last point I take to be an agreed requirement, not because it necessarily is but because without it all rights discourse is meaningless. In fact, however, the long historic march from privilege to rights, from status to citizenship, from oligarchy to formal democracy, is not accepted by modern radical Toryism as either desirable or irreversible. One of the major battles still to be fought is against the resurgent notion that even the formal equality of citizens in a democracy is an extravagance. In a sense, the hard right in Britain is doing no more than arguing for Conservative theory to be brought into line with a reality in which increasingly the meaning of rights has become the power to exploit them. The defeat of this ideology will depend not on a resort to the inherited rhetoric of rights, which, though important, is no more than the starting point, but on the offer and delivery of *tangible* rights of citizenship; and that in turn means addressing the concentrations of power which stifle the rights that they cannot absorb.

Unless, therefore, the constitutional settlement on which Charter 88 is predicated is itself founded on the break-up of power oligopolies, the project will not succeed. It is not that one has to come before the other in time, but that each is indispensable to the other. Here, it seems to me, is the positive case for Charter 88. The constitutional control of power, people's power included, is something an egalitarian political movement cannot any longer assume. If the twenty-first century is to find a polity in which redistributed power does not pass into the hands of a new elite, it is citizens' experience and expectation of *real* rights which meet *real* needs that are likely to be the best guarantee against this. It is the law, no doubt, which will both express and legitimise it; but it is politics which will determine what we get and when.

Whose Rights of Citizenship?

Michael Rustin

The major movement for extending rights of citizenship in Britain today, Charter 88, has opted for a definition of citizenship that is concerned almost exclusively with civil and political rights, and scarcely at all with the social and economic rights of citizens. The Charter's aims fall in three categories. The first seek to entrench the rights of citizens against the arbitrary exercise of state power, though the rights to assembly and association also involve the exercise of individual rights in common and for collective purposes. The second proposes to subject executive powers to the rule of law, and to provide legal remedies to abuses of power by the state and its officials. This involves, in effect, strengthening the powers of a reformed judiciary over the executive branch. The third aim of the Charter is to extend positive political citizenship by making government more representative – for example, through proportional representation and by establishing a democratic and non-hereditary second chamber.

How does the most significant new radical movement of the last two years come to have adopted a programme that would hardly have been out of place in Britain a century ago? T.H. Marshall, in his famous essay *Citizenship and Social Class*, identified three domains of 'rights' – civil, political and social. Working within an optimistic evolutionary perspective more widely shared in the 1950s than now, he located the struggle for civil rights as one primarily of the eighteenth century, the battle for political rights (in particular, the franchise) as that of the nineteenth century, and the movement for social and economic rights (social insurance, minimum income, full employment, rights to

228

education and health) as one of the twentieth century. We therefore seem to have returned – without noticing it – to the uncompleted liberal and radical agendas of the two previous centuries.

It is not that these agendas don't need to be completed. Indeed, the huge growth of governmental power (of whatever political colour) during this century has given a new importance to these goals – as citizens feel dwarfed or crushed by the Leviathan created to advance their various social ends. Civil citizenship was initially sought to defend bourgeois citizens against the powers of an aristocratic, landed class, creating freedom for individuals in the market-place. Limited representative democracy was first used as a means of dismantling restraints on the operation of markets, further increasing the vulnerability of the poor. But later, as the market economy became fully established, representative democracy was achieved for the majority: it was seen as the means of exercising a countervailing power, offering citizens some protection by the state against the uncertainties of the market. Demands for economic rights, which it now seems reached their culmination in the Beveridge Report, sought to make state power effective in these ways.

Given the distinctions of these historical phases in the discourse of rights, whose rights, in particular, are now being asserted by the Charter? Certainly, those who care most about freedom of information and communication – we might say those who live by the word. Also those offended or outraged by the abuse of parliamentary majority power practised by the Thatcher administrations, riding roughshod over all manner of established conventions and customary powers, from local government to the universities. Also those committed to a more pluralist, but also more consensual political system, who see electoral reform as a way of ending 'elective dictatorship' once and for all. This seems to amount to the programme of a sizeable, but still minoritarian intellectual and political class – the counter-establishments, we might say, which have felt excluded by the years of Thatcherism. It has little to say, however, about the circumstances of the urban underclass, about discrimination against women or blacks, about standards of public services in health, education, or community care, about low incomes or unemployment. This campaign for popular democracy in truth has a regrettably elitist flavour.

229

There is a theory behind the Charter which lends some conviction to the idea that these omissions are merely temporary and tactical. This is the idea, developed by Perry Anderson, Tom Nairn and Anthony Barnett in *New Left Review* and elsewhere over the last 25 years that the problem with British society is that it never had a proper democratic, bourgeois revolution. Until it does, the argument goes, the labour movement would remain hopelessly sunk in deferential habits of mind, trapped in the mystifications of the unwritten British constitution. The trouble is, we are now having our 'bourgeois revolution' – called Thatcherism. It is not especially democratic, and it is leading not to an alliance of a militant radical bourgeoisie with a powerful proletariat (as might just have been imaginable once upon a time) but to the determined efforts of a *resurgent* bourgeoisie to disperse, assimilate and divide what remains of a proletariat. It is possible, in a truly dreadful historical paradox, that Thatcherism, and the campaign for constitutional reform may even be two streams of the same historical current. The first institutes an individualism of property and private consumption; the second, if it succeeds, will give a legal and political endorsement to an equally individualist definition of rights and entitlements. It is a merit of the USA that it is in certain respects a more libertarian and democratic society than Britain, and the historic mission of constitutional reform could be, if we are not alert to the danger, merely to complete in the *civil and political* domain the 'Americanisation' of British society so keenly sought by Thatcherism on the economic and social plane.

The omission of an agenda of social and economic entitlements from the claims of the Charter may be more than merely a matter of tactical judgement, intended to focus attention more clearly on what are clearly important aims, and to win the widest political agreement on them from liberals and socialists. One of the problems is that the unrestrained powers of the state which radicals now wish to restrain and subject to redress have been developed in part in order to advance these very social and economic rights. The 'big state' is or was a 'welfare state'. Unfortunately, it was never so big and intimidating as in its role of administering 'welfare' to social security claimants, to the unemployed, to the clients of social services, housing, and even sometimes health and education. So passive a definition of 'citizenship' has been developed and enforced in the development of welfare services that it is indeed difficult to argue for more of these 'rights and entitlements' without apparently contradicting the whole libertarian ethos of the Charter: more economic and social rights for citizens, at least on the old model, would mean a stronger not a weaker state apparatus. As far as implementation is concerned, the Labour Party – whether in local or central government – has been little less authoritarian than the Conservatives. Indeed, one could say that some Thatcherite measures, in privatising services, imposing ballots, and giving autonomy to providers, have attempted to increase at least *some* citizens' rights in the welfare sphere (though with much damage to the rights of the worst-off).

Until radicals find some solution to the problem of how to combine social and economic entitlements with individual freedom, of how to define these as rights to which citizens are entitled rather than as benefits for which they are obliged to plead, one can understand why the Charter might choose to remain silent about them.

In the sphere of welfare, as in much else, the principle of 'consumerism' now reigns. The problem is, that if you can't afford the mortgage, or don't have an occupational pension, or you live in a place where there are no good schools to choose from, this kind of 'enfranchisement' is of little use. The left's traditional alternative is participatory democracy – making services more accountable and democratic by empowering both those who provide them, and citizens at large, in some collective process. This idea has also been exposed as full of contradictions. Workers in public services often tend to defend their own occupational interests, more than those of their clients. Far from welcoming participatory involvement by the latter (school parents, council tenants) they often prefer to keep them out. Participation in local, still more national politics, is so time-consuming and tedious for most people as to provide hardly any effective day-to-day means of change. Bureaucratic and professional administrative control is simply more efficient and powerful than voluntary action. So the market enfranchises only the more fortunate, whilst the democratic polity is too clumsy and remote to be an effective means of democratisation on the ground.

Governments thus exercise awesome power in the social sphere, taxing citizens, regulating their economic activity, recording and storing any number of facts about them, removing children from their parents' care where their protection demands it, compulsorily purchasing their property in the public interest. If the children's school is no good, the rubbish is not collected, the psychiatric patient is not treated, the ageing relative is left untended in a home, there is usually very little the citizen can do about it. Whereas, if the citizens' obligations to the state are not met, and the community charge bill is not paid, the authorities will be quick enough off the mark with their summonses and bailiffs.

Firstly, then, a 'new constitutional settlement' has to address itself to the rights of citizens to participate in the life of their society in a more than *formal* legal and political sense. The idea that 'constitutions' are concerned with these civil and political rights, rather than social and economic ones, is itself a contingent historical fact, rather than an absolute necessity. The Treaty of Rome, after all, concerned itself initially with economic freedoms, not civil or political entitlements. It was only subsequently that the European Community started to concern itself so much with civil rights, and has now moved on to a 'social charter' of workers' rights and perhaps soon to a fuller democratisation of its institutions. One could imagine a constitutional settlement founded on a 'social', not a merely civil contract, which specified in broad terms (subject to more detailed specification in law) rights to work, to subsistence and shelter, to educational opportunities, to equal rights for women and members of all ethnic and religious groups. Whilst this may seem wildly optimistic so far as political prospects in Britain is concerned, it is clearly more consistent with the direction of thinking in Europe.

Secondly, we have to develop ways in which 'rights' can be effective and enforceable in the social sphere. Public institutions must be open to individual redress for inefficient or inadequate services, even though this will involve substantial costs in establishing procedures through which grievances can be heard and remedies required. The civil courts provide redress for citizens in relation to malpractice by private firms. There needs to be some analogous 'social court' through which unacceptable deficiencies in public services are adjudicated. The point is not primarily to provide financial or material compensation (and thus further to monetise a society which is already too besotted with cash), but on the contrary to ensure accountability and that due public lessons are drawn from private grievances. In the higher education sector – a privileged domain it must be admitted – students are granted rights of redress in a quasi-judicial process against the maladministration of their courses and examinations. The existence of these procedures have undoubtedly altered the balance of rights and power in these institutions. even if few cases are brought, the possibility of appeal concentrates the mind of providers of courses, and makes them less likely to abuse their powers.

It should also be possible to strengthen the role of citizens in the collective monitoring and regulation of public services. Whilst it is impossibly costly in both time and money to involve large numbers of staff in the day-to-day management of organisations, it should be feasible to create forms of regular inspection and review of services which can achieve some of the same ends more efficiently. If schools, general practices, hospitals, social service area teams, council departments, were required to submit themselves to inspection at regular intervals, by boards which included customers, professionals from neighbouring organisations, expert advisers and professional inspectors, and ordinary citizens, (perhaps nominated on a random jury-service basis), they would become open institutions in a way that they currently are not. Such a system as this also operates in the 'public' (polytechnic and other colleges) sector of higher education, through the role of the Council for National Academic Awards in reviewing and accrediting courses and institutions, and has been vital in maintaining high educational standards throughout this system during twenty years of very rapid growth.

This proposal imagines the 'democratisation' of a system of institutional inspection invented in the nineteenth century through the development of the roles of factory and school inspectors. Traditional methods of inspection of 'public' institutions are closed and somewhat mandarin in nature: the experts inspect, and report to those at the top of the institutions' hierarchy for them to take note of any findings. There is no deliberate discussion, no need to formulate a common set of organisational objectives, no 'voice' given to clients, no involvement of the public. Nowadays, the main supplement to this system is the statistical audit, whether in financial terms or in measures of organisational output. This improves the factual but not the deliberative or democratic basis of assessment. When things go badly wrong, there is always recourse to the court or committee of inquiry, where lawyers (usually) take evidence and attempt to come to a balanced view. Sometimes useful, such inquiries are no substitute for what a more regular and accessible procedure could do.

What is proposed is a way of restoring 'public' institutions to the public, in a way which does not impose impossible costs of time and effort. The review of institutional performance every few years would require self-reflection by their members. Encouraging the formulation of institutional goals and the assessment of their performance will generally increase commitment to specific values and practices, strengthening the conception of social membership and public service when these are under grave threat from consumerist definitions of value. (The school development plans instituted by ILEA before its demise were one example of this practice.) Good public institutions will not be created by the power of 'exit' (that is, the right of consumer choice) alone. The idea of day-to-day participation by citizens in running organisations is a utopian myth – parents do not have time to run their children's schools! But participation in the regular monitoring and assessment of standards, in seeing at intervals what progress is being made, is a more feasible exercise of citizenship, and could make a significant difference. What we need are forms of democratic participation with large 'multiplier effects', both in symbolic and practical ways.

We can only hope to reconstruct an agenda of social and economic rights which is consistent with the principles of liberty and democracy if we develop new ways of managing the public sphere. First, we have to remove the immunity to public scrutiny and redress that governments confer on their own activities – this is a natural extension of the libertarian goals of the Charter. Then we have to find ways of letting citizens in, and finding for them a role in scrutinising and improving performance which both enhances standards and gives a new meaning to the exercise of social citizenship.

Sisters and Citizens

Caroline Ellis

> Access to things as they are, yes; to be taken on our own terms, that too. But more: to participate in defining the terms that create the standards, to be a voice in drawing the lines. This has been at the heart of every women's initiative for civil equality from suffrage to the Equal Rights Amendment: the simple notion that law – only words, words that set conditions as well as express them, words that are their own kind of art, words in power, words of authority, words in life – respond to women as well as men.[1]

Constitutional reform may not have been uppermost in the minds of second-wave feminists at the birth of the modern women's movement, concerned as they were with the basics of shared child-rearing, equal pay and consciousness-raising. Now in the 1990s with Britain facing considerable pressures (particularly from Scotland and Europe) to democratise and modernise its political system, it is not something feminists can afford to ignore.

However, the new citizenship debate presents huge problems for feminists and, as yet, there has been no coherent response. Socialist feminists have in the past perceived constitutional settlements as inevitably serving to reinforce women's subordination in the private and public spheres because such settlements have never addressed inequalities of social and economic power. In contrast, liberal feminism – while acknowledging the need for democratic and legal reforms – has failed to challenge the ideological and social structures of patriarchy through which men dominate and oppress women. Radical feminists, on the other hand, have challenged male power but not economic inequality. Eco-feminism has linked the exploitation of women with the exploitation of the earth's resources, but has been accused of an immobilising tendency towards essentialism. With such contrasting approaches and with the fragmentation of the women's movement,

235

how can British feminism possibly hope to develop a common strategy for achieving equal citizenship?

There are, however, two reasons for optimism on this score. Firstly, the history of the women's movement has often shown theoretical antagonisms to be less important than practical action to meet necessary goals. It has revealed the considerable capacity of women to find new ways of working together – co-operative, informal and non-hierarchical ways of organising. Secondly, the frustration of seeing struggles for women's rights set back by regressive policies imposed from above, has led those demanding social and economic empowerment to rethink the political and constitutional settlement within which this could be effected.

One of the essential questions of the 1990s for feminists is how the aspirations for a new political settlement can be reconciled with the apparent economic benefits of projected demographic changes. Between now and 1995, the number of young people on the labour market is expected to drop by about 25 per cent or one million, while the number of women entering the market in this period is likely to increase, so that women will account for about 80 per cent of an estimated 1.1 million new workers. While there is no compelling political reason why the government should respond positively to these new opportunities for women, the effect of these changes could be to increase our economic power substantially. More women will be moving into senior management positions and there will be strong pressures on employers to provide much improved maternity leave, child-care provision, more flexible working arrangements and more job-sharing.

However, if these economic changes are to be made to work for women, then there is an important lesson to be drawn from the history of women's struggles, namely that the attainment of political and civil rights is a necessary precondition for social emancipation. This point is emphasised in particular by Sylvia Walby who argues that first-wave feminism (1850-1930) was a much more important historical force than is usually perceived. The victories of political citizenship rights during this period gave women not only the vote, but education, access to the professions, property ownership and the chance to leave marriages. The unprecedented increase in women's paid employment after the Second

World War meant that most women were able to take advantage of their legal independence. Walby writes:

> The two changes, political and economic, had their impact as a result of their specific combination. In the absence of the political victory, the increase in women's wage labour would have been merely additional exploitation. It was only because of the citizenship rights that women were able to use the economic changes to broaden further their sphere of operation.[2]

Enter Charter 88, which has demanded an end to '300 years of unwritten rule from above' and a new constitutional settlement anchored in the principle of universal citizenship. Part of Charter 88's analysis is that the 'democratic deficit' in our political system and our lack of citizenship rights form a huge block against progressive social and economic change. But what has not been adequately appreciated in the wide-ranging discussion of the Charter's demands that is now taking place among commentators, politicians and academics, is that the constitution system the Charter attacks is one based on male traditions and male political supremacy. As Anna Coote and Polly Patullo vividly describe in *Power and Prejudice*:

> The machinery of British politics is an ancient cobwebby construction ... built up haphazardly over centuries by men with jewelled crowns on their heads, and men with clanking armour on their backs, and men with lace and velvet at their throats, and men with powder on their wigs, and men with pinstripes on their persons, and (just a few) men with flat caps.[3]

The body politic, as presently constituted is built on patriarchal hierarchies of power and the exclusion of women. Coote and Patullo recount how easily women's issues can be trivialised by male politicians in the House of Commons and how women of all backgrounds are alienated by the ethos and traditions of the body politic. Therefore, if there is the prospect of fundamental change to this alien body, women must stake their claim. But on what basis?

A recent report by the Hansard Society, 'Women at the Top', made the assumption that getting more women into top positions would necessarily break down barriers and discrimination throughout the system. It failed to question the hierarchical structures of the civil service, management or the polity. The concern in the report was with 'high fliers', the presumption being that most women will be willing to take on male values and climb the hierarchy in search of power and status. That may be so. But the culture of women's political organisation suggests that those who aspire to equal citizenship do not wish to see individual women set against each other. Rather they would like to see personal fulfilment in the context of the empowerment of all women and the development of new ways of working.

What, then, are the likely components of a new political citizenship deal for women? Firstly, the gross under-representation of women in Parliament needs to be addressed. The people who make the laws that frame our citizenship are not doing so from a woman's point of view. A key element is therefore to increase women's representation. As the Hansard Society report recognised, parliamentary procedures and internal party arrangements are a significant barrier to the entry of women into politics. Parliament still operates according to the archaic habits of a glorified men's club. Its hours and facilities make no concession to anyone with domestic commitments.

At least one long-standing pillar of the Establishment, the Labour Party, is on the move, impelled by an increasingly confident female membership and the need to catch the women's vote. It has now adopted a ten-year programme to achieve 50 per cent representation of women in the PLP and a policy of reserving places for women in the Shadow Cabinet, with MPs being required to vote for at least three women, guaranteeing minimum representation of 16 per cent. Advocacy of a Women's Ministry is a further indication that Labour is becoming serious about gender justice. Moreover, women across the political spectrum are anxious to get more women into Parliament and are now realising that it is, above all, the electoral system which stands in our way. With only 43 women MPs, or around 6 per cent, we are close to the bottom of the league of modern democracies, with West Germany on 15.4 per cent, Denmark 30.7 per cent and Sweden with 38 per cent. The Hansard Society declared that the unanimous finding of all the studies of legislative representation is that systems of proportional representation (PR) favour the election of women:

> The first-past-the-post electoral system is likely to be one of the main reasons for the low representation of women in the House of Commons.[4]

Furthermore, it explains that under PR it is the multi-member and/or party list element that favour women:

> In single-member constituencies, selection committees often hesitate to choose women candidates, while in constituencies with more than one member or a party list, there will be concern to secure a 'balanced ticket'. The absence of women from the shortlist is seen as likely to cause offence and narrow the party's appeal.[5]

But what will women do with this kind of political power once it has been secured? Will we use it differently to men, will we use it to help fellow women? As Catharine A. MacKinnon has written:

> The final issue is not whether biological males or females hold positions of power, although women must be there. The issue is: what are our identifications? What are our loyalties? To whom are we accountable?[6]

This particular problem is identified by socialist feminist Hilary Wainwright who writes that the proportion of women politicians does not necessarily mean a radical improvement in the state's ability to tackle the subordinate position of women:

> Successful challenges to male political power have not been invariably accompanied by effective challenges to the sexual division of labour. The Norwegian Parliament, for instance, is made up of over 40 per cent women and between 1986-89 over one third of the Cabinet were women, including the Prime Minister; yet Norway has one of the most gender-segregated occupational structures in Western Europe and child-care provisions are among the lowest.[7]

Wainwright, drawing on the experience of the Women's Committee of the Greater London Council before its abolition in 1986, argues the need for the 'economic and social struggles of women to be represented directly and democratically through the women's groups that promote them, in the political decision-making process'.[8]

This is precisely the approach adopted by a group of Scottish women drawn from different parties and movements, who seized the opportunity provided by the Scottish Constitutional Convention and its plans for a Scottish Parliament, to make their 'Claim of Right'. The demands of 'A Woman's Claim of Right' illustrate a new feminist politics of citizenship that goes beyond traditional liberal aims. They do not only want constitutional reform which guarantees equal representation for women in the political arena and positive action to enable women from all social backgrounds to be active in public life. They also call for a departure from the adversarial style of present-day politics and a move towards greater co-operation *in the cause of social justice*, which recognises the value of women's experience and wisdom. And they highlight the need for a future Parliament to deal with obstacles to women in housing, education, employment, child-care and personal safety. Their demands for equal representation have been favourably received by the (albeit male-dominated) Convention – 70 per cent of all respondents in a survey conducted by Emma Simpson supported special measures to increase women's membership of a future Scottish Parlaiment. In fact, Simpson concluded that:

> The initial rumblings of positive reform for women are turning into a political earthquake which will produce a seismic change in the make-up of a future government of Scotland.[9]

'A Woman's Claim of Right' has also developed radical ideas for a new kind of Parliament. It would work office hours, provide child-care facilities and offer care allowances for elderly dependants, thus making the political process more accessible to women. As Jackie Roddick has described, it would operate a system similar to that of Scottish local government, where the primary responsibility for initiating legislation and controlling executive departments lies with a committee of councillors. The minister would legally obtain her title by being convenor of the committee. Opposition members could thus initiate legislation with the approval of the committee and would be encouraged to co-operate across party lines rather than indulge in aggressive oppositional tactics.[10]

Such a format would be far more accessible to outside groups, and would enable women involved in other movements to use their expertise and see that the interests of groups of women are catered for. As Hilary Wainwright argues, effective action to challenge women's subordination should mean links between parliamentary representatives and women acting within civil society.

> The practical outcome is experimentation in a new form of democracy combining the representation of individual but socially and economically unequal citizens with that of groups through which citizens organise to overcome their unequal social position.[11]

A feminist agenda for constitutional reform does not end here. Devolution of power to the nations, regions and localities would give women more of an opportunity to shape their own futures. Statistical surveys have shown that women are more likely to be active in local politics and non-party campaigns in the community than national politics so the emergence of more autonomous and open local government will give women a more effective voice. Consequently, more of the decisions affecting women's daily lives, whether in housing, education and local finance, would be made at local level where need can best be assessed.

The achievement of a bill of rights, one of the most contentious aspects of the new constitutional reform proposals, could hardly in itself overturn inequalities of power. Yet a bill of rights, guaranteed by a written constitution, could provide women for the first time with a democratic forum within which to debate and claim their rights. At present we have to fight for rights that do not even exist on paper: getting them in writing would be the first step towards realising them in practice. Improving access to the law, and in particular creating precedents on constitutional claims – so that individual women could use their power to help wider groups of women – could equally strengthen the position of women in civil society. And if France and the Netherlands can achieve a judiciary with a near-perfect gender balance by means of a proper career structure and part-time appointments, perhaps a determined feminist politics of citizenship could achieve the same for Britain.

It is time for feminists in the UK to bury their differences and take up the constitutional challenge. Our demand for access to the political system must also be a demand for change. If Britain is to play a meaningful role in the new Europe, it will have to equip itself with a democratic constitution. Will women have the courage and imagination to help shape that constitution? Will the sisters become citizens?

Notes

[1] Catharine A. MacKinnon, *Feminism Unmodified: Discourses on Life and Law*, Harvard University Press, Cambridge Mass. 1987, p228.
[2] Sylvia Walby, *Theorising Patriarchy*, Blackwell, Oxford 1990, p190.
[3] Anna Coote and Polly Patullo, *Power and Prejudice*, Weidenfeld & Nicolson, London 1990, p20.
[4] The Report of the Hansard Society Commission on Women at the Top, 1990, p31.
[5] *Ibid.*, p31.
[6] MacKinnon, *op.cit.*, p26.
[7] Hilary Wainwright, 'New Forms of Democracy for Socialist Renewal', in David McLellan and Sean Sayers (eds), *Socialism and Democracy*, Macmillan, London (forthcoming).
[8] *Ibid.*
[9] Emma Simpson, *Radical Scotland*, no 44, April/May 1990.
[10] Jackie Roddick, *Socialist Citizen*, no 5, October 1989.
[11] Wainwright, *op.cit.*

Labour and the Constitutional Crisis

Paul Hirst

Labour's return to political credibility since the autumn of 1989 and the increasing probability that it will win the general election in 1992 must be welcomed by all who are sickened by the Thatcher governments' record of economic mismanagement and political authoritarianism. Yet Labour's success is also a cause for concern for radicals. If the diagnosis of Charter 88 is correct, then the British political system is in deep trouble and our institutions require thoroughgoing reform. However, Labour's success in the conventional political game weakens such pressure for reform. The Labour leadership remains sceptical about two central planks of the Charter's programme; electoral reform and a written constitution. If Labour can win by the old electoral system and rule as an exclusively party government, why bother with proportional representation or constitutional change?

Likewise, part of Labour's growing credibility is its willingness to downgrade its objectives in economic policy. John Smith, the shadow Chancellor, has adopted a cautious approach to macro-economic policy (reflected in the recent revised Policy Review document accepted by the NEC): Labour will be cautious about raising taxes; it rejects an incomes policy; it has abandoned the goal of full employment; it has begun to backtrack on the active industrial policy proposed by Bryan Gould when he was shadow spokesman on Trade and Industry; and John Smith has made clear that Labour will accept the disciplines imposed by the EMS and international financial markets on exchange

243

rates and monetary policy. Much of this is bowing to the inevitable and a pragmatist might well argue that unrealistic economic radicalism can only achieve one thing – losing Labour the election. Pragmatism might be appropriate if our economy were in good shape, but plainly it is not. Labour's cautious policy fits badly with its own repeated claims against Conservative economic management, that we face nothing less than an economic crisis created by the poor performance of our manufacturing sector. Our chronic balance of payments deficit stems from our poor industrial competitiveness and our restricted capacity in manufacturing output. Under-investment, wage inflation and tardy productivity growth all threaten to create a crisis in the early 1990s, just as competitive pressures in Europe intensify with the creation of a single market.

Labour's pragmatic caution is thus ill-adapted to meet the economic problems facing Britain. Labour has failed to develop a credible programme of economic revitalisation. This is because it has developed no new strategy for governance of the economy to replace either the Conservative's neo-liberal policies or its own previous commitment to Keynesian full-employment policies and a comprehensive welfare state. I shall argue that the Labour Party's political conservatism and its economic caution are linked; that an exclusive party government using our existing institutions cannot offer new ways of governing the economy. I shall also argue that political reform and economic revitalisation go together; that a change in our political institutions as envisaged by Charter 88 would have as an unintended consequence the possibility of creating new ways of responding to our economic difficulties.

Charter 88 has been attacked as an idealistic and utopian movement, seeking constitutional changes that stem from purely political principles divorced from the real concerns of the electorate. Whatever the truth of this claim in terms of the motives of the Charter's founders, it is completely mistaken about the likely outcomes of putting the Charter's principles into practice. Charter 88 can strengthen its advocacy of constitutional change if it can show that the reforms it proposes would have a very real and direct impact on both economic performance and the bread-and-butter interests of the ordinary voter.

In order to do this it is necessary to return to the record of the governments of the last 30 years in diagnosing and addressing the problems of the British economy. British policy since the early 1960s has been obsessed with economic failure and the ways to overcome it. Harold Wilson was elected in 1964 on the promise of a radical strategy to promote economic growth, and so was Edward Heath in 1970. Mrs Thatcher came to power in 1979 on the basis of a claim that the post-1945 consensus had failed in economic policy, that Britain needed a radical break with the past if competitiveness was to be restored and economic growth accelerated. Every government since 1964 has made similar claims about its economic objectives; even if the remedies proposed were very different. The issue of reversing industrial decline has dominated British politics, and yet we have failed to attain that objective. This failure cannot be a matter of chance. It goes to the heart of our governmental system and its relations to economic performance.

The failure is not due to a simple inattention to the issue of governance of the economy. Two reforming governments have put that issue at the core of their strategies: Harold Wilson's first administration and Mrs Thatcher's. Wilson wanted to accelerate growth through the intensification of Keynesian policy; indicative planning and corporatist co-ordination would unite industry, labour and the state in a common programme of managed growth. Mrs Thatcher saw this Labour policy not as a solution to our problems but as the intensification of one of the main sources of our failure.

It has been a commonplace on both left and right to treat Britain's industrial decline as a century-long process, with deep-seated cultural and social causes. This perception was explicit in the new Tory thinking of the late 1970s. Conservative arguments started from a variety of grounds: a major source was Hayek's critique developed in the early 1940s, emphasising the inevitable authoritarian consequences of centrally-planned state socialism, and the superior economic perform-ance of the free market and its central role in preserving political liberty; another source of Tory policy was Friedman's and others' advocacy of monetarism as a solution to the perceived inflationary effects of Keynesian policy in the postwar period. This was the international common core of the new economic liberalism. Conservatism also drew on specific diagnoses of British failure. Two are specially worthy of note since they tied poor British performance to features of the British political system. Keith Middlemas' *Politics in Industrial Society* (1979) argued the stifling effects of the growing role of state intervention and corporatism since the radical Liberal government of 1910. Marcur Olson's *The Rise and Decline of Nations* (1982), following on from his *Logic of Collective Action* (1965), argued that Britain, having enjoyed a long period of political stability and democratic government, suffered from the distorting effects of the gradual accumulation of accommodations to economic special interest groups by the state. This led to the growth of institutional rigidies which impede the working of markets and reduce the scope for action of entrepreneurs.

Conservative politicians adopted an analysis, bolstered by academic studies, which stressed the long-run growth of institutional impediments to effective market-based economic performance. The Conservatives argued that Britain failed to be competitive and dynamic because of too much state intervention and corporatism, which impeded the working of markets and reduced the scope for entrepreneurial enterprise. Trade unions had been too powerful and influential in the post-1945 period, and workers were therefore able both to obstruct changes in working practices and to maintain unrealistically high wage levels. Government and the civil service had been dominated by anti-business and anti-enterprise attitudes. The state had pursued collectivist, corporatist and redistributist policies to the detriment of industrial investment and the long-run efficient working of markets for capital and labour. The answer offered in 1979 was a radical dose of economic liberalism in order to demolish the institutional constraints to the workings of the free market. The Conservatives argued for the use of political power to increase the free working of social institutions and personal initiatives. The concentrated sovereignty of Westminster-style parliamentary government was to be exploited to destroy the accretions of the corporate state. The Conservatives saw no contradiction in using a strong state and concentrated power directed by an exclusive party government to restore the balance of social power toward the market. Their political analysis of economic failure led them to emphasise using the traditional powers of the executive and Parliament against the quasi-governmental institutions of economic co-operation and consultation that had grown up since 1945. However radical their social and economic objectives, the Conservatives saw the exercise of power in traditional terms: reform was to be delivered by bending Whitehall and Westminster in the direction of new policies.

We can now see that not only have more than ten years of neo-liberal policies failed to address a supposed century-long process of industrial and economic decline, but that the most serious period of decline in manufacturing ('de-industrialisation') has taken place in the years since 1979. Conservative policy has failed in its own terms and by the standard of its own objectives – to stage a British 'economic miracle'. This is now so self-evident that there is no need to rehearse the evidence of economic failure.[1] Even the international financial markets have learnt the lesson, and there is no inbuilt goodwill towards the Thatcher administration.

Actually, almost every proposition in the Conservative diagnosis of economic failure outlined above is substantially untrue. Britain has not been declining consistently in the same way and for the same basic causes since the 1880s.[2] Decline has been punctuated by periods of recovery and industrial revitalisation – the most impressive of which were the very decades singled out for Conservative criticism, the 1950s and 1960s. In fact, there has not been too much corporatism in Britain but too little. Britain, unlike its major European competitors, has lacked a co-operative and collaborative political culture in which industry, organised Labour and the state have worked consistently together to promote industrial development. Conservative policy has not failed for contingent reasons, but because its analysis of the sources of British economic decline was wrong and the methods to reverse decline therefore inappropriate. Britain has sought to remedy the defects of too much economic liberalism by a further dose of the same disease, rather than struggling to learn the lessons of our failures in economic co-ordination and co-operation, reforming and enhancing our corporatist institutions.

As David Marquand has shown in *The Unprincipled Society* (1988) and I have tried to underline in *After Thatcher* (1989), it was commitment to market liberalism on the part of entrepreneurs, to free collective bargaining on the part of the unions, and a commitment to traditional forms of policy formation and administrative action on the part of politicians and civil servants that prevented the creation of a 'developmental state'.

A 'developmental state' is defined by two main characteristics: firstly, its role in orchestrating the co-operation of the major social interests in acting toward common economic goals, and secondly, its adoption of consistent long-run policies in relation to the supply-side of the economy – such as promoting investment, providing collective services for industry, training the labour force, and so on. There is no fixed institutional model of a developmental state, and the concept does not imply rigid *dirigiste* state intervention. Most of the successful industrial countries have versions of such a state or substitute for it at the level of regional government. Britain, with the USA, is exceptional and, like the USA, has suffered most markedly from de-industrialisation and competitive failure.

In order to substantiate the thesis that Britain's economic performance has suffered because of long-standing commitments to forms of *laissez-faire* by the major social actors, I shall advance three propositions about the relationship between industrial management, organised labour and the state in twentieth-century Britain.

The economic role of government has been circumscribed by the limits of the 'Westminster Model'. This latter term has been used by David Marquand (adapted from John Mackintosh) to characterise the British system of government.[3] Modern democratic government developed in Britain by the piecemeal reform of pre-democratic political institutions, rather than as in other countries like France or West Germany by the creation of a new constitution after a revolution or the destruction of the existing state and the continuity of its institutions. Part of that price is the staggering complacency of our politicians, amounting to blindness to the faults of our system. Political democracy was grafted by successive reforms onto the powers of pre-democratic parliamentary institutions. British parliamentary sovereignty and executive power pre-date modern forms of political accountability, and the evolution of the British system has placed precious few limits on either the power to make laws or on executive action. Parallel with the extension of the franchise was the growth of a modern party system and with it the conversion of parliamentary government into disciplined party government. This means that the unlimited legislative sovereignty of

Parliament is placed in the hands of party leaders by their control of the party's majority in the House of Commons. Likewise, the core of executive accountability, the answerability of Ministers to the Commons, is subverted by those Ministers having a majority which is subject to party discipline at their disposal. Political office is thus the exclusive possession of the majority party. It is able to use the legislative primacy of the Commons and the executive's appropriation of the prerogative powers of the Crown to carry out its party programme with very little check if it has a sufficient majority.

Our electoral system has emphasised these defects; it makes majority government more probable than not, even in the absence of a genuine majority of the votes of the electorate. Both major parties, the Conservatives and Labour, have seen office as the prize of the electoral competition, and a period in office as an opportunity to pursue purely party policies. Neither party has put any great emphasis on the development of a collaborative rather than a competitive political culture. Even in the era of supposed 'consensus politics' in the 1950s and 1960s, the major parties were unable to work together to pursue a consistent long-run programme of economic development.

The modern British system of government concentrates power in the hands of the majority party's leaders, but it does so at a price. Power can only be exclusively possessed if it is confined to Westminster and Whitehall, limited to legislation and formal state action. This limits the policies that can be pursued – restricting the scope for governing through the co-operation and consultation of interests, for co-ordinating by bringing in a wide variety of agencies into partnership with government. The main focus of state intervention in the economy in the post-1945 period, 'Keynesian' macro-economic policies, show the political limits of the British state very clearly. Kenyesianism was the supposed core of the postwar consensus, and Keynesian policies have been savaged by Thatcherite Conservatives as both incompetently interventionist and inflationary. However, we should note how limited a form of intervention macro-economic Keynesianism was. It used established governmental means – fiscal and budgetary policy – to influence the behaviour of economic actors; stimulating effective demand or cooling down excessive demand by changing such key variables as the level of government expenditure, the level of public borrowing, tax rates and the supply of private credit. Such a policy is a politically neutral instrument, capable of being put into effect by the established civil service under Cabinet control. It was also conceived as economically neutral, acting on all economic agents rather than selectively targeting by administrative discretion certain key firms or groups of economic agents. Keynesianism was thus a form of 'liberal collectivism',[4] that is the utilisation of traditional insruments of state policy to new purposes rather than the state playing an active role in creating new relationships between the key economic actors. Keynes saw it as a virtue that his macro-economic policies changed neither the state nor the pattern of economic ownership, utilising the existing institutions of government and preserving the power of company managements to manage. Keynes' doctrine is a modification of economic liberalism designed to stave off thoroughgoing collectivism and more active state intervention. It left both the constitution and the institutions of private capitalism intact.

Keynesianism succeeded because it fitted the system of party government without difficulty. British macro-economic management was quite different from 'Keynesian' policies in other states like Sweden.[5] Britain limited the scope and instruments of state policy – concentrating above all on demand management. Its failure to change the underlying performance of the economy is emphasised by the success of those countries that refused post-1945 to follow the new Keynesian orthodoxy, West Germany and Japan. In both countries macro-economic policy was constrained by traditionalist commitments to a balanced budget and sound money. Yet, because of active industrial and supply-side policies, they were both able to achieve economic miracles while Britain sowed the seeds of competitive failure.[6]

In fact, one can argue that British Keynesianism came to grief in the later 1960s and early 1970s, not because it was too interventionist, but because it was not interventionist enough. The true alternative to Keynesianism was not the state socialism Keynes had feared, but the new forms of co-ordination of the economy by the active collaboration of the major economic interests developed in such countries as Sweden and West Germany. These new forms never developed in Britain to the extent necessary to change basic economic relationships because they threatened the existing constitutional settlement and the power of party government – hence the restricted agenda of British Keynesianism, and the destructive effects of 'stop/go' policies and the inflationary consequences of governing primarily by means of demand management. British Keynesianism invoked the supposition that, given the right macro-economic regime, private management in industry could be left to make the right decisions about levels of investment and manufacturing methods. When private managements on a wide scale failed to make the right decisions, then that strategy of neutrality was undermined and British industry was exposed to failure as the result of incompetence at the level of the firm. The primary loser was the Labour Party. Far from being socialist, Labour in the post-1945 period had staked all on a social-liberal strategy. The key assumptions of this strategy were the efficacy of neutral Keynesian macro-manipulation, a welfare system based on full employment and economic growth, and the continued efficiency of industry in the hands of private management. Labour's advocacy of corporatism was always a half-hearted and fitfully pursued supplement to these basic economic polices. The failure of these assumptions ruined Labour in the 1970s – leaving it with no credible strategy of economic management. Labour has still to discover an overall approach to economic and social policy to replace the marriage of Keynes and Beveridge; Labour stole the policies of radical liberalism after 1945 and has found no credible substitute to this day. The failure of the Thatcher experiment and the absence of any distinctive Labour alternative to it thus leaves us all with no credible doctrine of economic management.

The substitute for an active industrial policy has been the promotion of industrial concentration. Before 1914 British business failed to take full advantage of the new forms of corporate ownership, professional management and the economies of scale entailed in mass production. Most British industries were characterised by small units, technological backwardness and traditional entrepreneurial control. Britain was falling behind because capitalists clung to nineteenth-century conceptions of ownership and control. Industry was hampered by too great an adherence to the free market rather than too little, *pace* the Conservative case. It failed to adopt contemporary German or American standards in management and manufacturing technology. One of the main responses to competitive failure was cartellisation, which in the British case allowed small and inefficient production units to survive by protecting markets by price fixing and quotas.

After the First World War British industry began to merge and concentrate on a large scale; rationalisation and takeovers accelerating through the 1920s and 1930s.[7] In the 1930s British industry began haltingly to adopt and adapt to British conditions American mass production methods. Thereafter both government and management tended to see the modernisation of industry in terms of the concentration of ownership to gain economies of scale in manufacture. Both the Conservatives and Labour favoured concentration; the state passively accepting mergers or actively promoting them to create firms which would be 'national champions'. This was particularly the case with the 1966-70 Labour governments' Industrial Re-organisation Commission. As an industrial policy it amounted to little more than state indulgence to successive merger waves engineered through the stock market. By the early 1970s British industry was highly concentrated, and yet it had failed fully to adopt the internationally prevailing methods of standardised mass production. Many of the merged firms were made up of less than optimally sized plants that failed to exploit fully prevailing international norms of production organisation and productivity.[8]

At this point, relatively slow growth and competitive failure to match international levels of productivity and product design was reinforced by a series of hammer blows following in the wake of the 1973 OPEC oil price rise crisis. Industrial countries from the later 1960s onwards came to trade manufactured goods ever more intensively with one another. Britain failed to retain export markets and lost domestic market share in sector after sector to foreign import penetration. International markets in manufactured goods have become more competitive, volatile and differentiated, thereby undermining the advantages of long production runs and standardised products. As a consequence, economies of scale have become less and less realisable in sector after sector. Successful firms and national economies have responded to this by the adoption of more flexible methods of production, which emphasise a broader and adaptable mix of products, general purpose machine tools and more flexible and broadly skilled labour.[9] In response to this international turn to flexible specialisation,

Britain (a less than efficient mass producer) has largely stagnated. There is little evidence that British firms have adopted the new strategies, production techniques and working methods.[10] This shows in continuing high levels of import penetration and low market shares for British firms in many sectors.

The response of British firms to this development has been yet further concentration. The 1980s have witnessed the most prolonged and the largest of the successive British merger waves. Firms are merging and acquiring other firms less in order to gain economies of scale in production than to control defensively domestic market share by buying up the competition, and to acquire profitable subsidiaries in often unrelated industries to boost group profits. The logic of concentration is now dominated less by the needs of productive efficiency than by the state of the stock market. The result is the construction of conglomerate firms without industrial logic and often without any apparent underlying economic rationale. One of the effects of this is a massive diversion of top management energy from investment in new capacity and new processes. The Conservatives have simply accepted this merger boom with complete passivity. These developments in industrial concentration flatly contradict their claims as to the virtues of open and competitive markets and the superior enterprise of small businesses. Yet they have accepted such concentration by reference to a species of *laissez-faire* – management must be free to manage.

The problem is that concentration has *not* made British manufacturing more efficient nor adapted our firms' industrial organisation to foreign competitive pressures. The leading edge of foreign competition is marked by a number of features that stem from quite different political legacies and industrial policies. Such policies stress the collaboration of state, regional and municipal governments with the major economic interests, firms and organised labour, to promote new forms of efficiency and new services to sustain them.

The first major trend of the 1970s and 1980s in the re-emergence of regional economies with strong populations of small and medium-sized firms linked one to another by supportive institutional cultures based on public-private co-operation to supply key inputs like labour training, market information and low-cost finance which individual firms cannot hope to provide for themselves. Examples of such regions are Baden-Württemburg in West Germany and Emilia-Romagna in Italy.[11]

The second major trend is that such regions draw on legacies of artisan production and craft labour skill, on small firm traditions and on local collaborative institutions, which – far from being obsolete in the face of mass production – are enjoying a new lease of life as competitive pressures change. Britain's loss of distinctive regional economies as a result of industrial concentration and de-industrialisation, our wretched record in training skilled labour by the collaboration of government, management and the unions, and the weakness of our small-firm sector in manufacturing are now major liabilities. The centralisation of the 'Westminster Model' has prevented the emergence of regional government, so effective in regional economic regulation in West Germany and Italy. The collapse of local government autonomy and the abolition of the major metropolitan authorities as a result of Conservative centralisation has even further weakened local strategies for industrial revitalisation.

The third major trend is the increasing mirroring within large manufacturing multinationals abroad of these regional policies. Firms are decentralising to create families of co-operating sub-units with high autonomy and increasingly based upon the flexible production of a diversified product range.[12] Such firms have adopted strategies of co-operation with and consultation of labour within the operating units. British firms remain by contrast highly centralised, allowing low autonomy to subsidiaries. They remain managerially rigid – emphasising managements' control of labour – and they are dominated by short-term accounting criteria rather than by long-run strategic consideration of the conditions of manufacturing success. Centralised and authoritarian *political* control is mirrored by centralised and authoritarian *management* control. British management has caught the buzz word 'flexibility', but it interprets it as flexibility at the expense of labour, without any change in basic organisational structures and with the preservation of top managements' prerogative of control.

If this analysis is correct then Britain desperately needs an active industrial policy to revitalise the supply side of the economy. Our problem is that an active industrial policy – other than promoting concentration – has always meant a *dirigiste* 'alternative' strategy advocated by the left.[3] The classic left-Labour strategy, advocated through the 1970s into the early 1980s with disastrous results, was the control of industry through central government. The left, like the right, was wedded to the Westminster Model of political authority – a party government utilising Whitehall control would use its concentrated powers to coerce and control private firms to meet its objectives. This simply will not do: *dirigisme* implies greater centralisation and less flexibility, whereas we need both greater *de*centralisation and the promotions of greater co-operation. That implies a new political model, not dominated by Whitehall. Labour has been stumbling toward such a policy – as evidenced by the first two reports of the Policy Review Group 'A Productive and Competitive Economy' chaired by Bryan Gould. At the same time, labour has failed to see the wider agenda of political change implied in this model, to link economic and constitutional reform. The danger of Labour's new caution is that this link is further than ever from the centre of the Party's agenda.[14]

Trade unions, far from being bulwarks of the corporate state, have been committed to 'free collective bargaining'. The trade unions have always preferred to see wage determination as a private matter of direct negotiation between management and organised labour outside public co-ordination. Unions have always insisted that they are private voluntary bodies, not public agencies operating in the public sphere and responsible to a political community for their actions. They have always sought to avoid a positive labour law in favour of a system of legalised immunities for the actions of their members and officials. The Conservatives, contrary to this dominant perception among trade unionists, saw the unions as a state within the state. The unions have always refused this role, rejected power and influence in favour of their autonomy to bargain with management. Thus the unions rejected both Wilson's and Heath's attempts to reform industrial relations legislation, and they refused to support the proposals of the 1978 Bullock Report on industrial democracy.

The unions have always exploited legislation beneficial to them (like the Employment Protection Act, 1975); they have always been willing to use their opportunities for informal or quasi-formal influence whilst refusing publicly sanctioned responsibility; and they have refused to accept the need for regular and ongoing tripartite bargains about wage levels, productivity, etc. They have been unwilling to participate in a system of full and publicly codified corporation on the Swedish or West German models. Even when the Trade Union Congress (TUC) has moved toward corporatist bargains under the spur of economic necessity, as with the 1974-79 Labour government's Social Contract, individual unions and the rank and file have worked to subvert them. The TUC has lacked such power to co-ordinate union strategy and make bargains stick, as that possessed by the LO in Sweden, for example. The unions have seen incomes policies as at best short-term emergency measures to be followed by a return to the normal practices of 'free collective bargaining' as soon as possible. In the 1960s and 1970s they refused ongoing co-operation to both Wilson and Heath. They brought down the 1970-74 Heath government and in 1978-79 they destroyed the Labour Government for their perceived short-term advantage. If the unions were over-powerful it was not as the adjuncts but as the wreckers of the corporate state. Given such union organisation and attitudes, a fully corporatist system of wage determination could never take root. The co-ordination of economic policy by the major economic interests, fitfully pursued by Wilson and Heath in an attempt to move outside the Westminster Model, failed because of the unions' commitment to *laissez faire* in wage bargaining. A highly centralised government seeking to escape from economic problems by corporatism, yet conscious of its own party privilege to determine economic policy from above, and a highly concentrated industrial system controlled by managements jealous of the power to manage, were matched by the unions hostile to the concentration of power in the TUC and determined to maintain their autonomy and the private government of industrial relations.

If the Conservative analysis of the role of unions in the corporate state was in substance inaccurate, the willingness of the Conservatives to allow the concentration of 'free collective bargaining' within ever more restrictive legal limits as part of their own commitment to *laissez faire* has proved a disaster. The unions, battered in the early and mid-1980s, have recovered much of their strength in the private sector, legislation notwithstanding. Britain is moving into double digit inflation and a wage/price spiral. These are the very conditions Tory reforms were supposed to eliminate. The continuing legacy of union autonomy bodes ill for Labour. Labour is so cowed by the experience of 1978-79 that it has foresworn an incomes policy of any kind – senior party figures dismiss it out of hand as a political impossibility. But if that is true a sustained policy of economic expansion is impossible, as the recent years of the Thatcher administration prove. Wage/price inflation can only be controlled by low growth and restrictive macro-economic policies. But such policies cannot address, let alone solve, the growing economic crisis fuelled by the failure of British manufacturing. Labour has abandoned Keynesianism and it has also abandoned the only effective institutional check to its inflationary pressures – the corporatist determination of wages and incomes. A Labour government can survive without an incomes policy, but only as a conservative government with limited economic objectives in a period of growing economic crisis.[15] This is not merely depressing news for radicals, it is a disaster for Britain. Only radical policies are appropriate to the problems we now face and which will intensify in the 1990s. Labour pragmatism demonstrates all the vices of superficial realism.

The conclusion of this analysis is that not only were the policies of the Thatcher administration based on a complete mis-diagnosis – not too much corporatism but too little – but that it also reveals the continuing bankruptcy of Labour Party policy. Hostile to political reform, committed to the Westminster Model of majority party government, lacking a subsitute for Keynesianism in macro-economic policy, having no credible policy for wage determination, and having no effective means of instituting an industrial policy, Labour is ill-equipped to exploit the Conservative's failure by offering a new doctrine of economic governance. The issues involved in the development of such a doctrine are primarily political, rather than concerning the introduction of new economic theories or technical methods of economic management. The resistance to such development stems from the *political* conservatism of Labour's leadership.

Our real problems derive from crucial weaknesses in the social institutions in which our economic activity is embedded. No technical 'fix' by central government officials in macro-economic management and no 'working smarter' by management within the existing organisation of the firm can compensate for these weaknesses. To revitalise our economy and to reverse the decline in manufacturing, we need major political and institutional changes. These are radical and threatening, since they involve a new political culture based on collaboration and a new social politics of co-operation.

Constitutional change would help to create such a culture. Proportional representation, of all the changes proposed by Charter 88, would make the biggest dent in the Westminster Model. It would not prevent majority government or party government, but it would stimulate the powers of the opposition in the House of Commons and it would make possible the effective representation of smaller party opinion. It would be the greatest dent in our present drift towards electoral despotism. The codification and entrenchment of a Bill of Rights in a written constitution overseen by a constitutional court would not merely check the gradual erosion of civil liberties, it would also increase pressure for the general codification of citizen's rights. This would make the present position of industrial relations legislation all the more anomalous – half restrictive legislation and half the continuation of a system of legalised immunities.

Labour law is but one example of the need to codify and protect rights. Arguing for greater corporatism stems from pragmatic needs – to ensure both economic co-ordination and to mobilise consent for policy. Yet commitments by the major social interests can all too often ignore minority concerns. Corporatist bargains will be resisted if they ride roughshod over individual and group rights. The constitutional defence of individual liberty and the enhancement of rights by a new written constitution is essential if individuals are to be guaranteed the freedom to consent without excessive regimentation. It would make a positive labour law inescapable.

The creation of national self-government for Scotland and Wales, and the revitalisation of local government autonomy in England would both create pressures for the decentralisation and devolution of functions from Whitehall to the regions. Decentralisation would make possible the emergence of regional economic initiatives by public bodies and the construction of regional policies for economic renewal.

Formal constitutional charge would begin to unblock the rigidities of the British political system that serve as barriers to new economic policies and it would create the conditions for the emergence of a new spirit of co-operation between the political parties and the major social interests. Institutional change would encourage innovations in policy and changes in attitudes.

The first and overwhelming necessity for change is to switch national income from consumption to investment, from short-term considerations of financial dealing and commercial profit to long-run considerations of manufacturing competitiveness and success. Britain has been over-consuming, over-utilising consumer credit to sustain consumption by the household sector, and under-investing in new manufacturing capacity. The British manufacturing sector is too small to sustain our current level of consumption (about one third of West Germany's share of total EC output) and the proportion of GDP directed to investment in new machinery and plant is too low to close the disparities in productivity compared with our major competitors. This has to be achieved by a long-term and sustained programme, and no purely party government, using traditional techniques of macro-economic management and constrained by the pressures of the electoral cycle under the existing system, has the certainty of office and the consistency of public consent necessary to achieve this.[16]

The answer to this problem is not prolonged party government on the Westminster Model. Mrs Thatcher's decade in office on a minority of the votes cast has not won such consent or called forth such co-operation. A new political system cannot rely on governments of the same political complexion, but on continuity of policy through changes in the ruling party or ruling coalition. To achieve this we have to go beyond formal constitutional change towards changes in the style of governance that such new institutional arrangements make possible. If our diagnosis is that Britain has failed because of not too much corporatism but too little, then we must accept the consequences of such an analysis. We need a more open and ongoing form of co-operation between government and the major social interests – not short-term pacts between Labour governments and the Labour movement. We need a new style of government which bases its authority not on parliamentary sovereignty and Westminster centralism but on a continuing *social pact*. This has to come from a political source, but the Conservatives as present constituted are not prepared to act as a party of social leadership based on a coalition of the social interests for economic recovery. Neither business nor organised labour will sacrifice present powers and influence to support a purely party government, destined to last for a few years at best. If the opposition parties collaborated they could build a broad-based coalition that could survive transitory electoral pressures. If Labour, as the strongest of all these parties, were to adopt a role of social leadership, accepting the partnership of the Liberal Democrats and the light Greens, then it could (with PR) weld together a sustainable electoral bloc. It would have to abandon its commitment to Westminster political tradition. A strong coalition led by a major party committed to social collaboration would have the power to win changes in attitude and new commitments from the major social partners in such a pact – business and the unions. Both sides would have to change their existing stance – business to cede management prerogatives in order to secure the gains of collaboration from organised labour, labour to cede short-term strengths to bid up wages in the private sector in order to secure the long-run advantages of a collaborative drive to transform productivity.

Many leading business people in the manufacturing sector resent 'short termism', high-cost finance and the low priority given to making things over making money. They are the cinderellas of the Thatcher years to a degree only outmatched by the unions. Many leading trade unionists know that the present position is unsustainable; that our failures in industrial training, manufacturing investment and less than adequate productivity growth may well spell disaster for their members in the intensely competitive environment of European business in the 1990s. Both sides of industry agree we face a crisis in training, and that the skills shortage created by inaction will cripple business expansion and threaten competitiveness. The costs of a programme of training workers to international standards are immense: they can only be borne by a major commitment of public expenditure and by the public accepting the costs of this policy, recognising its priority as nothing less than a national emergency. A solution to the training crisis is only possible if industry, labour and the state actively co-operate. The same is true of funds for manufacturing investment. Increasing the supply of low-cost finance involves major institutional changes, shifts in priorities of public spending, and a willingness to create a new sector of industrial development decoupled from existing financial markets.[17]

Labour has not begun to give either of these objectives the attention or priority they require, and until it does it cannot hope to change public perceptions of these issues or win the support of the two sides of industry. If it did, and if it built a coalition with the other opposition parties, it would change the terms of political life. The Conservatives could not hope to govern whilst aiming to change these objectives and refusing to support publicly sponsored corporate collaboration.

A policy of collaboration by the major social interests at national level cannot succeed unless it is backed up by comprehensive measures of co-operation at the regional level. National co-operation can only create a climate conducive to collaboration, orchestrating consent for policies implemented by more specific forums and agencies. Change in the institutions of regional and local government would permit, given new powers and new sources of funding, the creation of public-private partnerships to promote training and industrial development. A centralised state industrial policy is beyond the capacity of British government and out of line with successful policies of regionalising collective services for industry elsewhere in the advanced industrial world. Regional regulation and intervention is the key to building successful industrial districts involving partnership between business, labour and local administration. The creation of a single market in the European Community and the growth of political and monetary union will promote the importance of regional economic regulation. National governments will cede certain macro-economic functions to the Community, although they will retain their saliency as forums to promote *political* consensus on economic policy issues. These countries, which can link such national orchestration of policy commitments with effective institutions of regional regulation, will profit most from the new Europe.

As part of a strategy of economic revitalisation any reforming government in the UK must enthusiastically embrace the new 'social Europe' which is an essential complement to the creation of a single market. The Conservatives have mindlessly resisted this as part of their hostility to corporatism and to dialogue with organised labour. A single market and a common monetary policy without strategies and institutions at Community level for economic consultation, social co-operation and aid to promote the development of the less favoured regions will promote greater inequality in Europe and the further centralisation of influence in the hands of unaccountable corporate capital. British traditionalists, with Mrs Thatcher in the lead, have resisted such developments because they imply the loss of parliamentary 'sovereignty'. Yet the new Europe will both inevitably weaken such sovereignty and, if we do not reform, leave us with an authoritarian, ineffective and over-centralised state. In Thatcher's Europe Britain would get the worst of both worlds, intensified competition without the means to respond to it, and the retention of the worst aspects of our national political system without effective means for compensating by policies at regional level.

My argument has been that Britain's failure can be traced to the absence of the institutions to sustain a collaborative political culture and the failure to develop other forms of corporate consultation that proved effective in other states' post-1945 strategies of economic developments. Without a programme of constitutional reform and without active efforts to build a more democratic European Community we shall lack the means to build the new institutions of national collaboration and regional regulation adapted to the circumstances of the new Europe and the new conditions of economic competition it imposes.

Notes

This is a revised version of a paper given on 13 October 1989 in the Charter 88 seminar series 'Issues of the Constitution'.

[1] For such evidence see the April-June 1989 special issue of *Political Quarterly*, 'The British Economy: Miracle or Collapse', especially the articles by Coutts and Godley, Hirst and Zeitlin, and Senker.
[2] This case for a punctuated history of decline and revival is argued in the introduction to P. Hirst and J. Zeitlin (eds), *Reversing Industrial Decline?*, Berg, Oxford 1989.
[3] See D. Marquand, *The Unprincipled Society*, Cape, London 1988.
[4] The concept of 'liberal collectivism' is advanced by T. Cutler, K. Williams and T. Williams in *Keynes, Beveridge and Beyond*, Routledge, London 1986.
[5] See M. Weir and T. Skocpol, 'State Structures and the Possibilities for 'Keynesian' Responses to the Great Depression in Sweden, Britain and the United States', in P.B. Evans, D. Rueschemeyer and T. Skocpol (eds), *Bringing the State Back In*, CUP, Cambridge 1985; and for a survey of national traditions and responses to

Keynesianism see P.A. Hall (ed.), *The Political Power of Economic Ideas: Keynesianism Across Nations*, Princeton University Press, Princeton 1989.

[6] See the essays by C.S. Allen (Ch.10) and E.M. Hadley (Ch.11) on West Germany and Japan respectively in Hall (ed.), *op.cit.*

[7] For an account of the successive merger waves in the UK until the 1970s see L. Hannah, *The Rise of the Corporate Economy*, Methuen, London 1976.

[8] On the strategy of building 'national champions' and the sources of failure in UK manufacturing generally see K. Williams, J. Williams and D. Thomas, *Why are the British Bad at Manufacturing*, Routledge, London 1983; and on the difference between concentration of ownership and plant size, see S.J. Prais, *The Evolution of Giant Firms in Britain*, CUP, Cambridge 1976.

[9] For an account of this trend toward 'flexible specialisation' see M. Piore and C. Sabel, *The Second Industrial Divide*, Basic Books, New York 1984.

[10] See P. Hirst and J. Zeitlin, 'Flexible Specialisation and the Competitive Failure of UK Manufacturing', in *Political Quarterly*, vol 60, no 2, April-June 1989.

[11] See C. Sabel, 'Flexible Specialisation and the Re-emergence of Regional Economies', in Hirst and Zeitlin (eds), *op.cit.*

[12] See Sabel, *op.cit.*

[13] In this analysis I have argued that in Britain concentration policy was the most consistent and widely employed substitute for an active industrial policy. I have thus neglected nationalisation, which the Conservatives have identified as the most damaging form of state intervention. Nationalisation was never intended as an active industrial policy, except within sections of the Labour left without effective policy influence. Post-1945 Labour remained committed to the 'mixed economy' and its attitude to nationalisation was dictated by two major principles.

Firstly, firms were to be taken into public ownership for two major reasons: a) the competitive failure of the private sector (eg, coal and the railways), with few exceptions successful firms in manufacturing were to be left free to manage (one exception is the special steel firms taken in with the bulk of the industry in the first nationalisation), thus nationalisation was not an industrial policy but a policy of rescue for employment and other social reasons; b) for welfare and public policy reasons (eg, to improve working conditions in the mines, to secure adequate standards of public service from monopoly utilities).

Secondly, firms that were nationalised were, under the Morrisonian conception of the public corporation, to be publicly owned but managed by a professional management, the government remaining at arms length.

Nationalisation was thus not intended to promote change in industrial structure by movement into new sectors or to direct the successful competitive firms in private manufacturing. For a critique of *dirigiste* industrial policies see P. Hirst and J. Zeitlin, 'Flexible Specialisation vs Post-Fordism: Theory, Evidence and Policy Implications', *Birkbeck Public Policy Centre Papers*, 1990.

[14] See my articles on the first and second stages of Labour's Policy review in *New Statesman* (20 May 1988), *New Statesman and Society* (19 May 1989).

[15] Incomes policies have become unfashionable and do raise formidable problems of institutionalisation. John Smith's current thinking seems to be that entering the EMS will provide sufficient anti-inflationary discipline through exchange rate constraints. I believe this is too simplistic since such regulation through monetary mechanisms is too far removed from the actual processes of wage determination which fuel wage/price inflation under expansionary conditions. Free collective bargaining, as practised in Berlin, is not readily subject to such remote monetary discipline. Key workers in successful firms have pushed for wage rises above the cost of living ever since Britain emerged from the trough of the depressions of the

1980s, they tend to set a target 'going rate' for other groups. This problem needs to be tackled at root. Monetarism was advocated by the Conservative Party as a form of control over inflation, yet it failed dismally.

[16] I have developed this point more fully in my *After Thatcher*, Collins, London 1989.

[17] I have considered how to create a low-cost financial sector for manufacturing in some detail in *After Thatcher*, *op.cit.*, and also set out in some detail the possible forms of regional institutions to revitalise manufacturing through new investment and collective services.

Notes on Contributors

Geoff Andrews was educated at the Open University, Ruskin College, Oxford and University College, Cardiff. He teaches politics and sociology 'A' level and is researching the egalitarian traditions of British socialism.

Sarah Benton, formerly political editor of the *New Statesman & Society*, is a freelance writer and journalist.

Jon Bloomfield is the author of *Passive Revolution: Politics and the Czechoslovak Working Class 1945-48* (1979). He reported on the Czechoslovak revolution of 1989 for *The Guardian*.

Caroline Ellis is a trainee journalist at the *New Statesman & Society*, a Charter 88 council member and the editor of *Socialist Citizen*.

David Held is a senior lecturer in social science at the Open University and the author of *Models of Democracy* (1986) and *Political Theory and the Modern State* (1989).

Paul Hirst is a Professor in social theory at Birkbeck College, University of London. He is author of *After Thatcher* (1989) and a Charter 88 council member.

Stephen Howe is tutor in development studies at Ruskin College, Oxford, a writer for the *New Statesman & Society* and a Charter 88 council member.

Michael Ignatieff is a historian and journalist. He is author of *The Needs of Strangers* (1984) and *The Russian Album* (1987), and is also an editorial columnist for *The Observer*.

Martin Kettle is editor of *The Guardian*'s European section, and is a regular contributor to *Marxism Today*.

Geoff Mulgan works as policy adviser to Gordon Brown MP, shadow spokesman for trade and industry. He is the co-author (with Ken Worpole) of *Saturday Night or Sunday Morning* (1986) and the author of *Communication and Control* (forthcoming).

John Osmond is author of *The Divided Kingdom* (1988), and producer of the Channel 4 series of the same name. He is currently a freelance writer.

Bhikhu Parekh is Professor of politics at the University of Hull, and deputy chair of the Commission for Racial Equality. He is the editor of *The Concept of Socialism* (1975).

Anne Phillips is Professor of politics at the City of London Polytechnic. She has written extensively on issues of feminism and socialism, and her latest book *Engendering Democracy* is due in early 1991.

Raymond Plant is Professor of politics at the University of Southampton, co-author with Andrew Vincent of *Philosophy, Politics and Citizenship* (1984) and a contributor to *The Alternative* (1990), edited by Ben Pimlott *et al.*

Michael Rustin is Professor of sociology at the Polytechnic of East London and author of *For a Pluralist Socialism* (1985). He is a Charter 88 council member.

Stephen Sedley is a QC specialising in civil rights cases; his publications include an anthology of British folksongs and a volume of Spanish prison poetry in translation.

David Selbourne was until 1986 a tutor in politics at Ruskin College, Oxford. He is the author of *Against Socialist Illusion: A Radical Argument* (1984), *Left Behind: Journeys into British Politics* (1987) and most recently *Death of a Dark Hero: Eastern Europe 1987-90* (1990).

Fred Steward is a lecturer in innovation and management at Aston University, a member of *Marxism Today*'s editorial board and a contributor to *New Times* (1989), edited by Stuart Hall and Martin Jacques.

Simon Watney is a director of the National Aids Manual. He chairs the Health Education Group of the Terrence Higgins Trust. His most recent book is *Taking Liberties: AIDS and Cultural Politics* (1989), which he co-edited with Erica Carter. He is a contributor to *Identity: Community, Culture, Difference* (1990), edited by Jonathan Rutherford.

Index

ACT UP, 168-75

'active citizenship', 12, 20, 50, 77, 84, 127, 215-6, 218; and the dependency culture, 13; and property, 26-7; and republicanism, 125-6

AIDS, 164-81; and cultural politics, 168-75

altruism, 34

American Civil Liberties Union (ACLU), 170

Arendt, Hannah, 79, 127, 181

Ashdown, Paddy, 50

assimilationism, 189-94

Beveridge, William, 251

Beveridge Report (1942), 229

bill of rights, 12, 22, 50, 55, 176, 178, 213, 219-27, 258; and cultural difference, 202; and subjecthood, 216; and women, 241

'Britishness', 136-42, 185-204

Bullock Report (1978), 255

Canadian Charter of Rights and Freedoms, 223-5

Charter 77, 108, 109, 226

Charter 88, 12-3, 50, 55, 86, 136-42, 178, 207-64

Charter of Rights, 12

citizenship, 25, 28, 56-60, 71-5, 129, 177-81, 234; and altruism, 26-36; and corporatism, 243-64; and cultural difference, 183-204; and democracy 23-4, 125-34; and the environment, 25, 35, 65-75; and Europe, 107-48; and the family, 82, 164; and gender, 76-87, 127-8, 151-63, 235-42; and interest groups, 53-4; and the market, 29-30, 59-60; and the nation state, 11, 24, 115-22; and responsibility, 37-49; and sex-

uality, 151-81; and socialist ideology, 13-4, 24, 50-4, 91-104; and the welfare state, 29, 31-3, 230-4

civic brotherhood, 160

civic duty, 42, 60-3, 65, 96-7, 197, 214-8; see also responsibility

Civic Forum (Czechoslovakia), 107-12, 127; see also Eight Rules of Dialogue

civic friendship, 203-4

civic virtue, 60-1, 77, 131

civil society, 19-25, 68, 133

Claim of Right for Scotland, 136, 146, 147; see also Woman's Claim of Right

Clause 28 (of 1988 Local Government Bill), 164, 167, 175

collective bargaining, 255-6

Communism, 28, 40; collapse of, 38, 124

consensus politics, 249

conservatism, 12, 27, 29, 32-3, 35, 52, 59, 231, 252-3, 261; and 'active citizenship', 12, 26; and bill of rights, 225; and consumer choice, 52; and Europe, 115; see also Thatcherism

corporatism, 243-64

cultural difference, 183-204

Delors, Jacques, 121

democratic deficit, 122, 237

developmental state, 248

Dewar, Donald, 142

Dubcek, Alexander, 110

duties, see civic duty and responsibility

Eight Rules of Dialogue (Civic Forum), 113-4

electoral system, 12, 238-9, 249

empowerment, 31, 47, 68, 94-6, 178, 236, 238

—